BY DAVID BROOKS

How to Know a Person

The Second Mountain

The Road to Character

The Social Animal

On Paradise Drive

Bobos in Paradise

HOW TO KNOW A PERSON

HOW

TO

KNOW

A

PERSON

The Art of SEEING OTHERS DEEPLY
and BEING DEEPLY SEEN

DAVID

BROOKS

RANDOM HOUSE
NEW YORK

Published in the United States by Random House, an imprint and division of Penguin
Random House LLC, New York.

RANDOM HOUSE and the HOUSE colophon are registered trademarks of Penguin
Random House LLC.

Portions of this work were originally published in different form in
The New York Times.

Hardback ISBN 9780593230060
Ebook ISBN 9780593230084

Printed in the United States of America on acid-free paper

randomhousebooks.com

6 8 10 9 7 5

Book design by Casey Hampton

To Peter Marks

Contents

PART 3: I SEE YOU WITH YOUR STRENGTHS

Part 1

———

I

SEE

YOU

ONE

The Power of Being Seen

f you ever saw the old movie *Fiddler on the Roof,* you know how warm and emotional Jewish families can be. They are always hugging, singing, dancing, laughing, and crying together.

I come from the other kind of Jewish family.

The culture of my upbringing could be summed up by the phrase "Think Yiddish, act British." We were reserved, stiff-upper-lip types. I'm not saying I had a bad childhood—far from it. Home was a stimulating place for me, growing up. Over our Thanksgiving dinner tables, we talked about the history of Victorian funerary monuments and the evolutionary sources of lactose intolerance (I'm not kidding). There was love in the home. We just didn't express it.

Perhaps unsurprisingly, I became a bit detached. When I was four, my nursery school teacher apparently told my parents, "David doesn't always play with the other children. A lot of the time he stands off to the side and *observes* them." Whether it was nature or nurture, a certain aloofness became part of my personality. By high school I had taken up long-term residency inside my own head. I felt most alive when I was engaged in the solitary business of writing. Junior year I wanted to date a woman named Bernice. But after doing some intel gathering, I discovered she wanted to go out with another guy. I was shocked. I remember telling myself, "What is she *thinking*? I write way better than that guy!" It's quite possible that I had a somewhat constrained view of how social life worked for most people.

Then, when I was eighteen, the admissions officers at Columbia, Wesleyan, and Brown decided I should go to the University of Chicago. I love my alma mater, and it has changed a lot for the better since I was there, but back then it wasn't exactly the sort of get-in-touch-with-your-feelings place that would help thaw my emotional ice age. My favorite saying about Chicago is this one: It's a Baptist school where atheist professors teach Jewish students Saint Thomas Aquinas. The students there still wear T-shirts that read, "Sure it works in practice, but does it work in theory?" And so into this heady world I traipsed and . . . shocker, I fit right in.

If you had met me ten years out of college, I think you would have found me a pleasant enough guy, cheerful but a tad inhibited—not somebody who was easy to get to know or who found it easy to get to know you. In truth, I was a practiced escape artist. When other people revealed some vulnerable intimacy to me, I was good at making meaningful eye contact with their shoes and then excusing myself to keep a vitally important appointment with my dry cleaner. I had a sense that this wasn't an ideal way of being. I felt painfully awkward during those moments when someone tried to connect with me. I inwardly wanted to connect. I just didn't know what to say.

Repressing my own feelings became my default mode for moving through the world. I suppose I was driven by the usual causes: fear of intimacy; an intuition that if I really let my feelings flow, I wouldn't like what bubbled up; a fear of vulnerability; and a general social ineptitude. One seemingly small and stupid episode symbolizes this repressed way of living for me. I'm a big baseball fan, and though I have been to hundreds of games, I have never once caught a foul ball in the stands. One day about fifteen years ago, I was at a game in Baltimore when a hitter's bat shattered, and the whole bat except the knob helicoptered over the dugout and landed at my feet. I reached down and grabbed it. Getting a bat at a game is a thousand times better than getting a ball! I should have been jumping up and down, waving my trophy in the air, high-fiving the people around me, becoming a temporary jumbotron celebrity. Instead, I just placed the bat at my feet and sat, still-faced, as everyone stared at me. Looking back, I want to scream at myself: "Show a little joy!" But when it came to spontaneous displays of emotion, I had the emotional capacity of a head of cabbage.

Life has a way of tenderizing you, though. Becoming a father was an emotional revolution, of course. Later, I absorbed my share of the blows that any adult suffers: broken relationships, public failures, the vulnerability that comes with getting older. The ensuing sense of my own frailty was good for me, introducing me to deeper, repressed parts of myself.

Another seemingly small event symbolizes the beginning of my ongoing journey toward becoming a full human being. As a commentator and pundit, I sometimes get asked to sit on panel discussions. Usually, they are at Washington think tanks and they have exactly as much emotional ardor as you'd expect from a discussion of fiscal policy. (As the journalist Meg Greenfield once observed, Washington isn't filled with the wild kids who stuck the cat in the dryer; it's filled with the kind of kids who tattled on the kids who stuck the cat in the dryer.) But on this particular day, I was invited to appear on a panel at the Public Theater in New York, the company that would later launch the musical *Hamilton*. I think we were supposed to talk about the role of the arts in public life. The actress Anne Hathaway was on the panel with me, along with a hilarious and highbrow clown named Bill Irwin and a few others. At this panel, D.C. think-tank rules didn't apply. Backstage, before the panel, everybody was cheering each other on. We gathered for a big group hug. We charged out into the theater filled with camaraderie and purpose. Hathaway sang a moving song. There were tissues on the stage in case anybody started crying. The other panelists started emoting things. They talked about magical moments when they were undone, transported, or transformed by some artwork or play. Even I started emoting things! As my hero Samuel Johnson might have said, it was like watching a walrus trying to figure skate—it wasn't good, but you were impressed that you were seeing it at all. Then, after the panel, we celebrated with another group hug. I thought, "This is fantastic! I've got to be around theater people more!" I vowed to alter my life.

Yes, I'm the guy who had his life changed by a panel discussion.

Okay, it was a *little* more gradual than that. But over the years I came to realize that living in a detached way is, in fact, a withdrawal from life, an estrangement not just from other people but from yourself. So I struck out on a journey. We writers work out our stuff in public, of course, so I wrote books on emotion, moral character, and spiritual growth. And it kind of worked. Over the years, I altered my life. I made myself more vulnerable with people and more emotionally expressive in public. I tried to become the sort of person people would confide in—talk with me about their divorces, their grief over the death of their spouse, worries about their kids. Gradually, things began to change inside. I had these novel experiences: "What are these tinglings in my chest? Oh, they're *feelings*!" One day, I'm dancing at a concert: "Feelings are great!" Another day, I'm sad that my wife is away on a trip: "Feelings suck!" My life goals changed, too. When I was young, I wanted to be knowledgeable, but as I got older, I wanted to be wise. Wise people don't just possess information; they possess a compassionate understanding of other people. They know about life.

I'm not an exceptional person, but I am a grower. I do have the ability to look at my shortcomings, then try to prod myself into becoming a more fully developed human being. I've made progress over these years. Wait, I can prove this to you! Twice in my life I've been lucky enough to have appeared on Oprah's show *Super Soul Sunday,* once in 2015 and once in 2019. After we were done taping the second interview, Oprah came up to me and said, "I've rarely seen someone change so much. You were so blocked before." That was a proud moment for me. I mean, she should know—she's Oprah.

I learned something profound along the way. Being open-hearted is a prerequisite for being a full, kind, and wise human being. But it is not enough. People need social skills. We talk about the importance of "relationships," "community," "friendship," "social connection," but these words are too abstract. The real act of, say, building a friendship or creating a community involves performing a series of small, concrete social actions well: disagreeing without poisoning the relationship; revealing vulnerability at the appropriate pace; being a good listener; knowing how to end a conversation gracefully; knowing how to ask for and offer forgiveness; knowing how to let someone down without breaking their heart; knowing how to sit with someone who is suffering; knowing how to host a gathering where everyone feels embraced; knowing how to see things from another's point of view.

These are some of the most important skills a human being can possess, and yet we don't teach them in school. Some days it seems like we have intentionally built a society that gives people little guidance on how to perform the most important activities of life. As a result, a lot of us are lonely and lack deep friendships. It's not because we don't want these things. Above almost any other need, human beings long to have another person look into their face with loving respect and acceptance. It's that we lack practical knowledge about how to give each other the kind of rich attention we desire. I'm not sure Western societies were ever great at teaching these skills, but over the past several decades, in particular, there's been a loss of moral knowledge. Our schools and other institutions have focused more and more on preparing people for their careers, but not on the skills of being considerate toward the person next to you. The humanities, which teach us what goes on in the minds of other people, have become marginalized. And a life spent on social media is not exactly helping people learn these skills. On social media you can have the illusion of social contact without having to perform the gestures that actually build trust, care, and affection. On social media, stimulation replaces intimacy. There is judgment everywhere and understanding nowhere.

In this age of creeping dehumanization, I've become obsessed with social skills: how to get better at treating people with consideration; how to get better at understanding the people right around us. I've come to believe that the quality of our lives and the health of our society depends, to a large degree, on how well we treat each other in the minute interactions of daily life.

And all these different skills rest on one foundational skill: the ability to understand what another person is going through. There is one skill that lies at the heart of any healthy person, family, school, community organization, or society: the ability to see someone else deeply and make them feel seen—to accurately know another person, to let them feel valued, heard, and understood.

That is at the heart of being a good person, the ultimate gift you can give to others and to yourself.

———

Human beings need recognition as much as they need food and water. No crueler punishment can be devised than to *not* see someone, to render them unimportant or invisible. "The worst sin towards our fellow creatures is not to hate them," George Bernard Shaw wrote, "but to be indifferent to them: that's the essence of inhumanity." To do that is to say: You don't matter. You don't exist.

On the other hand, there are few things as fulfilling as that sense of being seen and understood. I often ask people to tell me about times they've felt seen, and with glowing eyes they tell me stories about pivotal moments in their life. They talk about a time when someone perceived some talent in them that they themselves weren't even able to see. They talk about a time when somebody understood exactly what they needed at some exhausted moment—and stepped in, in just the right way, to lighten the load.

Over the past four years I've become determined to learn the skills that go into seeing others, understandings others, making other people feel respected, valued, and safe. First, I've wanted to understand and learn these skills for pragmatic reasons. You can't make the big decisions in life well unless you're able to understand others. If you are going to marry someone, you have to know not just about that person's looks, interests, and career prospects but how the pains of their childhood show up in their adulthood, whether their deepest longings align with your own. If you're going to hire someone, you have to be able to see not just the qualities listed on their résumé but the subjective parts of their consciousness, the parts that make some people try hard or feel comfortable with uncertainty, calm in a crisis, or generous to colleagues. If you're going to retain someone in your company, you have to know how to make them feel appreciated. In a 2021 study, McKinsey asked managers why their employees were quitting their firms. Most of the managers believed that people were leaving to get more pay. But when the McKinsey researchers asked the employees themselves why they'd left, the top reasons were relational. They didn't feel recognized and valued by their managers and organizations. They didn't feel seen.

And if this ability to truly see others is important in making the marriage decision or in hiring and retaining workers, it is also important if you are a teacher leading students, a doctor examining patients, a host anticipating the needs of a guest, a friend spending time with a friend, a parent raising a child, a spouse watching the one you love crawl into bed at the end of the day. Life goes a lot better if you can see things from other people's points of view, as well as your own. "Artificial intelligence is going to do many things for us in the decades ahead, and replace humans at many tasks, but one thing it will never be able to do is to create person-to-person connections. If you want to thrive in the age of AI, you better become exceptionally good at connecting with others."

Second, I wanted to learn this skill for what I think of as spiritual reasons. Seeing someone well is a powerfully creative act. No one can fully appreciate their own beauty and strengths unless those things are mirrored back to them in the mind of another. There is something in being seen that brings forth growth. If you beam the light of your attention on me, I blossom. If you see great potential in me, I will probably come to see great potential in myself. If you can understand my frailties and sympathize with me when life treats me harshly, then I am more likely to have the strength to weather the storms of life. "The roots of resilience," the psychologist Diana Fosha writes, "are to be found in the sense of being understood by and existing in the mind and heart of a loving, attuned, and self-possessed other." In how you see me, I will learn to see myself.

And third, I wanted to learn this skill for what I guess you'd call reasons of national survival. Human beings evolved to live in small bands with people more or less like themselves. But today, many of us live in wonderfully pluralistic societies. In America, Europe, India, and many other places, we're trying to build mass multicultural democracies, societies that contain people from diverse races and ethnicities, with different ideologies and backgrounds. To survive, pluralistic societies require citizens who can look across difference and show the kind of understanding that is a prerequisite of trust—who can say, at the very least, "I'm beginning to see you. Certainly, I will never fully experience the world as you experience it, but I'm beginning, a bit, to see the world through your eyes."

Our social skills are currently inadequate to the pluralistic societies we are living in. In my job as a journalist, I often find myself interviewing people who tell me they feel invisible and disrespected: Black people feeling that the systemic inequities that afflict their daily experiences are not understood by whites, rural people feeling they are not seen by coastal elites, people across political divides staring at each other with angry incomprehension, depressed young people feeling misunderstood by their parents and everyone else, privileged people blithely unaware of all the people around them cleaning their houses and serving their needs, husbands and wives in broken marriages who realize that the person who should know them best actually has no clue. Many of our big national problems arise from the fraying of our social fabric. If we want to begin repairing the big national ruptures, we have to learn to do the small things well.

———

In every crowd there are Diminishers and there are Illuminators. Diminishers make people feel small and unseen. They see other people as things to be used, not as persons to be befriended. They stereotype and ignore. They are so involved with themselves that other people are just not on their radar screen.

Illuminators, on the other hand, have a persistent curiosity about other people. They have been trained or have trained themselves in the craft of understanding others. They know what to look for and how to ask the right questions at the right time. They shine the brightness of their care on people and make them feel bigger, deeper, respected, lit up.

I'm sure you've experienced a version of this: You meet somebody who seems wholly interested in you, who gets you, who helps you name and see things in yourself that maybe you hadn't even yet put into words, and you become a better version of yourself.

A biographer of the novelist E. M. Forster wrote, "To speak to him was to be seduced by an inverse charisma, a sense of being listened to with such intensity that you had to be your most honest, sharpest, and best self." Imagine how good it would be to be that guy.

Perhaps you know the story that is sometimes told of Jennie Jerome, who later became Winston Churchill's mother. It's said that when she was young, she dined with the British statesman William Gladstone and left thinking he was the cleverest person in England. Later she dined with Gladstone's great rival, Benjamin Disraeli, and left that dinner thinking *she* was the cleverest person in England. It's nice to be like Gladstone, but it's better to be like Disraeli.

Or consider a story from Bell Labs. Many years ago, executives there realized that some of their researchers were far more productive, and amassed many more patents, than the others. Why was this? they wondered. They wanted to know what made these researchers so special. They explored every possible explanation—educational background, position in the company—but came up

empty. Then they noticed a quirk. The most productive researchers were in the habit of having breakfast or lunch with an electrical
engineer named Harry Nyquist. Aside from making important
contributions to communications theory, Nyquist, the scientists
said, really listened to their challenges, got inside their heads, asked
good questions, and brought out the best in them. In other words,
Nyquist was an Illuminator.

So what are you most of the time, a Diminisher or an Illuminator? How good are you at reading other people?

I probably don't know you personally, but I can make the following statement with a high degree of confidence: You're not as
good as you think you are. We all go through our days awash in
social ignorance. William Ickes, a leading scholar on how accurate
people are at perceiving what other people are thinking, finds that
strangers who are in the midst of their first conversation read each
other accurately only about 20 percent of the time and close friends
and family members do so only 35 percent of the time. Ickes rates
his research subjects on a scale of "empathic accuracy" from 0 to
100 percent and finds great variation from person to person. Some
people get a zero rating. When they are in conversation with someone they've just met, they have no clue what the other person is
actually thinking. But other people are pretty good at reading others and score around 55 percent. (The problem is that people who
are terrible at reading others think they are just as good as those
who are pretty accurate.) Intriguingly, Ickes finds that the longer
many couples are married, the less accurate they are at reading
each other. They lock in some early version of who their spouse is,
and over the years, as the other person changes, that version stays

fixed—and they know less and less about what's actually going on in the other's heart and mind.

You don't have to rely on an academic study to know that this is true. How often in your life have you felt stereotyped and categorized? How often have you felt prejudged, invisible, misheard, or misunderstood? Do you really think you don't do this to others on a daily basis?

The purpose of this book is to help us become more skilled at the art of seeing others and making them feel seen, heard, and understood. When I started research on this subject, I had no clue what this skill consisted of. But I did know that exceptional people in many fields had taught themselves versions of this skill. Psychologists are trained to see the defenses people build up to protect themselves from their deepest fears. Actors can identify the core traits of a character and teach themselves to inhabit the role. Biographers can notice the contradictions in a person and yet see a life whole. Teachers can spot potential. Skilled talk show and podcast hosts know how to get people to open up and be their true selves. There are so many professions in which the job is to see, anticipate, and understand people: nursing, the ministry, management, social work, marketing, journalism, editing, HR, and on and on. My goal was to gather some of the knowledge that is dispersed across these professions and integrate it into a single practical approach.

So I embarked on a journey toward greater understanding, a journey on which I still have a long, long way to go. I gradually realized that trying to deeply know and understand others is not just about mastering some set of techniques; it's a way of life. It's like what actors who have gone to acting school experience: When they're onstage, they're not thinking about the techniques they learned in school. They've internalized them, so it is now just part of who they are. I'm hoping this book will help you adopt a different posture toward other people, a different way of being present with people, a different way of having bigger conversations. Living this way can yield the deepest pleasures.

One day, not long ago, I was reading a dull book at my dining room table when I looked up and saw my wife framed in the front doorway of our house. The door was open. The late afternoon light was streaming in around her. Her mind was elsewhere, but her gaze was resting on a white orchid that we kept in a pot on a table by the door.

I paused, and looked at her with a special attention, and had a strange and wonderful awareness ripple across my mind: "I *know* her," I thought. "I really know her, through and through."

If you had asked what it was exactly that I knew about her in that moment, I would have had trouble answering. It wasn't any collection of facts about her, or her life story, or even something expressible in the words I'd use to describe her to a stranger. It was the whole flowing of her being—the incandescence of her smile, the undercurrent of her insecurities, the rare flashes of fierceness, the vibrancy of her spirit. It was the lifts and harmonies of her music.

I wasn't seeing pieces of her or having specific memories. What I saw, or felt I saw, was the wholeness of her. How her consciousness creates her reality. It's what happens when you've been with someone for a while, endured and delighted together, and slowly grown an intuitive sense for how that person feels and responds. It might even be accurate to say that for a magical moment I wasn't seeing her, I was seeing out from her. Perhaps to really know another person, you have to have a glimmer of how they experience the world. To really know someone, you have to know how they know you.

The only word I can think of in the English language that captures my mental processes at that instant is "beholding." She was at the door, the light blazing in behind her, and I was beholding her. They say there is no such thing as an ordinary person. When you're beholding someone, you're seeing the richness of this particular human consciousness, the full symphony—how they perceive and create their life.

I don't have to tell you how delicious that moment felt—warm, intimate, profound. It was the bliss of human connection. "A lot of brilliant writers and thinkers don't have any sense for how people operate," the therapist and author Mary Pipher once told me. "To be able to understand people and be present for them in their experience—that's the most important thing in the world."

TWO

How Not to See a Person

A few years ago, I was sitting at a bar near my home in Washington, D.C. If you'd been there that evening, you might have looked at me and thought, "Sad guy drinking alone." I would call it "diligent scholar reporting on the human condition." I was nursing my bourbon, checking out the people around me. Because the bar was in D.C., there were three guys at a table behind me talking about elections and swing states. The man with his laptop at the table next to them looked like a junior IT officer who worked for a defense contractor. He had apparently acquired his wardrobe from the garage sale after the filming of *Napoleon Dynamite*. Down the bar there was a couple gazing deeply into their phones. Right next to me was a couple apparently on a first date, with the guy droning on about himself while staring at a spot on the wall about six feet over his date's head. As his monologue hit its tenth minute, I sensed that she was silently praying that she might spontaneously combust, so at least this date could be over. I felt the sudden urge to grab the guy by the nose and scream, "For the love of God—just once ask her a question!" I think this impulse of mine was justified, but I'm not proud of it.

In short, everybody had their eyes open, and nobody seemed to be seeing each other. We were all, in one way or another, acting like Diminishers. And in truth, I was the worst of them, because I was doing that thing I do: the size-up. The size-up is what you do when you first meet someone: You check out their look, and you immediately start making judgments about them. I was studying the bartender's Chinese-character tattoos and drawing all sorts of conclusions about her sad singer/indie rock musical tastes. I used to make a living doing this. Just over two decades ago I wrote a book called *Bobos in Paradise.* Doing research for that book, I followed people around places like the clothing and furniture store Anthropologie, watching them thumb through nubby Peruvian shawls. I'd case people's kitchens, checking out the Aga stove that looked like a nickel-plated nuclear reactor right next to their massive Sub-Zero fridge, because apparently mere zero wasn't cold enough for them. I'd make some generalizations and riff on the cultural trends.

I'm proud of that book. But now I'm after bigger game. I'm bored with making generalizations about groups. I want to see people deeply, one by one. You'd think this would be kind of easy. You open your eyes, direct your gaze, and see them. But most of us have all sorts of inborn proclivities that prevent us from perceiving others accurately. The tendency to do the instant size-up is just one of the Diminisher tricks. Here are a few others:

EGOTISM. The number one reason people don't see others is that they are too self-centered to try. I can't see you because I'm all about myself. Let *me* tell *you* my opinion. Let me entertain you with this story about myself. Many people are unable to step outside of their own points of view. They are simply not curious about other people.

ANXIETY. The number two reason people don't see others is that they have so much noise in their own heads, they can't hear what's going on in other heads. *How am I coming across? I don't think this person really likes me. What am I going to say next to appear clever?* Fear is the enemy of open communication.

NAÏVE REALISM. This is the assumption that the way the world appears to you is the objective view, and therefore everyone else must see the same reality you do. People in the grip of naïve realism are so locked into their own perspective, they can't appreciate that other people have very different perspectives. You may have heard the old story about a man by a river. A woman standing on the opposite shore shouts to him: "How do I get to the other side of the river?" And the man shouts back: "You *are* on the other side of the river!"

THE LESSER-MINDS PROBLEM. University of Chicago psychologist Nicholas Epley points out that in day-to-day life we have access to the many thoughts that run through our own minds. But we don't have access to all the thoughts that are running through other people's minds. We just have access to the tiny portion they speak out loud. This leads to the perception that I am much more complicated than you—deeper, more interesting, more subtle, and more high-minded. To demonstrate this phenomenon, Epley asked his business school students why they were going into business. The common answer was "I care about doing something worthwhile." When he asked them why they thought other students at the school were going into business, they commonly replied, "For the money." You know, because other people have lesser motivations . . . and lesser minds.

OBJECTIVISM. This is what market researchers, pollsters, and social scientists do. They observe behavior, design surveys, and collect data on people. This is a great way to understand the trends among populations of people, but it's a terrible way to see an individual person. If you adopt this detached, dispassionate, and objective stance, it's hard to see the most important parts of that person, her unique subjectivity—her imagination, sentiments, desires, creativity, intuitions, faith, emotions, and attachments—the cast of this unique person's inner world.

Over the course of my life, I've read hundreds of books by academic researchers who conduct studies to better understand human nature, and I've learned an enormous amount. I've also read hundreds of memoirs and spoken with thousands of people about their own singular lives, and I'm here to tell you that each particular life is far more astounding and unpredictable than any of the generalizations scholars and social scientists make about groups of people. If you want to understand humanity, you have to focus on the thoughts and emotions of individuals, not just data about groups.

ESSENTIALISM. People belong to groups, and there's a natural human tendency to make generalizations about them: Germans are orderly, Californians are laid-back. These generalizations occasionally have some basis in reality. But they are all false to some degree, and they are all hurtful to some degree. Essentialists don't recognize this. Essentialists are quick to use stereotypes to categorize vast swaths of people. Essentialism is the belief that certain groups actually have an "essential" and immutable nature. Essentialists imagine that people in one group are more alike than they really are. They imagine that people in other groups are more different from "us" than they really are. Essentialists are guilty of "stacking." This is the practice of learning one thing about a person, then making a whole series of further assumptions about that person. If this person supported Donald Trump, then this person must also be like this, this, this, and this.

THE STATIC MINDSET. Some people formed a certain conception of you, one that may even have been largely accurate at some point in time. But then you grew up. You changed profoundly. And those people never updated their models to see you now for who you really are. If you're an adult who has gone home to stay with your parents and realized that they still think of you as the child you no longer are, you know exactly what I'm talking about.

———

I'm breaking out these Diminisher proclivities to emphasize that seeing another person well is the hardest of all hard problems. Each person is a fathomless mystery, and you have only an outside view of who they are. The second point I'm trying to make is this:

The untrained eye is not enough. You'd never think of trying to fly a plane without going to flight school. Seeing another person well is even harder than that. If you and I are relying on our untrained ways of encountering others, we won't be seeing each other as deeply as we should. We'll lead our lives awash in social ignorance, enmeshed in relationships of mutual blindness. We'll count ourselves among the millions of emotional casualties: husbands and wives who don't really see each other, parents and children who don't really know each other, colleagues at work who might as well live in different galaxies.

It's disturbingly easy to be ignorant of the person right next to you. As you'll discover over the course of this book, I like to teach through examples, so let me tell you about a case that illustrates how you can think you know someone well without really knowing them. It's from Vivian Gornick's classic 1987 memoir *Fierce Attachments*. Gornick was thirteen when her father died of a heart attack, and her mother, Bess, was forty-six. Bess had always enjoyed the status of seeming to be the one woman in her working-class Bronx apartment building in a happy, loving marriage. Her husband's death undid her. At the funeral parlor she tried to climb into the coffin with him. At the cemetery she tried to throw herself into the open grave. For years after she would be deranged by paroxysms of grief, suddenly thrashing around on the floor, veins bulging, sweat flying.

"My mother's grief was primitive and all-encompassing: it sucked the oxygen out of the air," Gornick wrote in that memoir. Her mother's grief consumed everybody else's grief, gathered the world's attention on her, and reduced her children to props in her drama. Afraid to sleep alone, Bess would pull Vivian close, but

Vivian, repelled, would lie like a granite column, in this intimacy without togetherness that would last a lifetime. "She made me sleep with her for a year, and for twenty years afterward I could not bear a woman's hand on me."

For a while it seemed that Bess would grieve herself to death; instead, grief became her way of living. "Widowhood provided Mama with a higher form of being," Gornick wrote. "In refusing to recover from my father's death she had discovered that her life was endowed with a seriousness her years in the kitchen had denied her. . . . Mourning Papa became her profession, her identity, her persona."

Vivian spent her adult years trying to win some measure of independence from this dominating, difficult, and thoroughly mesmerizing mother. But she kept getting drawn back. The two Gornick women would take long walks through New York City. They were both highly critical, vehement, dismissive—masters of the New York verbal put-down. They were intimate antagonists, both angry. "My relationship with my mother is not good, and as our lives accumulate it seems to worsen," Vivian wrote. "We are locked into a narrow channel of acquaintance, intense and binding." In Vivian's memoir, part of what divides them is personal— the record of hurts they've inflicted on each other. "She's burning and I'm glad to let her burn. Why not? I'm burning too." But part of it is also generational. Bess is a woman of the 1940s and 1950s urban working class and sees the world through that prism. Vivian is a woman of 1960s and 1970s liberal arts academia and sees the world through that prism. Vivian thinks Bess and her generation of women should have fought harder against sexism all around them. Bess thinks Vivian's generation has taken the nobility out of life.

One day while they're walking, Bess blurts out, "A world full of crazies. Divorce everywhere.... What a generation you all are!"

Vivian shoots back, "Don't start, Ma. I don't want to hear that bullshit again."

"Bullshit here, bullshit there. It's still true. Whatever else we did, we didn't fall apart in the streets like you're all doing. We had order, quiet, dignity. Families stayed together, and people lived decent lives."

"That's a crock," Vivian responds. "They didn't live decent lives, they lived hidden lives."

They eventually agree that people were equally unhappy in both generations, but, Bess observes, "The unhappiness is so *alive* today." They both pause, startled, and enjoy the observation. Vivian is briefly proud of when her mother says a clever thing, comes close to loving her.

Still, Vivian is struggling to be recognized, to have the kind of mother who understands the effect she has on her own daughter. "She doesn't know I take her anxiety personally, feel annihilated by her depression. How can she know this? She doesn't even know I'm there. Were I to tell her that it's death to me, her not knowing I'm there, she would stare at me out of her eyes crowding up with puzzled desolation, this young girl of seventy-seven, and she would cry angrily, 'You don't understand! You have never understood!'"

When Bess is eighty, the tenor of their relationship softens as they both seem more aware that death is closing in. Bess even shows some self-awareness: "I had only your father's love. It was the only sweetness in my life. So I loved his love. What could I have done?"

Vivian is angry. She reminds her mother that she was only forty-six when her husband died. She could have created another life.

"Why don't you go already?" Bess snaps. "Why don't you walk away from my life? I'm not stopping you."

But their attachment is unbreakable. Vivian's retort is the final sentence of the book: "I know you're not, Ma."

Fierce Attachments is a brilliant description of seeing but not really seeing. Here are two smart, dynamic, highly verbal women in lifelong communication who are never quite able to understand each other. Gornick's book is so good because it illustrates that even in cases where we're devoted to a person, and know a lot about them, it's still possible to not see them. You can be loved by a person yet not be known by them.

Part of the reason the Gornicks can't see each other is because they pay attention only to the effect the other has on them. Vivian and Bess are belligerents locked in a struggle over where the blame is going to lie. Part of the problem is Bess. Bess is so involved in her own drama that she never sees from her daughter's point of view, or even notices the effect she has on her daughter. But some of the problem lies with Vivian, too. Her intent in writing *Fierce Attachments* had been to create a voice that could finally stand up to her mother, and to figure out a way to detach from her. But Vivian is so busy trying to break free, she never really asks, Who is my mother, apart from her relationship with me? What was her childhood like and who were her parents? We never get to see how Bess experiences the world, who she might be outside of her relationship with her daughter. In essence, mother and daughter are so busy making their own case, they can't get inside the other's perspective.

I'm haunted by a phrase Vivian uses in the book: "She doesn't even know I'm there." Her own mother doesn't know she's there. How many people suffer through this feeling?

Being an Illuminator, seeing other people in all their fullness, doesn't just happen. It's a craft, a set of skills, a way of life. Other cultures have words for this way of being. The Koreans call it *nunchi,* the ability to be sensitive to other people's moods and thoughts. The Germans (of course) have a word for it: *herzensbildung,* training one's heart to see the full humanity in another.

What exactly are these skills? Let's explore them, step by step.

THREE

Illumination

A few years ago, I was in Waco, Texas. I was there to find and interview Weavers, the kind of community builders who knit towns and neighborhoods together, who drive civic life. It's not hard to find such people. You simply go to a place and ask residents, "Who is trusted around here? Who makes this place run?" People will start offering you the names of the people they admire, the people who hold up and work for the community.

In Waco, a number of people told me about a ninety-three-year-old Black woman named LaRue Dorsey. I reached out, and we arranged to get together over breakfast at a diner. She'd spent her career mostly as a teacher, and I asked her about her life and the communities she was part of in Waco.

Every journalist has their own interviewing style. Some reporters are seducers. They lure you into giving them information by showering you with warmth and approval. Some are transaction-alists. Their interviews are implicit bargains: If you give me information about this, I'll give you information about that. Others are simply delightful, magnetic personalities. (I have a theory that my friend Michael Lewis has been able to write so many great books because he's just so damn likable that people will divulge anything simply to keep him hanging around.) My mode, I suppose, is that of a student. I'm earnest and deferential, not overly familiar. I ask people to teach me things. I generally don't get too personal.

That morning over breakfast, Mrs. Dorsey presented herself to me as a stern drill sergeant type, a woman, she wanted me to know, who was tough, who had standards, who laid down the law. "I loved my students enough to discipline them," she told me. I was a bit intimidated by her.

In the middle of the meal, a mutual friend named Jimmy Dor-rell entered the diner. Jimmy is a teddy-bearish white man in his sixties who built a church for homeless people under a highway overpass, who leads a homeless shelter by his house, who serves the poor. He and Mrs. Dorsey had worked together on various community projects over the years.

He saw her across the room and came up to our table smiling as broadly as it is possible for a human face to smile. Then he grabbed her by the shoulders and shook her way harder than you should ever shake a ninety-three-year-old. He leaned in, inches from her face, and cried out in a voice that filled the whole place: "Mrs. Dorsey! Mrs. Dorsey! You're the best! You're the best! I love you! I love you!"

I've never seen a person's whole aspect transformed so suddenly. The old, stern disciplinarian face she'd put on under my gaze vanished, and a joyous, delighted nine-year-old girl appeared. By projecting a different quality of attention, Jimmy called forth a different version of her. Jimmy is an Illuminator.

At that moment, I began to fully appreciate the power of attention. Each of us has a characteristic way of showing up in the world, a physical and mental presence that sets a tone for how people interact with us. Some people walk into a room with an expression that is warm and embracing; others walk in looking cool and closed up. Some people first encounter others with a gaze that is generous and loving; other people regard those they meet with a formal and aloof gaze.

That gaze, that first sight, represents a posture toward the world. A person who is looking for beauty is likely to find wonders, while a person looking for threats will find danger. A person who beams warmth brings out the glowing sides of the people she meets, while a person who conveys formality can meet the same people and find them stiff and detached. "Attention," the psychiatrist Iain McGilchrist writes, "is a moral act: it creates, brings aspects of things into being." The quality of your life depends quite a bit on the quality of attention you project out onto the world.

The moral of my Waco story, then, is that you should attend to people more like Jimmy and less like me.

Now, you may think this is an unfair comparison. Jimmy had known Mrs. Dorsey for years. Of course he was going to be more familiar with her than I was going to be. Jimmy has a big, boisterous personality. If I tried to greet people the way Jimmy does, it would feel fake. It's just not me.

But the point I'm trying to make is more profound than that. Jimmy's gaze when he greets a person derives from a certain conception of what a person is. Jimmy is a pastor. When Jimmy sees a person—any person—he is seeing a creature who was made in the image of God. As he looks into each face, he is looking, at least a bit, into the face of God. When Jimmy sees a person, any person, he is also seeing a creature endowed with an immortal soul— a soul of infinite value and dignity. When Jimmy greets a person, he is also trying to live up to one of the great callings of his faith: He is trying to see that person the way Jesus would see that person. He is trying to see them with Jesus's eyes—eyes that lavish love on the meek and the lowly, the marginalized and those in pain, and on every living person. When Jimmy sees a person, he comes in with the belief that this person is so important that Jesus was willing to die for their sake. As a result, Jimmy is going to greet people with respect and reverence. That's how he's always greeted me.

Now, you may be an atheist, an agnostic, a Christian, a Jew, a Muslim, a Buddhist, or something else, but this posture of respect and reverence, this awareness of the infinite dignity of each person you meet, is a precondition for seeing people well. You may find the whole idea of God ridiculous, but I ask you to believe in the concept of a soul. You may just be chatting with someone about the weather, but I ask you to assume that the person in front of you contains some piece of themselves that has no weight, size, color, or shape yet gives them infinite value and dignity. If you consider that each person has a soul, you will be aware that each person has some transcendent spark inside them. You will be aware that at the deepest level we are all equals. We're not equal in might, intelligence, or wealth, but we are all equal on the level of our souls. If you see the people you meet as precious souls, you'll probably wind up treating them well.

If you can attend to people in this way, you won't be merely observing them or scrutinizing them. You'll be illuminating them with a gaze that is warm, respectful, and admiring. You'll be offering a gaze that says, "I'm going to trust you, before you trust me." Being an Illuminator is a way of being with other people, a style of presence, an ethical ideal.

When you're practicing Illuminationism, you're offering a gaze that says, "I want to get to know you and be known by you." It's a gaze that positively answers the question everybody is unconsciously asking themselves when they meet you: "Am I a person to you? Do you care about me? Am I a priority for you?" The answers to those questions are conveyed in your gaze before they are conveyed by your words. It's a gaze that radiates respect. It's a gaze that says that every person I meet is unique, unrepeatable, and, yes, superior to me in some way. Every person I meet is fascinating on some topic. If I approach you in this respectful way, I'll know that you are not a puzzle that can be solved but a mystery that can never be gotten to the bottom of. I'll do you the honor of suspending judgment and letting you be as you are. Respect is a gift you offer with your eyes.

In the previous chapter, I listed some of the qualities that make it hard to see others: egotism, anxiety, objectivism, essentialism, and so on. In this one I'd like to list some of the features of the Illuminator's gaze:

TENDERNESS. If you want to see a stellar example of how to illuminate people, go back and look at how Mister Rogers used to interact with children. Look at how Ted Lasso looks at his players on that TV show. Look at how Rembrandt rendered faces. When you are in the presence of a Rembrandt portrait, you're seeing the warts and wounds of the subject, but you're also peering into their depths, seeing their inner dignity, the immeasurable complexity of their inner lives. The novelist Frederick Buechner observed that not all the faces Rembrandt painted were remarkable. Sometimes the subject is just an old man or an elderly lady we wouldn't look at twice if we passed them on the street. But even the plainest faces "are so remarkably seen by Rembrandt that we are jolted into seeing them remarkably."

"Tenderness is deep emotional concern about another being," the novelist Olga Tokarczuk declared in her Nobel Prize acceptance speech. "Tenderness perceives the bonds that connect us, the similarities and the sameness between us." Literature, she argued, "is built on tenderness toward any being other than ourselves." And so is seeing.

RECEPTIVITY. Being receptive means overcoming insecurities and self-preoccupation and opening yourself up to the experience of another. It means you resist the urge to project your own viewpoint; you do not ask, "How would *I* feel if *I* were in your shoes?" Instead, you are patiently ready for what the other person is offering. As the theologian Rowan Williams put it, we want our minds to be slack and attentive at the same time, the senses relaxed, open, and alive, the eyes tenderly poised.

ACTIVE CURIOSITY. You want to have an explorer's heart. The novelist Zadie Smith once wrote that when she was a girl, she was constantly imagining what it would be like to grow up in the homes of her friends. "I rarely entered a friend's home without wondering what it might be like to never leave," she wrote. "That is, what it would be like to be Polish or Ghanaian or Irish or Bengali, to be richer or poorer, to say these prayers or hold those politics. I was an equal-opportunity voyeur. I wanted to know what it was like to be everybody. Above all, I wondered what it would be like to believe the sorts of things I didn't believe." What a fantastic way to train your imagination in the art of seeing others.

AFFECTION. We children of the Enlightenment live in a culture that separates reason from emotion. Knowing, for us, is an intellectual exercise. When we want to "know" about something, we study it, we collect data about it, we dissect it.

But many cultures and traditions never fell for this nonsense about the separation between reason and emotion, and so they never conceived of knowing as a brain-only, disembodied activity. In the biblical world, for example, "knowing" is also a whole-body experience. In the Bible, "knowing" can involve studying, having sex with, showing concern for, entering into a covenant with, being familiar with, understanding the reputation of. God is described as the perfect knower, the seer of all things, the one who sees not only with the objective eye of a scientist but with the grace-filled eye of perfect love.

The human characters in the Bible are measured by how well they can imitate this affectionate way of knowing. They often fail during these dramas of recognition. In the parable of the Good Samaritan, an injured Jew lies beaten and left for dead on the side of the road. At least two other Jews, one of them a priest, pass him by, crossing to the other side of the street, not doing anything to help. They see him strictly intellectually. Only the Samaritan, a man from an alien and hated people, truly sees him. Only the Samaritan enters into the injured man's experience and actually does something to help him. In these biblical cases, where someone sees another without really seeing, these failures of knowledge are not intellectual failures; they are failures of the heart.

GENEROSITY. Dr. Ludwig Guttmann was a German Jew who escaped Nazi Germany in 1939 and found a job in a hospital in Britain that served paraplegics, mostly men injured in the war. When he first started working there, the hospital heavily sedated these men and kept them confined to their beds. Guttmann, however, didn't see the patients the way the other doctors saw them. He cut back on the sedatives, forced them out of bed, and started throwing balls at them and doing other things to get them active. As a result, he was summoned to a tribunal of his peers, where his methods were challenged.

"These are moribund cripples," one doctor asserted. "Who do you think they are?"

"They are the best of men," Guttmann replied.

It was his generosity of spirit that changed how he defined them. He continued organizing games, first at the hospital, then for paraplegics around the nation. In 1960 this led to the Paralympic Games.

A HOLISTIC ATTITUDE. A great way to mis-see people is to see only a piece of them. Some doctors mis-see their patients when they see only their bodies. Some employers mis-see workers when they see only their productivity. We must resist every urge to simplify in this way. The art historian John Richardson, Pablo Picasso's biographer, was once asked if Picasso was a misogynist and a bad guy. He would not let his subject be oversimplified or robbed of his contradictions. "That's a lot of nonsense," he replied. "Whatever you say about him—you say that he's a mean bastard—he was also an angelic, compassionate, tender, sweet man. The reverse is always true. You say he was stingy. He was also incredibly generous. You say that he was very bohemian, but also he had a sort of up-tight bourgeois side. I mean, he was a mass of antitheses." As are we all.

As the great Russian novelist Leo Tolstoy once wrote:

One of the commonest and most generally accepted delusions is that every man can be qualified in some particular way— said to be kind, wicked, stupid, energetic, apathetic and so on. People are not like that. We may say of a man that he is more often kind than cruel, more often wise than stupid, more often energetic than apathetic or vice versa; but it could never be true to say of one man that he is kind or wise, and of another that he is wicked or stupid. Yet we are always classifying mankind in this way. And it is wrong. Human beings are like rivers; the water is one and the same in all of them but every river is narrow in some places, flows swifter in others; here it is broad, there still, or clear, or cold, or muddy or warm. It is the same with men. Every man bears within him the germs of every human quality, and now manifests one, now another, and frequently he is quite unlike himself, while still remaining the same man.

Being an Illuminator is an ideal, and one that most of us will fall short of a lot of the time. But if we try our best to illuminate people with a glowing gaze that is tender, generous, and receptive, we'll at least be on the right track. We will see beyond the cliché character types we often lazily impose on people: the doting grandmother, the tough coach, the hard-charging businessperson. We will be on our way toward improving how we show up in the world.

"Every epistemology becomes an ethic," the educator Parker J. Palmer once observed. "The shape of our knowledge becomes the shape of our living; the relation of the knower to the known becomes the relation of the living self to the larger world." Palmer is saying that the way we attend to others determines the kind of person we become. If we see people generously, we will become generous, or if we view them coldly, we will become cold. Palmer's observation is essential, because he is pointing to a modern answer to an ancient question: How do I become a better person?

Over the centuries, male writers and philosophers—think of Immanuel Kant—have built these vast moral systems that portray moral life as something that disinterested, rational individuals do by adhering to abstract universal principles: always treat human beings as an end in themselves, and not as a means to something else. That emphasis on abstract universal principles is fine, I suppose, but it's impersonal and decontextualized. It's not about how this one unique person should encounter another unique person. It's as if these philosophers were so interested in coming up with coherent abstract principles and philosophically impregnable systems that they became afraid of particular people—messy creatures that we are, and the messy situations we find ourselves in—and the personal encounters that are the sum and substance of our daily existence.

Along comes the philosopher and novelist Iris Murdoch in the second half of the twentieth century, offering us something else. She argues that morality is not mostly about abstract universal principles, or even about making big moral decisions during climactic moments: Do I report fraud when I see it at work? Morality is mostly about how you pay attention to others. Moral behavior happens continuously throughout the day, even during the seemingly uneventful and everyday moments.

For Murdoch, the essential immoral act is the inability to see other people correctly. Human beings, she finds, are self-centered beings, anxiety-ridden and resentful. We are constantly representing people to ourselves in self-serving ways, in ways that gratify our egos and serve our ends. We stereotype and condescend, ignore and dehumanize. And because we don't see people accurately, we treat them wrongly. Evil happens when people are unseeing, when they don't recognize the personhood in other human beings.

By contrast, the essential moral act for Murdoch is being able to cast a "just and loving attention" on another person. "Love is knowledge of the individual," she writes. That doesn't mean you have to romantically swoon for everybody you meet. It means that a good person tries to look at everyone with a patient and discerning regard, tries to resist self-centeredness and overcome prejudice, in order to see another person more deeply and with greater discernment. The good person tries to cast a selfless attention and to see what the other person sees. This kind of attention leads to the greatness of small acts: welcoming a newcomer to your workplace, detecting anxiety in somebody's voice and asking what's wrong, knowing how to host a party so that everyone feels included. Most of the time, morality is about the skill of being considerate toward others in the complex situations of life. It's about being a genius at the close at hand.

But this kind of attention also does something more profound. To use grand, old-fashioned language, casting this kind of attention makes you a better person. In her celebrated lecture "The Sovereignty of Good over Other Concepts," Murdoch describes a mother-in-law, whom she calls M, who has contempt for her daughter-in-law, D. The mother-in-law is always perfectly polite to D, but inside, she looks down on her.

But M is aware that she can be a bit superior, conventional, and old-fashioned. M is also aware that she probably harbors some sense of rivalry with D; they're competing for her son's time and affections, after all. Perhaps, she realizes, she is seeing D in a way that is unworthy. So one day, as an act of intellectual charity and moral self-improvement, she decides she's going to change the way she sees D. Before she saw D as "coarse," but now she resolves to see her as "spontaneous." Before she thought D was "common," but now she will see her as "fresh." M is trying to purge herself of her snobbery and become a better person. This has nothing to do with her outer behavior, which has remained exemplary. It has to do with the purification of who she is inside. Good and evil, Murdoch believes, begin in the inner life, and M wants her inner life to be a little nicer and a little less mean.

Murdoch's emphasis on how we attend to people is personal, concrete, and very actionable. "Nothing in life is of any value except the attempt to be virtuous," Murdoch writes. We can, Murdoch writes, "grow by looking." I find this philosophy of moral development tremendously attractive and compelling.

————

Let me give you an example of somebody who embodies the "just and loving attention" that Murdoch is writing about. I've interviewed a therapist and author named Mary Pipher a couple of times over the past few years, to get a better idea of how she goes about the business of getting to know people. Pipher has had professional training, of course, but she told me that her trick when doing therapy is to have no tricks, to just engage in a conversation with the patient. Being a therapist, she argues, is less about providing solutions and more "a way of paying attention, which is the purest form of love."

She grew up in a town on the Nebraska prairie, amid clashing points of view. She had a rich aunt who was a liberal and a farmer uncle who was a conservative. Her family members ran the gamut from the emotional to the reserved, the travelers to the stay-putters, the sophisticates to the provincials. An education in human variety prepares you to welcome new people into your life.

"In therapy, as in life, point of view is everything," Pipher writes in her book *Letters to a Young Therapist*. In her practice, she projects a happy realism. The old grand masters of her field, like Freud, saw people driven by dark drives, repressions, and competitive instincts, but Pipher, who cut her professional teeth as a waitress, sees vulnerable, love-seeking people sometimes caught in bad situations. She tries to inhabit each person's point of view and see them, sympathetically, as those who are doing the best they can. Her basic viewpoint is charitable to all comers.

Some therapists try to separate patients from their families. Pipher says that they are quick to see the problems in a family, give it a label—dysfunctional—and then blame the family for whatever is afflicting the patient. And, of course, in many cases, families really are abusive and the victims need to break free. But Pipher, characteristically, looks for the good. "While families are imperfect institutions, they are also our greatest source of meaning, connection, and joy," she writes. "All families are a little crazy, but that is because all humans are a little crazy." After one difficult family session, she overheard a father offering to take his family out for ice cream. Pipher called them back into her office to congratulate him on being so generous and kind and watched his eyes well up with tears.

She doesn't feel the need to fill the air with a constant stream of words. "Inspiration is very polite," she writes. "She knocks softly and then goes away if we don't answer the door." The questions she asks are intended to steer people toward the positive: Isn't it time you forgave yourself for that? When you and your parents are close again, what will you want them to understand about this time in your life? Early in her career, she tried to understand people by asking how others treated or mistreated them. As she matured, she found it more useful to ask, How do you treat others? How do you make them feel?

She is offering the kind of attention that can change people.

Pipher tells the story of another therapist who was working with a mother and daughter who were chronically furious with each other. During one session, they were again going after each other hammer and tong, their comments laced with resentment, criticism, and blame. Then there was a brief silence. The mother broke it by saying, "I'm thinking of the phrase 'paint oneself into a corner.'" The daughter was shocked. That was the exact phrase that had been circling around in her own mind as she'd tried to think about how she and her mother had gotten themselves into this situation. At that moment, after all the strife, they both cast down their weapons and saw each other differently. The therapist congratulated the mother and said, "I'll just leave you two alone to talk about this further." That's a moment of illumination.

FOUR

Accompaniment

Loren Eiseley, an American naturalist, was doing some fieldwork on the Platte River, which runs through Mary Pipher's Nebraska and then flows into the Missouri and eventually down into the Gulf of Mexico. He was trekking through thick brush when suddenly he broke through a willow thicket and found himself standing ankle-deep in the river, his feet drenched. He was hot and thirsty after miles of walking and there was no one around, so he took off his clothes and sat down in the water.

At that moment, he experienced what he called an "extension of the senses," an awareness that this river he was immersed in was a part of the whole North American watershed, starting with the cold little streams in snow-covered glaciers and flowing south into mighty rivers and then into oceans, and that he, too, was part of this vast flow. A thought came to him: "I was going to float."

If you know anything about the Platte River, you know the saying that the Platte is a mile wide and an inch deep. It's a shallow river, about knee-deep where Eiseley was. But to him, this was no trivial depth. For he did not know how to swim. A childhood near-death experience had given him a permanent fear of water, and the Platte, while shallow, does have its swirls, holes, and patches of quicksand, so the thought of floating in it came wrapped in fear, nervousness, and exhilaration.

Still, he lay on his back on the water and began to drift, savoring the sensation of it, asking, What does it feel like to be a river? He was washing away the boundaries between himself and the river he was now part of. "The sky wheeled over me. For an instant, as I bobbed into the main channel, I had the sensation of sliding down the vast tilted face of the continent. It was then that I felt cold needles of the alpine springs at my fingertips, and the warmth of the Gulf pulling me southward," he wrote later. "I was streaming over ancient sea-beds thrust aloft where giant reptiles had once sported; I was wearing down the face of time and trundling cloud-wreathed ranges into oblivion. I touched my margins with the delicacy of a crayfish's antennae, and felt great fishes glide about their work."

Eiseley's essay about this experience is called "The Flow of the River." In it, he's not only describing the Platte; he's describing how he felt he was merging with the river. He recounts a sort of open awareness of the connections between all creatures, all nature. He wasn't swimming in the river. He wasn't investigating the river. He was accompanying the river.

After the illuminating gaze, accompaniment is the next step in getting to know a person.

Ninety percent of life is just going about your business. It's a meeting at work, a trip to the supermarket, or small talk with another parent while dropping the kids off at school. And usually there are other people around. In these normal moments of life, you're not staring deeply into another's eyes or unveiling profound intimacies. You're just doing stuff together—not face-to-face but side by side. You are accompanying each other.

When you're first getting to know someone, you don't want to try to peer into their souls right away. It's best to look at something together. What do you think of the weather, Taylor Swift, gardening, or the TV series *The Crown*? You're not studying a person, just getting used to them. Through small talk and doing mundane stuff together your unconscious mind is moving with mine and we're getting a sense of each other's energy, temperament, and manner. We're attuning with each other's rhythms and moods and acquiring a kind of subtle, tacit knowledge about each other that is required before other kinds of knowledge can be broached. We're becoming comfortable with each other, and comfort is no small thing. Nothing can be heard in the mind until the situation feels safe and familiar to the body.

Small talk and just casually being around someone is a vastly underappreciated stage in the process of getting to know someone. Sometimes you can learn more about a person by watching how they talk to a waiter than by asking some profound question about their philosophy of life. Even when you know someone well, I find that if you don't talk about the little things on a regular basis, it's hard to talk about the big things.

This chapter is about how to get to know people a bit better during the daily routines of everyday life. There are ways of showing up that deepen connection and trust, and ways that do not. If you go through life with an efficiency/optimization mindset, you're just going to drop off your kids at nursery school in the shortest time possible and you and the other parents will be ships passing in the night. But I believe that Eiseley's float down the river gives us a different model for how to be present with other people.

Obviously, floating down a river is not the same as being in a meeting with someone or having coffee with an acquaintance. But there is something about Eiseley's attitude that is instructive and inspiring. Accompaniment, in this meaning, is an other-centered way of moving through life. When you're accompanying someone, you're in a state of relaxed awareness—attentive and sensitive and unhurried. You're not leading or directing the other person. You're just riding alongside as they experience the ebbs and flows of daily life. You're there to be of help, a faithful presence, open to whatever may come. Your movements are marked not by willfulness but by willingness—you're willing to let the relationship deepen or not deepen, without forcing it either way. You are acting in a way that lets other people be perfectly themselves.

The first quality I associate with accompaniment is *patience*. Trust is built slowly. The person who is good at accompaniment exercises what the philosopher Simone Weil called "negative effort." This is the ability to hold back and be aware of the other person's timetable. "We do not obtain the most precious gifts by going in search of them but by waiting for them," Weil wrote. The person who is good at accompaniment is decelerating the pace of social life. I know a couple who treasure friends who are what they call "lingerable." They are the sort of people you want to linger with at the table after a meal or in chairs outside by the pool, to let things flow, to let the relationship emerge. It's a great talent—to be someone others consider lingerable.

Getting to know someone else is always going to be a vulnerable proposition. Personal truths resent approaches that are too aggressive, too intense, too impatient. People rightly guard their own psychological space and erect gates that can be passed through only in their own good time. Before a person is going to be willing to share personal stuff, they have to know that you respect their personal stuff. They have to know that you see their reserve as a form of dignity, their withholding as a sign that they respect themselves.

Accompaniment is a necessary stage in getting to know a person precisely because it is so gentle and measured. As D. H. Lawrence put it:

> Whoever wants life must go softly towards life, softly as one would go towards a deer and fawn that are nestling under a tree. One gesture of violence, one violent assertion of self-will and life is gone. . . . But with quietness, with an abandon of self-assertion and a fullness of the deep true self one can approach another human being, and know the delicate best of life, the touch.

The next quality of accompaniment is *playfulness*. When Eiseley was floating down that river, he wasn't wearing his scientific hat. He was off on a lark. He was playing, enjoying an activity he found spontaneous and fun. When the hosts of retreats and workshops want the participants to get to know each other quickly, they encourage them to play together—whether by means of croquet, cards, music, charades, taking a walk, arts and crafts, or even floating down a river.

We do this because people are more fully human when they are at play. As the essayist Diane Ackerman notes in her book *Deep Play,* play isn't an activity; it's a state of mind.

For some, tennis is work. They're locked in that achievement mentality, trying to make progress toward some proficiency goal. But for others, tennis is play—a movement that feels fun and absorbing in itself. Their whole manner is loose; they celebrate happily when they hit a good volley, cheer when their opponent does. For some, science is work—winning status and getting grants. But I know an astronomer for whom science is play. When she's talking about black holes or distant galaxies, she sounds like an eleven-year-old bubbling over with excitement: She's got these cool telescopes and she gets to look at cool things!

When I'm playing basketball with my friends, the quality of our game may be wanting, but we're at play and it brings us together. We're coordinating movements. We're passing the ball to each other and weaving in and out, trying to get open. There's a kind of spontaneous communication: the cheering, the high fives, the strategizing, the trash talk. I know some guys who've been in a monthly basketball game together for years. They may never have had a deep conversation, but they'd lay down their lives for one another, so deep are the bonds between them—bonds that were formed by play.

In the midst of play, people relax, become themselves, and connect without even trying. Laughter is not just what comes after jokes. Laughter happens when our minds come together and something unexpected happens: We feel the ping of common recognition. We laugh to celebrate our shared understanding. We see each other.

In her memoir *Let's Take the Long Way Home,* the writer Gail Caldwell describes how her deep friendship with a woman named Caroline was formed. It happened during play, either rowing sculls on the Charles River in Boston or going out in the woods to train their dogs together. Gail and Caroline would spend hours working with their dogs, dissecting the different meanings the word "no" can have when spoken to a canine. "If the two of us had had our trust shaken in lousy relationships, it was being rebuilt here, with tools we hadn't quite been aware we possessed," she writes. "For us, dog training was a shared experience of such reward that the education was infused throughout the friendship. Much of training a dog is instinctive; it is also a complex effort of patience and observation and mutual respect." Through the rhythms of this kind of play, Gail and Caroline passed through a series of intimacy gradients. They went from "mutual caution to inseparable ease, and so much of it now seems like a careful, even silent exchange."

It's amazing how much you can come to know someone, even before any deep conversations happen. When my oldest son was an infant, he woke up every morning at around four. At the time, we were living in Brussels, where it doesn't get light in wintertime until almost nine. So I'd have four or five hours each morning in the dark to play—to bounce him on my chest, to run his wooden trains, to tickle him and laugh. One day as I was lying on the couch, holding his hands, and he was bouncing on my stomach with his shaky legs, it occurred to me that I knew him best of any person on the planet, and that of all the people on the planet, he probably knew me best, because while innocently playing with him I'd been so emotionally open and spontaneous. It also occurred to me that though we knew each other so well, we had never had a conversation, because he could not yet talk. All of our communication was through play, touch, and glance.

The third quality of accompaniment I should mention is the *other-centeredness* of it. Eiseley wasn't thinking about himself or his ego in that river. He was partially losing his self and transcending his ego. He was letting the river lead.

In normal life, when you're accompanying someone, you're signing on to another person's plan. We're most familiar with the concept of accompaniment in the world of music. The pianist accompanies the singer. They are partners, making something together, but the accompanist is in the supportive role, subtly working to embellish the beauty of the song and help the singer shine. The accompanist is sensitive to what the singer is doing, begins to get a feel for the experience she is trying to create. Accompaniment is a humble way of being a helpful part of another's journey, as they go about making their own kind of music.

The accompanist is not controlling the journey, but neither is she a passive bystander. Let me try to illustrate this delicate balance by describing a time when I screwed it up, drawn from the mundane circumstances of everyday life. My two sons both played baseball at a high level. One boy is eight years older than the other, so by the time the younger was about twelve, I'd been around youth baseball for about a decade, watching the professional coaches the league had hired to manage the older boy's squads. My younger son's coach on his club team that year was another dad, not a pro, and I volunteered to assist. It quickly became clear, at least to me, that I knew a lot more about coaching youth baseball than the coach, simply because I had a lot more experience around the sport.

So I began peppering him with my genius ideas about how to run practice, throw batting practice, make mid-game adjustments. Obviously, this was purely a case of selfless me being of service to the team. Obviously, it wasn't about any latent desire to show how much I knew, or to attract attention, or to be in control. Obviously, my behavior could have had *nothing* to do with the male ego in the presence of competitive sports.

The coach immediately sensed that I was getting inside his zone and threatening his authority. So of course his defensive walls went up. What could have been our mutual play with the boys turned into a subtle rivalry for power. Our relationship, which could have been warm, because he was a good guy, cooled. He rarely accepted the brilliant pointers I was offering.

If I'd been better schooled back then in the art of accompaniment, I would have understood how important it is to honor another person's ability to make choices. I hope I would have understood, as good accompanists do, that everybody is in their own spot, on their own pilgrimage, and your job is to meet them where they are, help them chart their own course. I wish I had followed some advice that is rapidly becoming an adage: Let others voluntarily evolve. I wish I had understood then that trust is built when individual differences are appreciated, when mistakes are tolerated, and when one person says, more with facial expressions than anything else, "I'll be there when you want me. I'll be there when the time is right."

Accompaniment often involves a surrender of power that is beautiful to behold. A teacher could offer the answers, but he wants to walk with his students as they figure out how to solve a problem. A manager could give orders, but sometimes leadership means assisting employees as they become masters of their own task. A writer could blast out her opinions, but writers are at their best not when they tell people what to think but when they provide a context within which others can think. Pope Paul VI said it wonderfully: "Modern man listens more willingly to witnesses than teachers, and if he does listen to teachers, it's because they are witnesses."

Finally, a person who is good at accompaniment understands the art of *presence*. Presence is about showing up. Showing up at weddings and funerals, and especially showing up when somebody is grieving or has been laid off or has suffered some setback or humiliation. When someone is going through a hard time, you don't need to say some wise thing; you just have to be there, with heightened awareness of what they are experiencing at that moment.

I recently read about a professor named Nancy Abernathy who was teaching first-year med students, leading a seminar on decision-making skills, when her husband, at age fifty, died of a heart attack while cross-country skiing near their Vermont home. With some difficulty, she managed to make it through the semester and carried on with her teaching. One day she mentioned to the class that she was dreading teaching the same course the next year, because each year, during one of the first sessions of the course, she asks everybody to bring in family photos so they can get to know one another. She wasn't sure if she could share a photo of her late husband during that session without weeping.

The course ended. Summer came and went, and fall arrived and, with it, the day she dreaded. The professor entered the lecture hall, full of trepidation, and sensed something strange: The room was too full. Sitting there, along with her current class, were the second-year students, the ones who had taken her class the year before. They had come simply to lend their presence during this hard session. They knew exactly what she needed, and didn't need to offer anything more. "This is compassion," Abernathy later remarked. "A simple human connection between the one who suffers and one who would heal."

When I was teaching at Yale, I had a student, Gillian Sawyer, whose father died of pancreatic cancer. Before he died, she and her father talked about the fact that he would miss her major life events—a wedding she might have someday, her children growing up. After he died, she was the bridesmaid at a friend's wedding. The father of the bride gave a beautiful speech about his daughter's curiosity and spirit. When it came time for the father-daughter dance, Gillian excused herself to go to the restroom and have a cry. As she emerged, she saw that all the people from her table, many of them friends from college, were standing there by the door. She gave me permission to quote from her paper describing this moment: "What I will remember forever is that no one said a word. I am still amazed at the profoundness that can echo in silence. Each person, including newer boyfriends who I knew less well, gave me a reaffirming hug in turn and headed back to their seats. No one lingered or awkwardly tried to validate my grief. They were there for me, just for a moment, and it was exactly what I needed."

———

In his book *Consolations,* the essayist and poet David Whyte observed that the ultimate touchstone of friendship "is not improvement, neither of the other nor of the self, the ultimate touchstone is witness, the privilege of having been seen by someone and the equal privilege of being granted the sight of the essence of another, to have walked with them and to have believed in them, sometimes just to have accompanied them for however brief a span, on a journey impossible to accomplish alone."

Loren Eiseley, during his float down the Platte River, models for us a way of accompaniment in the natural environment. I've tried to capture his attitude during that float and show how it can inspire a way of being in the social environment. Eiseley's core point in his essay describing that event is that everything in nature is connected with everything else, and that you can understand this if you simply lie back and let that awareness wash over you. In social life, too, everybody is connected to everybody else by our shared common humanity. Sometimes we need to hitch a ride on someone else's journey, and accompany them a part of the way.

FIVE

What Is a Person?

On December 26, 2004, the French writer Emmanuel Carrère; his girlfriend, Hélène; and their respective sons were vacationing at a cliff-top hotel in Sri Lanka. The trip, frankly, was proving to be a bit of a dud. Carrère had thought that Hélène might be the love of his life, the one he'd grow old with. But it occurred to him that he was impressed by her but had never really loved her. It was clear that they were growing apart. Just the night before, on Christmas, they had talked seriously about separating. "We were simply watching ourselves draw apart, without hostility, but with regret," Carrère wrote. "It was too bad. For the umpteenth time I spoke of my inability to love, all the more remarkable in that Hélène is truly worthy of love."

As he awoke the next morning, Carrère found himself in a pessimistic, disillusioned state of mind. It was his fault the relationship was ending. He was self-absorbed, unable to open his heart. He reviewed his history of failed relationships and realized, with a pang of self-pity, that he was destined to become a lonely old man. A passage in the novel he was reading hit home: "I would have liked, this morning, a stranger's hand to close my eyes; I was alone, so I closed them myself."

Unsurprisingly, a kind of pall settled over Carrère, Hélène, and their boys. Sri Lanka's beauty failed to enchant. Three days into the trip, they were ready to go home. Feeling listless, they decided to cancel the scuba-diving lesson they'd scheduled for that morning.

It turned out to be a consequential decision, for that was the morning the tsunami hit.

Two days earlier, Carrère had met another French family at the hotel restaurant—Jérôme, Delphine, and their lovely four-year-old daughter, Juliette. The morning of the tsunami, Jérôme and Delphine had gone into town to get supplies, leaving Juliette playing on the beach with her grandfather. Juliette was splashing in the surf while her grandfather read the paper in a beach chair. Suddenly, the old man felt himself swept up in a wall of swirling black water, pretty sure that he would die, and certain that his granddaughter already had.

The wave carried him inland. He passed over houses, trees, a road. Then the wave reversed itself and the vast force of the receding water threatened to sweep him out into open ocean. He grabbed onto a palm tree and held on. A section of fence, carried in the water, pinned him to the trunk. Furniture, people, animals, wooden beams, and chunks of concrete rushed by.

When the water receded, he opened his eyes and realized that he was alive—and that the real nightmare had just begun. He slid down the tree trunk and stood in what was now shallow water. A woman's body floated past. He understood his mission was to get to town and find Juliette's parents. When he spotted them at last, he was struck by the realization that they were experiencing their last moments of pure happiness. He told them that Juliette was dead.

"Delphine screamed; Jérôme didn't," Carrère writes in his memoir. "He took Delphine in his arms and hugged her as tightly as he could while she screamed and screamed, and from then on he had only one objective: *I can no longer do anything for my daughter, so I will save my wife.*"

The task now was to cope with the devastation: to find Juliette's body and bring her home for burial. Carrère and his group had dinner with Delphine and Jérôme that night, the night of Juliette's death, then breakfast the next day, then lunch and then dinner again, and over and over. The two families clung to one another for the next several days, eating together, searching the hospitals for Juliette, comforting the other victims of the tsunami. Carrère watched Delphine absorb the blow over these meals. She was no longer crying or screaming. She stared into space. She ate very little. Her hand shook as she brought a forkful of rice to her mouth. Her entire model of the world had been organized around her relationship with her daughter. That model had just been blown apart. Jérôme watched her constantly, willing her to keep herself together.

Hélène, Carrère's girlfriend, leapt into action, was everywhere at once, offering practical and emotional help to the broken and devastated survivors who had dragged themselves back to the hotel. Hélène was a woman with a mission. She called the insurance companies and airlines, made travel arrangements, and sat with the mourners. She felt that she and Carrère were united by the same mission: to help the survivors. He, though, was having a different experience. He was still walled in on himself, and saw himself as useless. "I see myself rather as the insipid husband," he writes. In bed that first night, the night of the tsunami, he reached out for Hélène's fingertips in bed but didn't quite make contact. "It's as if I no longer exist," he thinks at one point.

Later Carrère went to the nearby hospital to help search for Juliette's body, dragging himself through rooms reeking with the stench of the corpses laid out in rows, bloated and gray. He and Delphine met a twenty-five-year-old Scottish woman, Ruth, who was on her honeymoon, and had been standing ten feet from her husband near the beach when the wave lifted them up and separated them. She waited day after day at the hospital, convinced that if she fell asleep she would miss him, and he would never come back to her alive. She hadn't eaten or slept in days. "Her determination is frightening," Carrère writes. "You can sense that she's quite close to passing to the other side, into catatonia, living death, and Delphine and I understand that our role is to prevent this."

There were practical details to look after, but there was also a lot of waiting, times when they were just sitting with each other and talking. Instinctively, they told each other their life stories. Delphine told Carrère about her family's life back in France, about how Jérôme would come home from work every day to have lunch with his wife and daughter, about Juliette's love for animals and the way she insisted on feeding the rabbits. Delphine described it as if that life was now centuries in the past.

Jérôme was still on his mission to save his wife. At meals, he tried to bear everyone up, telling stories, talking loudly, smoking, pouring drinks, refusing to let silence envelop them. At the same time, Carrère watched Jérôme watching Delphine: "Out of the corner of his eye, he kept watch over Delphine, and I remember thinking, there it is, real love, a man who truly loves his wife. There's nothing more beautiful. But Delphine remained silent, absent, horribly calm."

They were all circling around Delphine, implicitly begging: Don't leave. Stay with us. During dinner at a restaurant one night, Delphine watched a little boy slide into his mother's lap, stared as she petted him. Carrère put himself in Delphine's mind as this happened and imagined what she must have been seeing and thinking: how she will never again sit on her daughter's bed and read her to sleep with a story. Delphine watched the boy and his mother go off to their room. She met Carrère's eyes and with a slight smile murmured, "He's so little."

Ruth was finally able to use Hélène's phone to call her parents in Scotland, to tell them that she was alive. Carrère and Hélène were looking on as she talked on the phone. She began crying. Her tears became convulsive sobs. Her parents had just told her that her husband was in fact alive, and her tears morphed into laughter. Delphine, weeping, rushed up and enfolded Ruth in her arms.

The members of this small community, Carrère writes, were by then intimately connected and radically separated: connected by grief and separated by the blow that had hit one couple and spared the others. Carrère was certainly not self-absorbed now. He looked at the others across the dinner table. "I know that we loved them and I believe they loved us," he remembers later. He had entered the minds of each of the people around him, feeling their feelings, seeing a bit through their eyes, understanding the things they did to survive. His searing memoir is called *Lives Other Than My Own,* for that is the thing he has learned to see in this crisis: other people, other perspectives.

As they embarked on their long trip back to France, Carrère began to view Hélène differently. Before he had seen her as a bit glum. Now he envisioned her "as the heroine of a novel or an adventure film, the brave and beautiful journalist who in the heat of the action holds nothing back." They were taken in a van to a school where they could shower and gather their things. Carrère reflected on how fragile their bodies were. "I looked at Hélène's, so lovely, so weighed down with horror and fatigue. I felt not desire but a searing pity, a need to care, to cherish, to protect forever. I thought, She might have died. She is precious to me. So precious. I'd like her to be old someday. I'd like her flesh to be old and flabby, and I'd like still to love her. . . . A dam opened, releasing a flood of sorrow, relief, love, all mixed together. I hugged Hélène and told her, I don't want to break up anymore, not ever. She said, I don't want to break up anymore either." Carrère had made a resolution: He must spend his life with her. "I tell myself that this long life together *must* happen," he writes. "If I need to succeed at one thing before I die, it's this." What Carrère remembers about the next days is his fear that Hélène will leave him. What Hélène remembers is that those were the days when they truly came together. They ended up marrying and having a little girl of their own.

I tell you this story to make two points. The first is that it shows, in a concrete way, how different people can experience the same event in profoundly different ways. Each of the people in the Carrère vignette has been hit by a terrible blow, but each one feels it differently, depending on how the event has affected them, depending on their life history, and depending on the task the situation has thrown before them.

For Jérôme, it's straightforward: The tsunami launches him on a desperate mission to save his wife. He doesn't have to deliberate about that. The moment he hears of his daughter's death, he knows that his only job is to save Delphine. For Delphine, the task is simply to withstand the blow. For Hélène, the tsunami means coming into herself—being the person who serves others in a crisis. For Ruth, the task is to stand guard and will her husband back to life. At first Carrère experiences the tsunami through the prism of his own haplessness. He is the self-enclosed loner who hasn't risen to the occasion.

Events happen in our lives, but each person processes and experiences any given event in their own unique way. Aldous Huxley captured the core reality: "Experience is not what happens to you, it's what you do with what happens to you."

In other words, there are two layers of reality. There is the objective reality of what happens, and there is the subjective reality of how what happened is seen, interpreted, made meaningful. That second subjective layer can sometimes be the more important layer. As the Yale psychologist Marc Brackett puts it, "Well-being depends less on objective events than on how those events are perceived, dealt with, and shared with others." This subjective layer is what we want to focus on in our quest to know other people. The crucial question is not "What happened to this person?" or "What are the items on their résumé?" Instead, we should ask: "How does this person interpret what happened? How does this person see things? How do they construct their reality?" This is what we really want to know if we want to understand another person.

An extrovert walks into a party and sees a different room than an introvert does. A person who has been trained as an interior designer sees a different room than someone who's been trained as a security specialist. The therapist Irvin Yalom once asked one of his patients to write a summary of each group therapy session they did together. When he read her reports, Yalom realized that she experienced each session radically differently than he did. She never even heard the supposedly brilliant insights Yalom thought he was sharing with the group. Instead, she noticed the small personal acts—the way one person complimented another's clothing, the way someone apologized for being late. In other words, we may be at the same event together, but we're each having our own experience of it. Or, as the writer Anaïs Nin put it, "We do not see things as they are, we see things as we are."

The second reason I've told you this story is that it shows how a person's whole perspective, his or her way of seeing and interpreting and experiencing the world, can be transformed. In normal times our subjective consciousness changes gradually, but in the wake of shocking events it can change all at once.

At the start of the story Carrère believes himself to be a morose, self-absorbed, hapless man. He regards Hélène as an impressive woman he does not love. But the tsunami breaks him open and revolutionizes how he sees himself, how he sees Hélène, and how he experiences the world. A self-absorbed perspective is replaced with a more other-absorbed perspective. He sees himself as a man with a new task: to commit to this love that has welled up inside him, to ensure that he and Hélène spend the rest of their lives together. It isn't so much that he makes a rational decision to change how he sees Hélène and himself. Something erupts from deep within him, a transformation of his whole point of view.

Delphine's transformation is even more dramatic. As any parent can tell you, when a child is born you find that your perspective on life gets transformed. It is transformed again if a child is ripped from your life. Delphine had gotten used to living in a certain way—hugging Juliette, feeding Juliette, playing with Juliette. She had models in her head built around those common experiences. Now Juliette is gone, and the models in her mind don't accord with her new reality. Her life story will now be organized around Before and After. Before the tsunami, she had one perspective on life. After it, she will have to develop another perspective. She will have to go through a process of grief, with its moments of shocking pain, moments when old memories intrude into her mind. She will probably suffer from recurring bouts of agony and anguish as she contemplates the terror that must have descended on Juliette in her final seconds. But slowly, slowly, the models in her mind will re-form. Her point of view will adjust to her new external reality. Delphine will construct a perspective that incorporates Juliette as a presence in her memories and in her heart, forever part of how the post-tsunami Delphine sees the world. This process of grief and mental re-formation is also not something that can be consciously controlled. It flows along its own surprising and idiosyncratic course—again from somewhere deep within. Each mind is relentlessly remaking itself.

———

If you want to see and understand people well, you have to know what you are looking at. You have to know what a person *is*. And this traumatic vignette highlights a central truth about what human beings are: A person is a point of view. Every person you meet is a creative artist who takes the events of life and, over time, creates a very personal way of seeing the world. Like any artist, each person takes the experiences of a lifetime and integrates them into a complex representation of the world. That representation, the subjective consciousness that makes you you, integrates your memories, attitudes, beliefs, convictions, traumas, loves, fears, desires, and goals into your own distinct way of seeing. That representation helps you interpret all the ambiguous data your senses pick up, helps you predict what's going to happen, helps you discern what really matters in a situation, helps you decide how to feel about any situation, helps shape what you want, who you love, what you admire, who you are, and what you should be doing at any given moment. Your mind creates a world, with beauty and ugliness, excitement, tedium, friends, and enemies, and you live within that construction. People don't see the world with their eyes; they see it with their entire life.

Cognitive scientists call this view of the human person "constructionism." Constructionism is the recognition, backed up by the last half century of brain research, that people don't passively take in reality. Each person actively constructs their own perception of reality. That's not to say there is not an objective reality out there. It's to say that we have only subjective access to it. "The mind is its own place," the poet John Milton wrote, "and in itself / Can make a Heaven of Hell, a Hell of Heaven."

As we try to understand other people, we want to be constantly asking ourselves: How are they perceiving this situation? How are they experiencing this moment? How are they constructing their reality?

Let me dip briefly into brain science to try to show you how radical this process of construction is. Let's take an example as simple as the act of looking around a room. It doesn't feel like you're creating anything. It feels like you're taking in what's objectively out there. You open your eyes. Light waves flood in. Your brain records what you see: a chair, a painting, a dust bunny on the floor. It feels like one of those old-fashioned cameras—the shutter opens and light floods in and gets recorded on the film.

But this is not how perception really works. Your brain is locked in the dark, bony vault of your skull. Its job is to try to make sense of the world given the very limited amount of information that makes it into your retinas, through the optic nerves, and onto the integrative layer of the visual cortex. Your senses give you a poor-quality, low-resolution snapshot of the world, and your brain is then forced to take that and construct a high-definition, feature-length movie.

To do that, your visual system constructs the world by taking what you already know and applying it to the scene in front of you. Your mind is continually asking itself questions like "What is this similar to?" and "Last time I was in this situation, what did I see next?" Your mind projects out a series of models of what it expects to see. Then the eyes check in to report back about whether they are seeing what the mind expected. In other words, seeing is not a passive process of receiving data; it's an active process of prediction and correction.

Perception, the neuroscientist Anil Seth writes, is "a generative, creative act." It is "an action-oriented construction, rather than a passive registration of an objective external reality." Or as the neuroscientist Lisa Feldman Barrett notes, "Scientific evidence shows that what we see, hear, touch, taste, and smell are largely simulations of the world, not reactions to it." Most of us non-neuroscientists are not aware of all this constructive activity, because it happens unconsciously. It's as if the brain is composing vast, complex Proustian novels, and to the conscious mind it feels like no work at all.

Social psychologists take a wicked delight in exposing the flaws of this prediction-correction way of seeing. They do this by introducing things into a scene that we don't predict will be there and therefore don't see. You probably know about the invisible gorilla experiment. Researchers present subjects with a video of a group of people moving around passing a basketball and ask the subjects to count the number of passes by the team wearing white. After the video, the researchers ask, "Did you see the gorilla?" Roughly half the research subjects have no idea what the researchers are talking about. But when they view the video a second time, with the concept "gorilla" now in their heads, they are stunned to see that a man in a gorilla suit had strolled right into the circle, stood there for a few seconds, and then walked out. They didn't see it before because they didn't predict "gorilla."

In my favorite experiment of this sort, a researcher asks a student for directions to a particular place on a college campus. The student starts giving directions. Then a couple of "workmen"—actually, two other researchers—rudely carry a door between the directions asker and the directions giver. As the door passes between them, the directions asker surreptitiously trades places with one of the workmen. After the door has passed, the directions giver finds himself giving directions to an entirely different human being. And the majority of these directions givers don't notice. They just keep on giving directions. We don't expect one human being to magically turn into another, and therefore we don't see it when it happens.

In 1951 there was a particularly brutal football game between Dartmouth and Princeton. Afterward, fans of both teams were furious because, they felt, the opposing team had been so vicious. When psychologists had students rewatch a film of the game in a calmer setting, the students still fervently believed that the other side had committed twice as many penalties as their own side. When challenged about their biases, both sides pointed to the game film as objective proof that their side was right. As the psychologists researching this phenomenon, Albert Hastorf and Hadley Cantril, put it, "The data here indicate that there is no such 'thing' as a 'game' existing 'out there' in its own right which people merely 'observe.' The 'game' 'exists' for a person and is experienced by him only insofar as certain things have significances in terms of his purpose." The students from the different schools constructed two different games depending on what they wanted to see. Or as the psychiatrist Iain McGilchrist puts it, "The model we choose to use to understand something determines what we find."

Researchers like exposing the flaws in our way of seeing, but I'm constantly amazed at how brilliant the human mind is at constructing a rich, beautiful world. For example, in normal conversation, people often slur and mispronounce words. If you heard each word someone said in isolation, you wouldn't be able to understand 50 percent of them. But because your mind is so good at predicting what words probably should be in what sentence, you can easily create a coherent flow of meaning from other people's talk.

The universe is a drab, silent, colorless place. I mean this quite literally. There is no such thing as color and sound in the universe; it's just a bunch of waves and particles. But because we have creative minds, we perceive sound and music, tastes and smells, color and beauty, awe and wonder. All that stuff is in here in your mind, not out there in the universe.

I've taken this dip into neuroscience to give the briefest sense of just how much creative artistry every person is performing every second of the day. And if your mind has to do a lot of constructive work in order for you to see the physical objects in front of you, imagine how much work it has to undertake to construct your identity, your life story, your belief system, your ideals. There are roughly eight billion people on Earth, and each one of them sees the world in their own unique, never-to-be-repeated way.

If I want to see you, I want to see, at least a little bit, how you see the world. I want to see how you construct your reality, how you make meaning. I want to step, at least a bit, out of my point of view and into your point of view.

How do you do that? Constructionism suggests a way forward, a method to engage with others. In this approach, the last thing I want to do is pin you down and inspect you, as if you were some lab sample. I will not reduce you to a type or restrict you to a label, like many of those human-typology systems do—Myers-Briggs, the Enneagram, the zodiac, and so on.

Instead, I want to receive you as an active creator. I want to understand how you construct your point of view. I want to ask you how you see things. I want you to teach me about the enduring energies of old events that shape how you see the world today.

I'm going to engage *with* you. Looking at a person is different from looking at a thing because a person is looking back at you. I'm going to get to know you at the same time you're going to get to know me. Quality conversation is the essence of this approach.

If we're going to become Illuminators, we need to first ask questions and engage with answers. We need to ask: How does this look to you? Do you see the same situation I see? Then we need to ask: What are the experiences and beliefs that cause you to see it that way? For example, I might ask, What happened to you in childhood that makes you still see the world from the vantage point of an outsider? What was it about your home life that makes celebrating holidays and hosting dinner parties so important to you? You hate asking for favors. Why is that such an issue for you? You seem to have it all, and yet you are insecure. Why is that?

As we have these conversations, we're becoming more aware of the models we use to construct reality. We're getting to know each other better. We're also getting to know ourselves better.

———

Before the tsunami, Emmanuel Carrère saw himself as an isolated, loveless man. He viewed life through the prism of his ambition: "I who live in dissatisfaction, constant tension, running after dreams of glory and laying waste to my loves because I always imagine that one day, somewhere else, I'll find something better." He was imprisoned by a set of models that made him feel perpetually unsatisfied with his own life, perpetually unable to see the beauty of the people right around him.

The trauma of the tsunami rearranged his models. He was pushed into intimate contact with others' minds as they suffered great loss and endured great pain. He sat with these people, talked with them, entered into their experiences. He got to know others in powerful new ways and became something of an Illuminator.

When he entered into lives other than his own, his perspectives widened and deepened. He saw others differently, himself differently. He was humanized. He felt with more affection and saw the world with more wisdom. This is the effect that seeing others deeply tends to have on people. As the Harvard psychologist Robert Kegan has observed, what the eye sees more deeply the heart tends to love more tenderly.

The greatest thing a person does is to take the lessons of life, the hard knocks of life, the surprises of life, and the mundane realities of life and refine their own consciousness so that they can gradually come to see the world with more understanding, more wisdom, more humanity, and more grace. George Bernard Shaw got it right: "Life isn't about finding yourself. Life is about creating yourself."

SIX

Good Talks

Now we're really getting into it. So far, we've been exploring how to pay attention to a person, how to accompany a person, and what a person is. Now we're going to get into what it's like to really engage, to probe the deep recesses of another person's mind. This is one of the most crucial and difficult things a person can do. If you succeed at this task, you'll be able to understand the people around you, and if you fail, you will constantly misread them and make them feel misread. So where can you go to perform this grand, portentous, and life-altering endeavor?

Well, a park bench is nice.

The epic activity I'm describing is called . . . having a conversation. If a person is a point of view, then to know them well you have to ask them how they see things. And it doesn't work to try to imagine what's going on in their head. You have to ask them. You have to have a conversation.

The subtitle of this book is "The Art of Seeing Others Deeply and Being Deeply Seen." I chose that specifically because I wanted you to immediately get what I was writing about. But it's not quite accurate, if I'm being honest. If what we're doing here is studying how to really get to know another person, it should probably be "The Art of Hearing Others Deeply and Being Deeply Heard." Because getting to know someone else is usually more about talking and listening than about seeing.

Being a mediocre conversationalist is easy. Being a good conversationalist is hard. As I've tried to understand how to become a better conversationalist, I've found that I've had to overcome weird ideas about what a good conversationalist is like. A lot of people think a good conversationalist is someone who can tell funny stories. That's a raconteur, but it's not a conversationalist. A lot of people think a good conversationalist is someone who can offer piercing insights on a range of topics. That's a lecturer, but not a conversationalist. A good conversationalist is a master of fostering a two-way exchange. A good conversationalist is capable of leading people on a mutual expedition toward understanding.

Arthur Balfour was a British statesman renowned for, among other things, the Balfour Declaration of 1917, which announced British support for a Jewish homeland in Palestine. "Unhesitatingly I should put him down as the best talker I have ever known," his friend John Buchan once observed. Balfour's particular skill was not that he was capable of uncorking brilliant monologues or spewing strings of epigrams. Instead, he created "a communal effort which quickened and elevated the whole discussion and brought out the best in other people."

Balfour, Buchan continued,

would take the hesitating remark of a shy man and discover in it unexpected possibilities, would probe it and expand it until its author felt he had really made some contribution to human wisdom. In the last year of the War, he permitted me to take American visitors occasionally to lunch with him in Carlton Gardens, and I remember with what admiration I watched him feel his way with the guests, seize on some chance word and make it the pivot of speculations until the speaker was not only encouraged to give his best, but that best was infinitely enlarged by his host's contribution. Such guests would leave walking on air.

A good conversation is not a group of people making a series of statements at each other. (In fact, that's a bad conversation.) A good conversation is an act of joint exploration. Somebody floats a half-formed idea. Somebody else seizes on the nub of the idea, plays with it, offers her own perspective based on her own memories, and floats it back so the other person can respond. A good conversation sparks you to have thoughts you never had before. A good conversation starts in one place and ends up in another.

Does everybody know how to have a good conversation? Not by a long shot. I was once on a call with a government official who was lecturing me about something or other when our call dropped. I expected he'd call me right back. Five minutes passed. Seven.

Finally, I called his office. His assistant said he couldn't talk because he was on the phone. I told her, "You don't understand. He's on the phone with me! He doesn't realize that our call dropped ten minutes ago. He's just blathering on!" Maybe I bring this out in people, but I often find myself on the receiving end of what the journalist Calvin Trillin calls bore bombs—people who think conversation is them giving you a lecture. I've had to make a resolution: If you call me up or invite me for coffee and then talk at me with not even a single molecule's worth of interest in what I might be thinking, we will not be enjoying each other's company again.

And when it comes to my own conversational skills, I'm probably like everybody else: I think I'm better than I am. In my defense, it's not all my fault. We should explicitly teach people, from a young age, how to be good conversationalists. But we don't. In an attempt to make up for this lack, I've spent some time talking with conversation experts and reading their books. I've put together a list of some of the nonobvious ways to become a better conversationalist:

TREAT ATTENTION AS AN ON/OFF SWITCH, NOT A DIM-MER. We've all had the experience of telling somebody something and noticing that they are not really listening. It feels like you're sending a message out to them and they're just letting it fly past. You become self-conscious, start stumbling, and finally trail off.

The problem is that the average person speaks at the rate of about 120 to 150 words a minute, which is not nearly enough data to occupy the brain of the person being spoken to. If you are socially anxious, you probably have so many thoughts about yourself dancing around in your head, they threaten to hijack your attention from whatever the person in front of you is saying. The solution as a listener is to treat attention as all or nothing. If you're here in this conversation, you're going to stop doing anything else and just pay attention to *this*. You're going to apply what some experts call the SLANT method: sit up, lean forward, ask questions, nod your head, track the speaker. Listen with your eyes. That's paying attention 100 percent.

BE A LOUD LISTENER. When another person is talking, you want to be listening so actively that you're practically burning calories. Watch Oprah Winfrey, a true master of conversation, as she interviews someone. You can see her feeling, in her highly reactive way, the emotions the other person is describing. Her mouth hangs open in surprise, her eyes light up with delight. When the conversation takes a happy turn, she volleys back musical verbal affirmations: "Aahh . . . oooh . . . eeee," a subtle chorus of encouragements. When the conversation takes a sad or serious turn, she wears a concerned look on her face and sits in attentive silence, allowing a slowing pause that invites deeper reflection.

Or consider my friend Andy Crouch, who listens to other people as if he were a congregant in a charismatic church. While you're talking, he fills the air with grunts and *aha*s, *amen*s, *hallelujah*s, and cries of "Preach!" I love talking to that guy.

Everyone in a conversation is facing an internal conflict between self-expression and self-inhibition. If you listen passively, the other person is likely to become inhibited. *Active* listening, on the other hand, is an invitation to express. One way to think of it is through the metaphor of hospitality. When you are listening, you are like the host of a dinner party. You have set the scene. You're exuding warmth toward your guests, showing how happy you are to be with them, drawing them closer to where they want to go. When you are speaking, you are like a guest at a dinner party. You are bringing gifts.

FAVOR FAMILIARITY. You might think that people love to hear and talk about things that are new and unfamiliar. In fact, people love to talk about the movie they have already seen, the game they already watched. The social psychologist Gus Cooney and others have found that there is a "novelty penalty" when we speak. People have trouble picturing and getting excited about the unfamiliar, but they love to talk about what they know. To get a conversation rolling, find the thing the other person is most attached to. If they're wearing a T-shirt from their kid's sports team, ask about that. If they've got a nice motorcycle, lead with a question about it.

MAKE THEM AUTHORS, NOT WITNESSES. People aren't specific enough when they tell stories. They tend to leave out the concrete details. But if you ask them specific questions—"Where was your boss sitting when he said that? And what did you say in response?"— they are likely to revisit the moment in a more vivid way.

Good conversationalists ask for stories about specific events or experiences, and then they go even further. They don't only want to talk about what happened, they want to know how you experienced what happened. They want to understand what you were feeling when your boss told you that you were being laid off. Was your first thought "How will I tell my family?" Was your dominant emotion dread, humiliation, or perhaps relief?

Then a good conversationalist will ask how you're experiencing now what you experienced then. In retrospect, was getting laid off a complete disaster, or did it send you off on a new path that you're now grateful for? Sometimes things that are hard to live through are very satisfying to remember. It's your job to draw out what lessons they learned and how they changed as a result of what happened.

DON'T FEAR THE PAUSE. In some conversations, it's fun when everything is rapid-fire. People are telling funny stories or completing each other's sentences. But other times, somebody says something important that requires reflection. For her book *You're Not Listening,* Kate Murphy spent some time with the Second City improv club to learn how improv comedians listen to one another. While there, she met the artistic director, Matt Hovde. While teaching his classes on how to do improv, Hovde holds his arm straight out and asks, "If a story someone is telling you starts at the shoulder and ends at the fingertips, where do we stop listening?" For most people, around the elbow is where they stop really listening and start formulating their response. This is a problem, because speaking and listening involve many of the same brain areas, so once you go into response mode, your ability to listen deteriorates. Like a good improv comedian, a good conversationalist controls her impatience and listens to learn, rather than to respond. That means she'll wait for the end of the other person's comment, and then pause for a few beats to consider how to respond to what's been said, holding up her hand, so the other person doesn't just keep on talking. Taking that extra breath creates space for reflection.

In her book, Murphy notes that Japanese culture encourages

people to pause and reflect before replying. A study of Japanese businesspeople found that they are typically comfortable with eight-second pauses between one comment and another, roughly twice as long as Americans generally tolerate. They're wise to take that pause.

DO THE LOOPING. Psychologists have a concept they call looping. That's when you repeat what someone just said in order to make sure you accurately received what they were trying to project. Conversation experts recommend this somewhat clumsy practice because people tend to believe they are much more transparent than they really are, and that they are being clearer than they really are. Somebody might say, "My mother can be a real piece of work" and assume that the other person knows exactly what she's talking about.

The experts suggest that when somebody expresses something important, you respond to their story with a question like "What I hear you saying is that you were really pissed at your mother." If you try this looping method, you will realize how often you are interpreting people incorrectly; that speaker might come back with "No, I wasn't angry at my mother. I just felt diminished by her. There's a difference."

Looping forces you to listen more carefully. Other people will sense the change in you. Looping is also a good way to keep the other person focused on their core point, rather than drifting away on some tangent. The problem is that some people, including me, feel a little phony when we're looping. If I say, "So what I hear you saying is . . ." six times in a twenty-minute conversation, I'm going to wind up sounding more like a shrink performing analysis than a friend having a conversation. So I try to do it, but in a less formal way. I find it more natural to paraphrase what they just said—"So you're really pissed at your mom?"—and pause to see if they agree with my paraphrase.

THE MIDWIFE MODEL. Many good conversations are reciprocal. Both people talk about half of the time. But some good conversations are, by necessity, lopsided. One person is going through a hard time or facing a big life decision, and the other person is accompanying them in their process of deliberation.

When ministering to others in such circumstances, good conversationalists adopt the posture of a midwife. A midwife is there not to give birth but simply to assist the other person in their own creation. In conversation, a midwife is there not to lead with insights but to receive and build on the insights the other person is developing. The midwife is there to make the person feel safe, but she is also there to prod. There are always ways we're not fully honest with ourselves. The midwife is there to encourage a deeper honesty.

Parker J. Palmer is a prominent Quaker educator and the author of *To Know as We Are Known,* which I quoted in chapter 3. In the 1970s he was offered the chance to become a college president. In order to think through the decision, he engaged in a Quaker practice that involves a body called a clearness committee. The committee is a group of peers who simply pose questions and allow the person to come to their own conclusions. Somebody asked Palmer why he wanted to be a college president. He went on to list all the things he didn't like about the president's role—the fundraising, the politics, not being able to teach. Another person said, "I get what you *don't* like, but what *do* you like?"

Palmer mentioned that what he would like about being a college president was having a desk with a plaque that said "President" on it. Finally, somebody in the clearness committee asked him, "Can you think of an easier way to get your picture in the paper?" Palmer laughed and realized that he didn't actually want the job. He was grateful to the clearness committee for giving him an opportunity to listen to himself. Sometimes we can't understand personal truths until we hear ourselves say them.

KEEP THE GEM STATEMENT AT THE CENTER. In the midst of many difficult conversations, there is what the mediator Adar Cohen calls "the gem statement." This is the truth underneath the disagreement, something you both agree on: "Even when we can't agree on Dad's medical care, I've never doubted your good intentions. I know we both want the best for him." If you can both return to the gem statement during a conflict, you can keep the relationship between you strong.

FIND THE DISAGREEMENT UNDER THE DISAGREEMENT. When arguing, the natural thing is to restate your point of view until the other person sees the issue the way you do. The more interesting thing to do is to ask, "Why, at heart, do we disagree? What is the values disagreement underneath our practical disagreement?" Maybe you disagree on gun regulations because deep down you have radically different notions of public safety or of the role of government, or maybe one of you is from a rural town and the other is from a city.

When you search for the disagreement under the disagreement, you are looking for the moral, philosophical roots of why you each believe what you do. You're engaged in a mutual exploration. Suddenly, instead of just repeating our arguments, we're pulling stories out of each other. As the neuroscientist Lisa Feldman Barrett puts it, "Being curious about your friend's experience is more important than being right."

DON'T BE A TOPPER. If somebody tells you they are having trouble with their teenage son, don't turn around and say, "I know exactly what you mean. I'm having incredible problems with my Steven." You may think you're trying to build a shared connection, but what you are really doing is shifting attention back to yourself. You're saying, in effect, "Your problems aren't that interesting to me; let me tell you about my own, much more fascinating ones." If you want to build a shared connection, try sitting with their experience before you start ladling out your own.

Mónica Guzmán, a journalist who wrote a book called *I Never Thought of It That Way,* currently works for Braver Angels, a group that brings Republicans and Democrats together to talk with one another. The lesson she has drawn from her experience is the same lesson I have learned: "The experience of being *listened* to all the way on something—until your meaning is completely clear to another human being—is extremely rare in life."

Our goal is to make that less rare. The kinds of social skills I've tried to describe here can get us part of the way. But learning how to ask the right questions is also a vital skill in the repertoire of a good conversationalist. That's what we turn to next.

SEVEN

The Right Questions

have a friend named David Bradley who does this thing with index cards. You go to him with a problem. Maybe you have a job opportunity you're considering or you're wondering if you should get married—or divorced. When I went to him about a decade ago, I was feeling overwhelmed. I was responding to other people's requests for my time, and I wasn't able to focus my energies on the stuff I thought most important. I presented my problem to David, and he started by asking questions. In my case, he asked me about three topics: my ultimate goals (What do you want to offer the world?), my skills (What are you doing when you feel most alive?), and my schedule (How exactly do you fill your days?). These were questions that lifted me out of the daily intricacies of my schedule and forced me to look at the big picture.

After the questions, David handed me a newspaper and asked

me to read it while he digested my answers. Then, a few minutes later, he started writing notes on index cards. I found myself glancing at the newspaper but really trying to sneak a peek at whatever on earth he was writing on those cards. About ten or fifteen minutes later, he laid the cards before me. They didn't have the answer to my problem on them; instead, they offered me an analytic frame to help me think about my problem. In my case, he'd ranked the things I really wanted to do on one card and the things I was actually doing on another card. On a third card, he had written out a strategy for how I could get card B to look more like card A.

It's been years since David did his last index-card treatment on me, but I still keep the cards he gave me that day on a shelf in my office, as a reminder of the framework he offered me. David's questions helped me get distance from a problem I was too immersed in to see. David has performed this exercise with hundreds of people over the years. I know others who have David's cards tucked inside the frame of the mirror they look at each morning. People come up to David twenty years after they got the index-card treatment to tell him how transformative the experience was. I asked David why he thinks this is. "People often haven't had anyone tell them about themselves," he responded.

David acquired his skill while hiring people. In his professional life, he started two successful consulting firms and then bought and revived *The Atlantic* magazine. He succeeded because he's fantastic at seeing and choosing the right people.

Job interviews are notoriously unreliable, in part because many people aren't good at seeing others, and in part because job applicants often lie during them. David hires well because he's very focused. The first thing he is looking for when he hires someone, he says, is "extreme talent." He defines this narrowly. He doesn't want someone who says they love teaching in general; he wants to hear someone identify the specific teaching task they excel at: *I love writing out a lesson plan.* Or *I love working with remedial students.* Or *I love one-on-one tutoring.* "People love to do the thing they are wired to do," he says. A person can go a long way with a narrow skill set.

Second, David is looking for a "spirit of generosity." Will this person be kind to others? One way he tries to discern a person's character is with what he calls the "take me back" technique. When you ask people about their lives, David finds, they tend to start in the middle—with their career. So he'll ask, "Take me back to when you were born." In this way he can get people out of talking about their professional life and into talking about their personal life. He can begin to get a sense of how they treat others, who they love, what they do to make the world a better place.

"People answer better with narrative. When they are in the thread of a narrative, they get comfortable and will speak more fully," David says. In a job interview, he focuses especially on someone's high school experience. Did the person feel like an outcast in high school? Did they empathize with the poor and the unpopular? "The only thing you can be certain about every person is that nobody escapes high school. Whatever your high school fears were, they are still there." David's getting at a person's vulnerabilities, trying to see the person whole.

People like David Bradley are questioners. They are comfortable asking other people questions about themselves, at meetings or over a meal. Isn't everybody that way? Well, no, although most of us start out that way. The average child asks about forty thousand questions between the ages of two and five. And most kids are fantastic at questioning. Niobe Way is an educator who one day was teaching eighth-grade boys how to conduct interviews. She made herself their first interview subject and told them they could ask her anything. Here's how one of those interviews went:

STUDENT A: Are you married?

WAY: No.

STUDENT B: Are you divorced?

WAY: Yes.

STUDENT C: Do you still love him?

WAY: (Deep gasp of breath)

STUDENT D: Does he know that you still love him? Does he know?

WAY: (Tears in her eyes)

STUDENT E: Do your children know?

Kids aren't afraid to ask blunt question. But at some point during late childhood or adolescence, many of us begin to withdraw from intimacy. I'd say it's because society sends the message that we shouldn't show emotions, shouldn't get personal; or it sends the message that if we show the world who we really are, people won't like us. Asking good questions can be a weirdly vulnerable activity. You're admitting that you don't know. An insecure, self-protective world is a world with fewer questions.

While I've been on this journey of discovery, I've begun to pay close attention to which people are question askers and which are not. My estimate is that about 30 percent of the people I interact with are natural question askers. You're at lunch or on a Zoom call and they turn their curiosity on you with a series of questions. People in the other 70 percent can be charming people; they're just not questioners. They spend their conversational time presenting themselves. Sometimes I'll be walking out of a party and realize: "That whole time nobody asked me a single question."

———

I don't know if I'm innately a questioner or not, because I don't have a choice. I've been in journalism for forty years. Asking other people questions is the core of my profession. In my first real job, I was a police reporter for the City News Bureau of Chicago. I had two assignments my first day. A teenager had committed suicide, and I had to call the neighbors to ask them if they knew why. A city official had died in a car crash, and I had to ask his widow for a response. I hated those assignments. Since that day I've had a harder time taking the phrase "journalistic ethics" entirely seriously. But during my brief time on that job I also had to break through some reticence barrier. I trained myself to walk up to strangers and ask them questions at uncomfortable times.

I've learned that sometimes simple questions are best. One of the greatest interviews of my life happened in Moscow. It was 1991. Tanks were in the streets. The whole city was in turmoil, and the Democratic Reform Movement was vying with the Soviet old guard. I met a ninety-four-year-old woman named Valentina Kosieva. I asked about her life story. She told me about the pogroms in 1905 when the Cossacks shot members of her family; the events around the 1917 revolution when she was nearly executed by a firing squad; the time in 1937 when the police raided her apartment, seized her husband, and sent him off to Siberia, never to be seen again; the time in 1944 when the Nazis beat her son to death; and on and on. Every trauma that had been inflicted on the Russian people had been inflicted on her. I just asked her the same question over and over again: And then what happened?

I learned another valuable lesson about asking good questions from Condoleezza Rice. When she was secretary of state, she would invite me to her office every other month or so for an off-the-record conversation. I didn't cover foreign policy much, or know much about her day-to-day activities, so my questions were ill-informed and kind of dumb. I finally asked her why she kept inviting me back. She said it was because my questions were so broad and general that they helped her step back from the minutiae of her job and see the big picture. Sometimes a broad, dumb question is better than a smart question, especially one meant to display how well-informed you are.

I've come to think of questioning as a moral practice. When you are asking a good question, you are adopting a posture of humility. You're confessing that you don't know and you want to learn. You're also honoring a person. We all like to think we are so clever that we can imagine what's going on in another's mind. But the evidence shows that this doesn't work. People are just too different from one another, too complicated, too idiosyncratic.

As the psychologist Nicholas Epley observes, perspective *taking* is untrustworthy, but perspective *receiving* works quite well. If I'm going to get to know you, it's not because I have the magical ability to peer into your soul; it's because I have the skill of asking the sorts of questions that will give you a chance to tell me about who you are.

The worst kinds of questions are the ones that don't involve a surrender of power, that evaluate: Where did you go to college? What
neighborhood do you live in? What do you do? They imply, "I'm
about to judge you."

Closed questions are also bad questions. Instead of surrender-
ing power, the questioner is imposing a limit on how the question
can be answered. For example, if you mention your mother and I
ask, "Were you close?," then I've limited your description of your
relationship with your mother to the close/distant frame. It's better
to ask, "How is your mother?" That gives the answerer the freedom to go as deep or as shallow as he wants.

A third sure way to shut down conversations is to ask vague
questions, like "How's it going?" or "What's up?" These questions
are impossible to answer. They're another way of saying, "I'm
greeting you, but I don't actually want you to answer."

Humble questions are open-ended. They're encouraging the
other person to take control and take the conversation where they
want it to go. These are questions that begin with phrases like
"How did you . . . ," "What's it like . . . ," "Tell me about . . . ," and
"In what ways . . ." In her book *You're Not Listening,* Kate Murphy
describes a focus group moderator who was trying to understand
why people go to the grocery store late at night. Instead of directly
asking, "Why do you go to grocery stores late," which can sound
accusatory, she asked, "Tell me about the last time you went to the
store after 11:00 P.M." A shy, unassuming woman who had said
little up to that point raised her hand and responded, "I had just
smoked a joint and was looking for a *ménage à trois*—me, Ben, and
Jerry." Because the moderator asked an open question, the unassuming woman felt empowered to go way beyond the narrow

topic of grocery stores and tell us something about her pleasures and her wider life.

Sometimes you're at a neighborhood barbecue or a work function with people you don't know or barely know at all. When an Illuminator is in those situations, he'll ask questions that probe for commonalities. I've learned to sometimes ask, "Where did you grow up?" which gets people talking about their hometown. I travel a lot for work, so there's a good chance I'll know something about their place. Other easy introductory questions are things like "That's a lovely name. How did your parents choose it?" That prompts conversations about cultural background and family history. Those conversations often go off in good directions.

At a party years ago I found myself in conversation with a stranger, but we quickly discovered what we had in common. We were both writers, though he was a novelist and I write nonfiction. We started talking about differences and similarities between our writing processes, and he asked me, "Do you ever have a glass of wine when you write?" I told him that I couldn't. I need to keep my mind sharp while I'm writing. Then he asked if I ever had a drink *after* I was done writing. Yes, I said, I might have a glass of wine. So did he. He asked me why. I told him that writing nonfiction is such a focused, disciplined activity, I often felt the need to loosen up afterward. He told me that writing fiction is such an uninhibited, emotional activity, he often needed to pull himself back together afterward. We had the same practice but for opposite reasons, and our exchange made me think about how the jobs we fall into shape the way we are in the world. If I'd become a novelist, I'd probably be more emotionally intense.

A conversation like that, based on an out-of-the-blue question and one thing we had in common, was a mutual exploration. We were using each other's experiences to come to know something about each other and ourselves.

Other times you'll be at a dinner table or a retreat with people you know at least decently well or want to know decently well. In this situation Illuminators ask *big questions*. It's easy to have a pleasant evening if only small questions are on the table, but it's possible to have a truly memorable dinner if someone asks a big question. Recently I was at a dinner with a political scientist who put down his fork and said to the four of us: "I'm eighty. What should I do with the rest of my life?" That was a really humble but big question to ask. Essentially, he was asking, "What is the best way to grow old?" We started talking about his values, the questions he wanted to ask in his future research, how anyone should spend the final years of their life. It was fantastic.

Big questions interrupt the daily routines people fall into and prompt them to step back and see their life from a distance. Here are some of my favorite questions that do that:

- "What crossroads are you at?" At any moment, most of us are in the middle of some transition. The question helps people focus on theirs.
- "What would you do if you weren't afraid?" Most people know that fear plays some role in their life, but they haven't clearly defined how fear is holding them back.
- "If you died tonight, what would you regret not doing?"
- "If we meet a year from now, what will we be celebrating?"

- "If the next five years is a chapter in your life, what is that chapter about?"

- "Can you be yourself where you are and still fit in?"

Peter Block is an author and consultant who writes about community development and civic engagement. He is a master at coming up with questions that lift you out of your ruts and invite fresh reevaluations. Here are some of his: "What is the no, or refusal, you keep postponing? . . . What have you said yes to that you no longer really believe in? . . . What forgiveness are you withholding? . . . How have you contributed to the problem you're trying to solve? . . . What is the gift you currently hold in exile?"

Mónica Guzmán, the journalist I quoted in the last chapter, asks people, "Why you?" Why was it *you* who started that business? Why was it *you* who felt a responsibility to run for the school board?

A few years ago, I met some guys who run a program for gang members in Chicago. These young men have endured a lot of violence and trauma and are often triggered to overreact. One of the program directors' common questions is "Why is that a problem for you?" In other words they are asking, "What event in your past produced that strong reaction just now?"

We too often think that deep conversations have to be painful or vulnerable conversations. I try to compensate for that by asking questions about the positive sides of life:

"Tell me about a time you adapted to change."

"What's working really well in your life?"

"What are you most self-confident about?"

"Which of your five senses is strongest?"

"Have you ever been solitary without feeling lonely?" or

"What has become clearer to you as you have aged?"

———

In modern society, we generally refrain from asking the kinds of big questions I've just laid out. I guess we're afraid of invading people's privacy, afraid that the conversation will get too heavy. It's a legitimate concern. But I've found in almost all cases that people are too shy about asking questions, not too aggressive. People are a lot more eager to have deep conversations than you think.

While doing the research for this book, I interviewed many people—seminar leaders, conversation facilitators, psychologists and focus group moderators, biographers and journalists—whose job it is to ask other people about their lives. I asked these experts how often somebody looks back at them and says, "None of your damn business." Every expert I consulted had basically the same answer: "Almost never." People are longing to be asked questions about who they are. "The human need to self-present is powerful," notes the psychologist Ethan Kross. A 2012 study by Harvard neuroscientists found that people often took more pleasure from sharing information about themselves than from receiving money. The Belgian psychologist Bernard Rimé found that people feel especially compelled to talk about negative experiences. The more negative the experience was, the more they want to talk about it.

Over the course of my career as a journalist I, too, have found that if you respectfully ask people about themselves, they will answer with a candor that takes your breath away. Studs Terkel was

a journalist who collected oral histories over his long career in Chicago. He'd ask people big questions and then sit back and let their
answers unfold. "Listen, listen, listen, listen, and if you do, people
will talk," he once observed. "They always talk. Why? Because no
one has ever listened to them before in all their lives. Perhaps
they've not ever even listened to themselves."

Each person is a mystery. And when you are surrounded by
mysteries, as the saying goes, it's best to live life in the form of a
question.

Part 2

—

I

SEE

YOU

IN

YOUR

STRUGGLES

EIGHT

The Epidemic of Blindness

And then the crisis of connection came.

So far I've been describing a process of getting to know someone as if we live in normal times. I've been writing as if we live in a healthy cultural environment, in a society in which people are enmeshed in thick communities and webs of friendship, trust, and belonging. We don't live in such a society. We live in an environment in which political animosities, technological dehumanization, and social breakdown undermine connection, strain friendships, erase intimacy, and foster distrust. We're living in the middle of some sort of vast emotional, relational, and spiritual crisis. It is as if people across society have lost the ability to see and understand one another, thus producing a culture that can be brutalizing and isolating.

Depression rates have been surging since the beginning of the twenty-first century. Between 1999 and 2019, American suicide rates increased by 33 percent. Between 2009 and 2019, the percentage of teens who reported "persistent feelings of sadness or hopelessness" rose from 26 percent to 37 percent. By 2021, it had shot up to 44 percent. The percentage of Americans who said they have no close friends quadrupled between 1990 and 2020. In one survey, 54 percent of Americans reported that no one knows them well. The number of American adults without a romantic partner increased by a third. More to the point, 36 percent of Americans reported that they felt lonely frequently or almost all of the time, including 61 percent of young adults and 51 percent of young mothers. People were spending much more time alone. In 2013, Americans spent an average of six and a half hours per week with friends. By 2019, they were spending only four hours per week with friends, a 38 percent drop. By 2021, as the Covid-19 pandemic was easing, they were spending only two hours and forty-five minutes per week with friends, a 58 percent decline. The General Social Survey asks Americans to rate their happiness levels. Between 1990 and 2018, the share of Americans who put themselves in the lowest happiness category increased by more than 50 percent.

These are statistics. We have all encountered this loneliness, sadness, and anxiety in the course of our daily lives. Almost every week, it seems, I speak to some parent with a child who is dealing with a mental health crisis. In 2021, I gave a talk in Oklahoma, and afterward, during the Q&A period, a woman sent up a question on an index card: "What do you do when you no longer want to be alive?" I was haunted by the question, not least because I didn't know how to answer her. I mentioned my embarrassment at a dinner the very next night, and one of the guests reported that her brother had committed suicide a few months before. I then re-counted these events to a group of friends on a Zoom call, and nearly half the people on the call said they had had some brush with suicide in their family.

Starting around 2018, a plethora of books have been published tracing the catastrophic decline in social relationships across society. They have titles like *Lost Connections, The Crisis of Connection,* and *The Lonely Century.* In different ways, they present us with the same baffling mystery: The thing we need most is relationships. The thing we seem to suck at most is relationships.

The effects of this are ruinous and self-reinforcing. Social disconnection warps the mind. When people feel unseen, they tend to shut down socially. People who are lonely and unseen become suspicious. They start to take offense where none is intended. They become afraid of the very thing they need most, which is intimate contact with other humans. They are buffeted by waves of self-loathing and self-doubt. After all, it feels shameful to realize that you are apparently unworthy of other people's attention. Many people harden into their solitude. They create self-delusional worlds. "Loneliness obfuscates," the interdisciplinary scientist Giovanni Frazzetto writes in his book *Together, Closer.* "It becomes a deceiving filter through which we see ourselves, others, and the world. It makes us more vulnerable to rejection, and it heightens our general level of vigilance and insecurity in social situations." We see ourselves as others see us, and when we feel invisible, well, we have a tendency to fall to pieces.

I recently asked a friend in publishing what kind of books are selling well these days. Books about healing, she said, adding that people want to find ways to heal. The psychiatrist Bessel van der

Kolk's book *The Body Keeps the Score* is one of the bestselling books of our era. It's about trauma—and healing from trauma—and has sold millions of copies. As Van der Kolk writes, "Knowing that we are seen and heard by the important people in our lives can make us feel calm and safe, and . . . being ignored or dismissed can precipitate rage reactions or mental collapse."

Sadness, lack of recognition, and loneliness turn into bitterness. When people believe that their identity is unrecognized, it feels like injustice—because it is. People who have been treated unjustly often lash out, seek ways to humiliate those who they feel have humiliated them.

Loneliness thus leads to meanness. As the saying goes, pain that is not transformed gets transmitted. The data I just cited about social isolation and sadness is, no surprise, accompanied by other sorts of data about rising hostility and callousness. In 2021, hate-crime reports surged to their highest levels in twelve years. In 2000, roughly two-thirds of Americans gave to charity; by 2021, fewer than half did. One restaurant owner recently told me that he has to ban somebody from his place for rude behavior almost every week these days. That didn't use to happen. A friend of mine who is a nurse says her number one problem is retaining staff. Her nurses want to quit because the patients have become so abusive, even violent. As the columnist Peggy Noonan put it, "People are proud of their bitterness now."

The social breakdown manifests as a crisis of distrust. Two generations ago, roughly 60 percent of Americans said that "most people can be trusted." By 2014, according the General Social Survey, only 30.3 percent did, and only 19 percent of millennials. High-trust societies have what Francis Fukuyama calls "spontaneous sociability," meaning that people are quick to get together and work together. Low-trust societies do not have this. Low-trust societies fall apart.

Distrust sows distrust. It creates a feeling that the only person you can count on is yourself. Distrustful people assume that others are out to get them, they exaggerate threats, they fall for conspiracy theories that explain the danger they feel.

Every society possesses what the philosopher Axel Honneth calls a "recognition order." This is the criteria used to confer respect and recognition on some people and not others. In our society, we confer huge amounts of recognition on those with beauty, wealth, or prestigious educational affiliations, and millions feel invisible, unrecognized, and left out. The crisis in our personal lives eventually shows up in our politics. According to research by Ryan Streeter of the American Enterprise Institute, lonely people are seven times more likely than non-lonely people to say they are active in politics. For people who feel disrespected and unseen, politics is a seductive form of social therapy. Politics seems to offer a comprehensible moral landscape. *We, the children of light, are facing off against them, the children of darkness.* Politics seems to offer a sense of belonging. *I am on the barricades with the other members of my tribe.* Politics seems to offer an arena of moral action. *To be moral in this world, you don't have to feed the hungry or sit with the widow. You just have to be liberal or conservative, you just have to feel properly enraged at the people you find contemptible.*

Over the past decade, everything has become politicized. Churches, universities, sports, food selection, movie awards shows, late-night comedy—they have all turned into political arenas. Except this was not politics as it is normally understood. Healthy societies produce the politics of distribution. How should the resources of the society be allocated? Unhappy societies produce the politics of recognition. Political movements these days are fueled largely by resentment, by a person or a group's feelings that society does not respect or recognize them. The goal of political and media personalities is to produce episodes in which their side is emotionally validated and the other side is emotionally shamed. The person practicing the politics of recognition is not trying to formulate domestic policies or to address this or that social ill; he is trying to affirm his identity, to gain status and visibility, to find a way to admire himself.

But, of course, the politics of recognition doesn't actually give you community and connection. People join partisan tribes, but they are not in fact meeting together, serving one another, befriending one another. Politics doesn't make you a better person; it's about outer agitation, not inner formation. Politics doesn't humanize. If you attempt to assuage your sadness, loneliness, or anomie through politics, it will do nothing more than land you in a world marked by a sadistic striving for domination. You may try to escape a world of isolation and moral meaninglessness, only to find yourself in the pulverizing destructiveness of the culture wars.

Ultimately, the sadness and dehumanization pervading society leads to violence, both emotional and physical. Look at many of the young men who commit these horrific mass shootings. They are ghosts. In school, no one knows them. Later, when journalists interview their teachers, they often don't remember them. These young men often have no social skills. *Why doesn't anybody like me?* As one researcher put it, they are not loners; they are failed joiners.

Love rejected comes back as hatred. The stressors build up: bad at school, bad at work, humiliating encounters with others. These young men contemplate suicide. And in their despair, they seem to experience something that feels like an identity crisis: *Is it my fault or is it the world's fault? Am I a loser or are they losers?*

And here's where victimhood turns into villainy. The ones who become mass shooters decide that they are supermen and it is the world that is full of ants. They decide to commit suicide in a way that will selfishly give them what they crave most: to be known, to be recognized, to be famous. They craft a narrative in which they are the hero. The guns seem to have some sort of psychological effect, too. For people who have felt impotent all their lives, guns can provide a narcotic sense of power. The guns are like serpents in the trees, whispering to the lonely.

In 2014, in *Esquire* magazine, the writer Tom Junod interviewed a young man who'd gotten the nickname Trunk, because when he'd been arrested, it was rumored that the police had found that he had a trunk full of guns. He had set out to commit a mass shooting, but he'd been caught just as he was about to commence. When Junod later asked him about his motive, he responded, "I wanted attention. If somebody would have come up to me and said, 'You don't have to do this, you don't have to have this strange strength, we accept you,' I would have broken down and given up." The essence of evil is the tendency to obliterate the humanity of another.

For his book *Machete Season,* the French journalist Jean Hatzfeld interviewed people who had participated in the Rwandan genocide. He spoke to one man who had murdered his neighbor of many years. "At that fatal instant I did not see in him what he had been before," the man recalled. His neighbor's face became blurry in the seconds before the machete swung. "His features were indeed similar to those of the person I knew, but nothing firmly reminded me that I had lived beside him for a long time." This man literally did not see.

———

Why, over the past two decades, have we seen this epidemic of loneliness and meanness, this breakdown in the social fabric? We can all point to some contributing factors: social media, widening inequality, declining participation in community life, declining church attendance, rising populism and bigotry, vicious dema- goguery from our media and political elites.

I agree that these factors have all contributed to produce what we are enduring. But as the years have gone by, I have increasingly fixated on what I see as a deeper cause of our social and relational crisis. Our problem, I believe, is fundamentally moral. As a society, we have failed to teach the skills and cultivate the inclination to treat each other with kindness, generosity, and respect.

I realize the phrase "moral formation" may sound stuffy and archaic, but moral formation is really about three simple, practical things. First, it is about helping people learn how to restrain their selfishness and incline their heart to care more about others. Second, it's about helping people find a purpose, so their life has stability, direction, and meaning. Third, it's about teaching the basic social and emotional skills so you can be kind and considerate to the people around you.

Over the centuries, our schools reflected the failings of our society—the racism, the sexism, and all the rest. But over those centuries, for all their many failings, schools really did focus on moral formation. They thought it was their primary job to turn out people of character, people who would be honest, gentle, and respectful toward those around them. But starting just after World War II, the focus on moral formation gradually fell away. In his history *Moral Education in America,* B. Edward McClellan argues that most elementary schools began to abandon moral formation in the 1940s and 1950s and "by the 1960s deliberate moral education was in full-scale retreat." He continues: "Educators who had once prided themselves on their ability to reshape character now paid more attention to the SAT scores of their students, and middle-class parents scrambled to find schools that would give their children the best chances to qualify for elite colleges and universities."

As schools became more fixated on career success, they stopped worrying about churning out students who would be considerate to others. As James Davison Hunter, the country's leading scholar on character education, put it, "American culture is defined more and more by an absence, and in that absence, we provide children with no moral horizons beyond the self and its well-being." Religious institutions, which used to do this, began to play a less prominent role in American life. Parents started practicing "acceptance parenting." They were less inclined to mold their children's moral lives, and more likely to just cheer them on for their academic and athletic achievements.

In a sense, American culture became demoralized. Moral talk and moral categories gradually came to occupy a smaller role in American life. Google's Ngram Viewer measures how often a word is used in published books. Over the course of the twentieth century, usage of morality-related words plummeted: "bravery" (down 66 percent); "gratitude" (down 49 percent); "humbleness" (52 percent). UCLA researchers have long surveyed entering college students about what they want from life. In 1966, nearly 90 percent said they were strongly motivated to develop a meaningful philosophy of life, the most popular of all life goals. In 2000, only 42 percent said that. Instead, the most important life goal was being well-off financially. In 2015, 82 percent of students said financial success was what school was primarily for. In 2018, the Pew Research Center asked Americans what gives them meaning in life. Only 7 percent said helping other people. Only 11 percent said that learning was a source of meaning in their life.

In short, several generations, including my own, were not taught the skills they would need in order to see, understand, and respect other people in all their depth and dignity. The breakdown in basic moral skills produced disconnection, alienation, and a culture in which cruelty was permitted. Our failure to treat each other well in the small encounters of everyday life metastasized and, I believe, led to the horrific social breakdown we see all around us. This is a massive civilizational failure. We need to rediscover ways to teach moral and social skills. This crisis helped motivate me to write this book.

NINE

Hard Conversations

As society grew more bitterly divided, I traveled. My job is to travel around the country and try to get a feel for what's going on. Most of the conversations I have had over the past few years have been warm and wonderful, but, befitting a time of great bitterness and distrust, many of them contained moments that were hard, fraught, and angry. In Greenville, South Carolina, I had dinner with an elderly Black woman who was filled with smoldering fury because the young Black girls in the neighborhood where she grew up have it even harder now than she did in the 1950s. At a baseball game, an ardent Trump supporter, stung by my anti-Trump stances, screamed in my face: "You're a fucking asshole! You're a fucking asshole!" About a year before that, my wife and I were welcomed with great hospitality by a Native American family in New Mexico, but the matriarch simmered with rage through the meal at the America we represented, and afterward, sitting in the living room, she finally vented her anger at the outrages visited on her people. I spent time with a seventy-year-old working-class Trump supporter in South Dakota who told me about the best day of his life. It happened when he was thirty-four and he was laid off from the factory where he worked as a foreman, because they'd upgraded the equipment and he was no longer skilled enough to do the job. He thought he was just going to leave quietly. He packed his stuff into a box, opened his office door, and found that the entire workforce—thirty-five hundred people—had formed a double line from his office door to his car door in the parking lot. He walked down the line as they applauded and cheered for him. He told me that every job he has had in the thirty-six years since has been worse, and that he and his wife have slid closer and closer to poverty. It was a sad recounting of a downward-sloping life.

Because I work at places like *The New York Times, The Atlantic,* and PBS, some people see me as a stand-in for the coastal elites, for the systems they believe have been crushing them down, and I get that. When those of us in positions of power in the establishment media and the larger cultural institutions of society tell stories that don't include you, it is disorienting and disenfranchising. It is as if you look into society's mirror and find that you are not there. People rightly get furious when that happens.

In the first part of this book, I've tried to describe the skills needed to see and be seen on a personal level—when two people happen to meet each other in normal, "healthy" circumstances. I think of that section as a college-level course on how to understand one another.

But we don't merely meet each other as unique individuals or in healthy social circumstances. We meet each other in the current atmosphere of disconnection and distrust. We meet each other as members of groups. We meet each other embedded in systems of power in which some groups have more and some groups have less. We meet each other in a society in which members of the red team and members of the blue team often stand apart and glare across metaphorical walls with bitterness and incomprehension. Our encounters are shaped by our historical inheritances—the legacies of slavery, elitism, sexism, prejudice, bigotry, and economic and social domination. You can't get to know another person while pretending not to see ideology, class, race, faith, identity, or any of the other fraught social categories.

These days, if you want to know someone well, you have to see the person in front of you as a distinct and never-to-be repeated individual. But you've also got to see that person as a member of their groups. And you've also got to see their social location—the way some people are insiders and other people are outsiders, how some sit on the top of society and some are marginalized to the fringes. The trick is to be able to see each person on these three levels all at once. That requires a graduate-level education in the process of understanding another, and that is what we're going to embark upon now. If the goal of Part 1 was to help you see people on a personal level, the goal of Part 2 is to help you understand and be present for people during harsh times, amid the social strife and bitter conflicts of our current age.

———

By now I've had plenty of experience with a certain kind of conversation—the hard conversations. By hard conversations, I mean conversations across differences and across perceived power inequalities. These hard conversations include the ones between family members who find themselves in different partisan tribes, managers whose authority is questioned by younger employees, students furious because they are inheriting such a broken world, populist outsiders who feel the coastal elite insiders are betraying them at every turn. These conversations often start with suspicion, animosity, resentment. People may want to connect, but their communications start off reserved, guarded.

One specific hard conversation lingers in my mind. It happened on a panel discussion in 2022. The subject was the "culture war." When I hear that phrase, I think of a wide variety of fights over everything from LGBTQ issues, to abortion, to religion in the public square, to what gets taught about sex and race in public classrooms. But one of my fellow panelists that particular day was a prominent Black intellectual—I'm not going to give you her name, because I don't want to make this personal—who heard the phrase "culture war" as an attack on the accurate teaching of Black history in schools. For her, the culture war was white supremacy rearing its ugly head once again.

I agreed that the attack on the teaching of African American history was an important part of the culture war these days, and I agreed with the obvious point that those attacks are often used as racial dog whistles by demagogues. But I tried to step back over the long history of culture wars to show how they were a broader clash between more progressive values, like the freedom to follow whatever lifestyle you choose, and more conservative values, like the need to preserve morally coherent communities. I tried to argue that at their best, both sides are defending legitimate moral traditions and expressing legitimate points of view, though I might favor one side more than the other. She countered that the attack on Black history today is like the reactionary attack on Black lives in the period after the Civil War—the period that saw the rise of lynching, the restoration of segregation, and the establishment of Jim Crow laws. Every time the United States takes a step forward, she argued, it takes two steps back, and that's what we're seeing right now. *That's* the culture war.

To be clear, there was no outright confrontation between us. Everyone stayed respectful. In fact, afterward, several of the audience members and some of the organizers told me they were disappointed that there wasn't more disagreement between us. But what lingers, for me, is that the emotional undercurrents between us were a complete mess. Every time I talked about the broader context of the culture war, she pulled a sour face that demonstrated her contempt for what I was saying—something several people mentioned to me later. I think she saw me as another clueless white guy who adopts this neutral thirty-thousand-feet view and can't possibly understand the fierce struggle she is in the middle of every day. Which is at least partly true.

In every conversation, there is some sort of power relationship between the participants. It's possible that she thought I had the power in that one. She's a radical academic fighting for justice, while I'm a member of the elite media establishment. I am implicated in systems, and have benefited from systems, that keep people down. But at the same time, I too felt powerless and afraid. I'm a white male talking about race with a Black woman who has spent her illustrious career writing and thinking about this issue. Do I even have a right to an opinion? I started watering down my views. I was acutely self-conscious, befogged, at sea. It was a hard conversation, and I did not navigate it well. I left it feeling like I should have done more to understand her point of view, but I also should have done more to assert my own, to clarify and explore any disagreements we might actually have.

Over the past few years, but especially after that panel discussion, I've tried to learn a few things about how to have hard conversations. I've talked to experts and read books on the subject, of which my favorites include *High Conflict* by Amanda Ripley, *I Never Thought of It That Way* by Mónica Guzmán, and, especially, *Crucial Conversations* by Kerry Patterson, Joseph Grenny, Ron McMillan, and Al Switzler.

The first thing I learned is that prior to entering into any hard conversation, it's important to think about conditions before you think about content. What are the conditions in which this conversation is going to take place? If you are a well-educated professional attending a conference in a nice hotel somewhere, you can show up in a room and just be yourself. But if you are a trucker from West Virginia with a high school education, you have to be much more aware of the social dynamics, much more discerning about what version of yourself you can present. Also, for members of dominant or majority groups, there's usually little or no gap between how others see you and how you see yourself. For people from marginalized or historically oppressed groups, there's usually a chasm between who you are and how you are perceived. Everybody has to walk into a hard conversation aware of these dynamics. If I meet a trucker at a conference in a luxury hotel, I'm going to show genuine curiosity about his work. I'm going to do whatever I can—and it may not be much—to let him know that he can be his full self with me.

When I walked into that panel discussion about our culture war, I was walking into four hundred years of race relations in America. Because of where I work and all the other advantages that have been bestowed upon me as a white guy in America, society conspires to make me visible. Because of my co-panelist's social coordinates, society conspires to make her invisible. The encounter between us was an encounter between visibility and invisibility. The situation was not changed by the fact that she's a prominent intellectual.

Ralph Ellison's words at the start of *Invisible Man* still rank as one of the most profound expressions of what it is like to not feel seen, heard, or understood, in this case because of race. "I am invisible, understand, simply because people refuse to see me," the nameless narrator declares. "It is as though I have been surrounded by mirrors of hard, distorting glass. When they approach me, they see only my surroundings, themselves, or figments of their imagination—indeed, everything and anything except me." Ellison writes that a person in this position wonders "whether you aren't simply a phantom in other people's minds." When you're put in this position, "you ache with the need to convince yourself that you do exist in the real world, that you're a part of all the sound and anguish, and you strike out with your fists, you curse and you swear to make them recognize you. And, alas, it's seldom successful."

The second crucial thing I learned, especially from the authors of *Crucial Conversations,* is that every conversation takes place on two levels: the official conversation and the actual conversation. The official conversation is represented by the words we say about whatever topic we are nominally discussing: politics, economics, workplace issues—whatever. The actual conversation occurs in the ebb and flow of underlying emotions that get transmitted as we talk. With every comment you are either making me feel a little more safe or a little more threatened. With every comment I am showing you either respect or disrespect. With every comment we are each revealing something about our intentions: *Here is why I am telling you this. Here is why this is important to me.* It is the volley of these underlying emotions that will determine the success or failure of the conversation.

The authors of *Crucial Conversations* also remind us that every conversation exists within a frame: What is the purpose here? What are our goals? A frame is the stage on which the conversation takes place. During that panel discussion, we were really having an argument about the frame of our conversation. I saw the culture war as one thing and wanted to analyze it from the detached perspective a journalist is trained to adopt. She saw the culture war entirely differently—as an assault on basic justice. She didn't want to analyze it from a detached point of view; she wanted to communicate it as an activist in the middle of the fight. In retrospect, I should have stayed within her frame a little longer, instead of trying to yank the conversation back to my frame. That would have shown her proper respect. It might have smoothed out the emotional undercurrents.

Let's say you're a college administrator and angry students have come to your office to demand extra time to take their final exams because of the stress they feel. Let's say you're a middle-aged manager and angry employees are in your office complaining because your company hasn't issued a statement on some piece of gun-control legislation. In either case, there's a temptation to get defensive. There's a temptation to try to yank the conversation back to your frame: *Here's how the situation looks to me. Here's what I'm doing to alleviate that problem. Here are all the other problems I have you might not be aware of.* There's a temptation, in other words, to revert to the frames you feel comfortable with.

It's best to avoid this temptation. As soon as somebody starts talking about times when they felt excluded, betrayed, or wronged, stop and listen. When somebody is talking to you about pain in their life, even in those cases when *you* may think their pain is performative or exaggerated, it's best not to try to yank the conversations back to your frame. Your first job is to stay within the other person's standpoint to more fully understand how the world looks to them. Your next job is to encourage them to go into more depth about what they have just said. "I want to understand your point of view as much as possible. What am I missing here?" Curiosity is the ability to explore something even in stressful and difficult circumstances.

Remember that the person who is lower in any power structure than you are has a greater awareness of the situation than you do. A servant knows more about his master than the master knows about the servant. Someone who is being sat on knows a lot about the sitter—the way he shifts his weight and moves—whereas the sitter may not be aware that the sat-on person is even there.

The Scots have a word that's useful in this context: "ken"; you may be familiar with it from the expression "beyond your ken." It comes from sailors who used the word to describe the area as far as they could see to the horizon. If you're going to have a good hard conversation with someone, you have to step into their ken. If you step into someone's ken, it shows that you at least want to understand. That's a powerful way to show respect. The authors of *Crucial Conversations* observe that in any conversation, respect is like air. When it's present nobody notices, but when it's absent it's all anybody can think about.

When you stand in someone else's standpoint—seeing the world from the other's point of view—then all participants in the conversation are contributing to a shared pool of knowledge. But very often in hard conversations, there is no shared pool of knowledge. One person describes their set of wrongs. The other person describes their own different set of wrongs. As the conversation goes on, they each go into deeper detail about their particular wrongs, but there's no shared pool. Pretty soon nobody is listening. It doesn't take much to create an us/them dynamic. This is a surefire way to do it.

When hard conversations go bad, everybody's motivations deteriorate. Two people at a company, for example, may be debating a new marketing strategy. At first their intentions are clear: They both want what's best for the firm. But as the conversation continues, their motivations shift: They each want to win the argument. They each want to show that they are smarter, more powerful. That's when they start pulling out the rhetorical dirty tricks. That's when, for example, they start labeling each other. Labeling is when you try to discredit another person by tossing them into some disreputable category: *You're a reactionary. You're the old establishment. You're woke.* Slapping a label on someone is a great way to render them invisible and destroy a hard conversation. Micah Goodman, who teaches at Hebrew University of Jerusalem, once told me, "A great conversation is between two people who think the other is wrong. A bad conversation is between those who think something is wrong with you."

I've learned that if you find yourself in a hard conversation that is going south, there are ways to redeem it. First, you step back from the conflict, and you try to figure out together what's gone wrong. You break the momentum by asking the other person, "How did we get to this tense place?" Then you do something the experts call "splitting." Splitting is when you clarify your own motives by first saying what they are not and then saying what they are. You say something like "I certainly wasn't trying to silence your voice. I was trying to include your point of view with the many other points of view on this topic. But I went too fast. I should have paused to try to hear your voice fully, so we could build from that reality. That was not respectful to you."

Then you try to reidentify the mutual purpose of the conversation. That's done by enlarging the purpose so that both people are encompassed by it. "You and I have very different ideas of what marketing plan this company should pursue. But we both believe in the product we are selling. We both want to get it before as many people as possible. I think we are both trying to take this company to the next level."

Finally, you can take advantage of the fact that a rupture is sometimes an opportunity to forge a deeper bond. You might say, "You and I have just expressed some strong emotions. Unfortunately, against each other. But at least our hearts are out on the table and we've both been exposed. Weirdly, we have a chance to understand each other better because of the mistakes we've made, the emotions we've aroused."

I've learned over these years that hard conversations are hard because people in different life circumstances construct very different realities. It's not only that they have different opinions about the same world; they literally see different worlds.

Allow me to take one final quick foray into the cognitive sciences to forcefully drive home this crucial point. Dennis Proffitt, a psychologist at the University of Virginia, studies perception. He wants to know how people construct their realities, sometimes at the most elementary level. For example, he has done extensive research on a curious phenomenon. People generally vastly overestimate how steep hills are, even in places like San Francisco, where the hills are, in fact, pretty steep. Proffitt was conducting experiments in which he asked groups of students to estimate the grade of various hills around UVA's campus. A hill on campus might actually have a 5 percent grade, but a typical participant would estimate that it had a 20 percent grade. One day Proffitt took a look at the most recent batch of experimental data and was stunned to find that suddenly the students had gotten much better at estimating the grade of a particular hill. Proffitt and his team delved into the mystery and discovered that the latest batch of questionnaires had been filled out by members of UVA's women's varsity soccer team. The hills didn't look so steep because these were extremely fit Division 1 athletes who would have relatively little trouble walking up them. How you see a situation depends on what you are capable of doing in a situation.

Since Proffitt first discovered this phenomenon, he and other researchers have found it again and again. People with heavy backpacks see steeper hills than people without backpacks, because it is harder for people with backpacks to walk up them. People who have just consumed energy drinks see less steep hills than people who have not. People who have listened to sad music (Mahler's Adagietto) see steeper hills than people who have listened to happy music. Overweight people see distances as longer than people who are not overweight. Baseball players on a hot streak see bigger balls coming at them than they do when they're in a slump. When tennis players are playing well, their opponents' serves seem significantly slower.

"We project our individual mental experience into the world, and thereby mistake our mental experience to be the physical world, oblivious to the shaping of perception by our sensory systems, personal histories, goals, and expectations," Proffitt and co-author Drake Baer later wrote in their book *Perception*.

Proffitt's work builds on an earlier theory developed by a psychologist named James J. Gibson. In 1942, Gibson, who also studied visual perception, was summoned by commanders of the U.S. Army Air Forces. They asked him basic questions: How do pilots land planes? How can we help them do it better? Gibson's insight was that as we enter a scene, we're looking for opportunities for action. How do I fit into this situation? What can I do here? What possibilities does this situation afford? In Gibson's language, we see "affordances." A hunter with a gun will see a much bigger field than a hunter with a spear because he has a much wider range of action. A police officer who is holding a gun is more likely to "see" other people holding guns than he would if he were holding a shoe, which is partly why 25 percent of police shootings involve unarmed suspects. Proffitt and Baer hammer home the point: "We perceive the world, not as it is but as it is for us."

The first time I read about this idea of affordances, it didn't seem very powerful. But then as I went on with my life, it dawned on me hour by hour that everywhere I went I was looking at each scene through some affordance. Unconsciously, you and I are always asking ourselves, What do my physical, intellectual, social, and economic capacities enable me to do in this situation? If you and I are out with a group contemplating a hike up a mountain, different members of the group are literally seeing different mountains, depending on how fit or unfit we are. Rich people walk into Neiman Marcus and see a different store than poor people do, because rich people actually have the capacity to buy things in that store. When I was teaching at Yale, my students saw a different campus than the less privileged people who lived in the New Haven neighborhoods nearby. My students had the capacity to take classes and use their ID badges to get into the buildings, so the campus looked to them like a collection of diverse buildings, each with its own purpose and possibilities. Meanwhile, the folks from town did not have the capacity to take classes or get inside most of the buildings, so the place looked more like an imposing and monolithic fortress. I would often see the neighborhood folks hanging around the New Haven Green, but I would almost never see them hanging around campus, even though it's just across the street.

One of the reasons hard conversations are necessary is that we have to ask other people the obvious questions—How do you see this?—if we're going to have any hope of entering, even a bit, into their point of view. Our differences of perception are rooted deep in the hidden kingdom of the unconscious mind and we're generally not aware how profound those differences are until we ask.

There is no way to make hard conversations un-hard. You can never fully understand a person whose life experience is very different from your own. I will never know what it is like to be Black, to be a woman, to be Gen Z, to be born with a disability, to be a working-class man, to be a new immigrant or a person from any of a myriad of other life experiences. There are mysterious depths to each person. There are vast differences between different cultures, before which we need to stand with respect and awe. Nevertheless, I have found that if you work on your skills—your capacity to see and hear others—you really can get a sense of another person's perspective. And I have found that it is quite possible to turn distrust into trust, to build mutual respect.

Like every writer, I am often the recipient of furious, insulting emails. Like every writer, I have found that if you respond to such emails in a way that is respectful and curious, the other person's tone almost always changes—immediately and radically. Suddenly they are civil, kinder, more human. Everybody wants to be heard. Most people are willing to make an extra effort to be kind, considerate, and forgiving when you give them the chance. Most people long to heal the divides that plague our society. At the foundation of all conversation lies one elemental reality: We all share a vast range of common struggles, common experiences, and common joys. Even in the midst of civil strife and hard conversations, I try to return to the great humanistic declaration made by the Roman dramatist Terence: "I am human, and nothing human is alien to me."

TEN

How Do You Serve a Friend
Who Is in Despair?

As public life has become more bitter, private life has become sadder. More and more, I've found myself having conversations with people suffering from depression, with people who are struggling, with people in the midst of grief. These conversations represent a different kind of hard conversations than the heavy-conflict situations I described in the last chapter. Over the next three chapters I'm going to try to share what I've learned about how to accompany someone through each of these trials—depression, struggle, and suffering. There's often little we can do to cure those who are afflicted, but there are ways we can make them feel deeply known.

My most searing encounter with depression came when the illness hit my oldest friend, Peter Marks. Starting at age eleven, Pete and I had built our friendship around play. We played basketball, softball, capture the flag, rugby. We teased each other, pulled pranks, made fun of each other's dance moves, romantic misalliances, and pretty much everything else. We could turn eating a burger into a form of play, with elaborate smacking of lips and operatic exclamations about the excellence of the cheese. We kept it up for five decades.

My wife has a phrase that got Pete just right: He was a rare combo of normal and extraordinary. He was masculine in the way you're supposed to be masculine, with great strength and great gentleness. A father in the way you're supposed to be a father, with endless devotion, a sense of fun and pride. A husband in the way you're supposed to be a husband, going home at night grateful that the one person in the whole world you most want to talk with is going to be sitting right there across the dinner table from you.

Over the years, Pete and I talked frequently about the stresses he was having with a couple of colleagues at work, but I didn't understand all that he was enduring until we spent a weekend with him in the spring of 2019. My wife noticed a change immediately. A light had gone out. There was a flatness in his voice, a stillness in his eyes. One bright June afternoon, he pulled us aside and told us what we knew already: He wasn't himself. He was doing what he loved most—playing basketball, swimming in the lake—but he couldn't enjoy anything. He was worried for his family and himself and asked for our continued friendship and support. It was the first time I had seen such pain in him—what turned out to be severe depression. I was confronted with a question I was unprepared to answer: How do you serve a friend when they are hit with this illness?

I tried the best I could, but Pete succumbed to suicide in April

2022. This chapter, based on an essay I wrote for the *Times,* attempts to capture what I learned from those agonizing three years and that senseless tragedy. It reflects a hard education with no panaceas.

———

First, I need to tell you more about Pete. We met as kids at Incarnation Camp in Connecticut, were campers and counselors together for a decade, and remained close for life. At camp, Pete was handsome, strong, athletic, and kind. There was an exuberant goofballism about him. Once, in a fit of high silliness, he started skipping around the dining hall, singing and leaping higher and higher with each skip. He tried to skip right out of the room, but there was a doorframe, probably about seven feet tall, and Pete slammed his forehead into the top of the frame and fell flat on his back. The rest of us, being sixteen-year-old junior counselors, found this utterly hilarious. Pete, also being sixteen, found it utterly hilarious, too. I remember him lying there in a fit of giggles, with a doorframe-shaped bruise forming on his brow.

One summer, Pete and I led a team of twelve- and thirteen-year-olds in a softball game against a team of fourteen- and fifteen-year-olds. Miraculously, our team won. In the celebration afterward, the boys, Pete, and I piled on one another on the pitcher's mound in a great wriggling heap of disproportionate ecstasy. We hugged and screamed and high-fived. I think our celebration lasted longer than the game—a volcano of male self-approval that is lodged in my memory as one of life's moments of pure joy.

As the years went by, Pete did well in college, joined the navy, went to medical school, and became an eye surgeon. On evenings before surgery Pete took great care of himself, didn't stay out, made sure he had enough sleep to do the job he loved. On evenings after surgery, he'd call his patients, to see how they were feeling. His wife, Jen, a dear friend who was also at camp with us, used to linger around just to hear the gentleness of his tone on those calls, the reassuring kindness of his manner.

He seemed, outwardly, like the person in my circle least likely to be afflicted by a devastating depression, with a cheerful disposition, a happy marriage, a rewarding career, and two truly wonderful sons, Owen and James. But he was carrying more childhood pain than I knew, and eventually the trauma overtook him.

At first, I did not understand the seriousness of the situation. That's partly temperamental. Some people catastrophize and imagine the worst. I tend to bright-icize and assume that everything will work out. But it's also partly because I didn't realize that depression had created another Pete. I had very definite ideas in my head about who Pete was, and depression did not figure into how I understood my friend.

Over the next months, severe depression was revealed to me as an unimagined abyss. I learned that those of us lucky enough never to have experienced serious depression cannot understand what it is like just by extrapolating from our own periods of sadness. As the philosophers Cecily Whiteley and Jonathan Birch have written, it is not just sorrow, it is a state of consciousness that distorts perceptions of time, space, and self.

The journalist Sally Brampton called depression a landscape that "is cold and black and empty. It is more terrifying and more horrible than anywhere I have ever been, even in my nightmares."

The novelist William Styron wrote brilliantly about his own depression in *Darkness Visible*. He described how "the madness of depression is, generally speaking, the antithesis of violence. It is a storm indeed, but a storm of murk. Soon evident are the slowed-down responses, near paralysis, psychic energy throttled back close to zero. . . . I experienced a curious inner convulsion that I can describe only as despair beyond despair. It came out of the cold night; I did not think such anguish possible."

During the Covid-19 pandemic, Pete and I spoke by phone. In the beginning, I made the mistake of trying to advise him about how he could recover from the illness. Years earlier, he had gone to Vietnam to perform eye surgeries for those who were too poor to afford them. I told him he should do that again, since he had found it so rewarding. I did not realize that it was energy and desire he lacked, not ideas about things to do. It was only later that I read that when you give a depressed person advice on how they can get better, there's a good chance all you are doing is telling the person that you just don't get it.

I tried to remind Pete of all the wonderful blessings he enjoyed, what psychologists call "positive reframing." I've since read that this might make the sufferer feel even worse about themselves for not being able to enjoy all the things that are palpably enjoyable.

I learned, very gradually, that a friend's job in these circumstances is not to cheer the person up. It's to acknowledge the reality of the situation; it's to hear, respect, and love them; it's to show them you haven't given up on them, you haven't walked away.

Time and again Pete would talk about his great fear that someday his skill as a surgeon would abandon him, that he would cease to be a healer, that he would lose his identity and self. As Pete spoke of his illness, it sometimes seemed as if there were two of him. There was the one enveloped in pain and the one who was observing all this and could not understand what was happening. That second self was the Pete I spoke to for those three years. He was analyzing the anguish. He was trying to figure it out. He was going to the best doctors. They were trying one approach after another. The cloud would not lift. I am told that one of the brutalities of the illness is the impossibility of articulating exactly what the pain consists of. Pete would give me the general truth: "Depression sucks." But he tried not to burden me with the full horrors of what he was going through. There was a lot he didn't tell me, at least until the end, or not at all.

There were moments during that hard plague year of 2020 that I feared my own mind was slipping. Cheerfulness is my normal default state, but that year my moods could be dark and troubled. When your oldest friend is battling his demons, it's natural to wonder about your own.

While I've devoted my life to words, I increasingly came up against the futility of words to help Pete in any meaningful way. The feeling of impotence was existential.

After a while, I just tried to be normal. I just tried to be the easygoing friend that I had always been to him and he had always been to me. I hoped this would slightly ease his sense of isolation. Intellectually, Pete knew that his wife and boys lavishly loved him, that his friends loved him, but he still felt locked inside the lacerating self-obsession that was part of the illness.

Since Pete's death, I've learned more about the power of just staying present. "If you know someone who's depressed, please resolve to never ask them why," the actor Stephen Fry once wrote.

"Be there for them when they come through the other side. It's hard to be a friend to someone who's depressed, but it is one of the kindest, noblest, and best things you will ever do."

Perhaps the most useful thing I did was send him a video. My friend Mike Gerson, the *Washington Post* columnist, had been hospitalized with depression in early 2019. He delivered a beautiful sermon at the National Cathedral about his experience before he died of complications from cancer in November 2022. Depression, he said, was a "malfunction of the instrument we use to determine reality." Then he talked about the lying voices that had taken up residence in his mind, spewing out their vicious clichés: You are a burden to your friends, you have no future, no one would miss you.

The video of Mike's sermon resonated with Pete and gave him a sense of validation. He, too, described the obsessive-compulsive voices that would attack him from inside his own head. Mike also talked about the fog eventually thinning, about the glimpses of beauty or of love, and reminded Pete that "there is something better on the far side of despair." I kept trying to reassure Peter that this would happen to him, too. Still, the clouds refused to lift.

Jen had some wise words when I asked her what she had learned from being around him during those years. "I was very aware this was not the real Pete," she said. "I tried not to take things personally." I wish I had bombarded Pete with more small touches. Just little notes and emails to let him know how much he was on my mind. Writing about his own depression in *The Atlantic,* Jeffrey Ruoff mentioned that his brother sent him more than seven hundred postcards over the years, from all fifty states, Central America, Canada, and Asia. Those kinds of touches say: I'm with you. No response necessary.

"There are moments in our lives," Honoré de Balzac wrote, "when the sense that our friend is near is all that we can bear. Our wounds smart under the consoling words that only reveal the depths of pain."

Pete developed theories to explain why this had happened to him. He pointed to a series of traumas and neglect he had suffered at home as a child—events he had vaguely referred to during our friendship but never really went into detail with me until his final years.

He thought part of his illness was just straight biology. Think of it like brain cancer, he'd say. A random physical disease. I agree with some of that, but I'm also haunted by the vast number of medications his doctors put him on. He always seemed to be getting on one or getting off another as he ran through various treatment regimes. His path through the mental healthcare system was filled with a scattershot array of different treatments and crushing disappointments.

Pete and his family joined us for Thanksgiving in 2021. By this point I was just trying to be as I always had been toward him, in hopes that he might be able to be as he always had been toward me. We all played basketball and board games and enjoyed the weekend. I felt some hope. But in one of the photos that were taken that weekend, Pete is sitting on the couch, still-faced, enveloped in shadow. One afternoon, he asked my wife to pray over him in the kitchen, plaintively, grasping for hope.

The experts say that if you know someone who is depressed, it's okay to ask them explicitly about suicide. The experts emphasize that you're not going to be putting the thought into their head. Very often it's already on their mind.

When Pete and I gestured toward the subject of suicide, we just talked about what a magnificent family he had, how much they all loved each other. Like Jen, I tried to tell him that this would lift, though as the years went by and the therapies failed, his faith in this deliverance waned.

Pete was always the braver of the two of us, the one who would go cliff diving or jump over bonfires without fear. And he was never more courageous than over his last three years. He fought with astonishing courage and steadfastness against a foe that would bring anybody to their knees. He fought it minute by minute, day by day—over a thousand days. He was driven by his selfless love for his family, which he cherished most of all in the world.

We had dinner a few days before he died. Jen and I tried to keep the conversation bouncing along. But apparently, their car ride home was heart-rending. "How can I not be able to talk to my oldest friend?" Pete asked. "Brooksie can talk to people. I can't."

I don't know what he was thinking on his final day, but I have read that depression makes it hard to imagine a time when things will ever be better. I have no evidence for this, but knowing Pete as I do, I strongly believe that he erroneously convinced himself that he was committing suicide to help his family and ease the hardship his illness had caused them. Living now in the wreckage, I can tell you if you ever find yourself having that thought, it is completely wrong.

"Little has been written about the fact that depression is ridiculous," Andrew Solomon, the author of *The Noonday Demon,* wrote.

"I can remember lying frozen in bed, crying because I was too frightened to take a shower and at the same time knowing that showers are not scary." I would add that depression is bitterly ridiculous. Pete died a few weeks before his younger son's college graduation, enmeshed by loving relationships and friendships, with so much to give.

If I'm ever in a similar situation again, I'll understand that you don't have to try to coax somebody out of depression. It's enough to show that you have some understanding of what they are enduring. It's enough to create an atmosphere in which they can share their experience. It's enough to offer them the comfort of being seen.

My friend Nat Eddy, who also accompanied Pete through those final years, wrote to me recently: "Do whatever it is you can do to give the wives and children a break—an hour or two when they don't have to worry that the worst will happen (and pray that it doesn't happen on your watch, because that isn't a given). Do whatever it is you do so you can look at yourself in the mirror. True friendship offers deep satisfactions, but it also imposes vulnerabilities and obligations, and to pretend it doesn't is to devalue friendship."

I feel sorrow that I didn't know enough to do this more effectively with Pete. I might have kept him company more soothingly; I might have made him better understand what he meant to me. But I do not feel guilt.

Pete had some of the world's great experts walking with him through this. He had his wonderful wife and kids, who accompanied him, lovingly and steadfastly, every day. Pete used to say he found talking to Jen more helpful than talking to any of the experts. So there is no reason for any of us to feel like failures because we could not alter what happened. Every case of depression is unique, and every case is to be fought with as much love and endurance and knowledge as can be mustered. But in this particular case, the beast was bigger than Pete; it was bigger than us.

I've read a lot about the grieving process for family members, but not so much about what grieving is like when your friends die. Death and I were too well acquainted in 2022. I lost three good friends—Pete, Mike Gerson, and my longtime *NewsHour* partner, Mark Shields—and each time I was surprised anew by how profound and lasting the inner aches were.

Pete's death disoriented me. He'd been a presence for practically my whole life, and suddenly the steady friendship I took for granted was gone. It's as if I went back to Montana and suddenly the mountains had disappeared.

One great source of comfort has been the chance to glimpse, from time to time, how heroically Pete's boys, Owen and James, have handled this loss. In their own grief, they have rallied around their mother. Two months after Pete's passing, my eldest son got married. To my great astonishment and gratitude, Jen and the boys were able to make the trip to attend. At the reception, the boys gently coaxed their mother to join us on the dance floor. It felt appropriate, since this was what we did at camp; dancing skeined through the decades of our lives. I have a sharp memory of those two fine young men dancing that evening, and a million memories of the parents who raised them so well.

Looking back now, I see the essential challenge. Each mind constructs its own reality. In normal circumstances, I can get a sense of my friend's perception of reality because it largely overlaps with my perception of reality. But depression changes that. In depression Andrew Solomon was experiencing a reality that was just bizarre. The guy thought showers were terrifying. Pete also experienced a reality that was bizarre. He saw a world without pleasure.

When we are trying to see a depressed person deeply, and make them feel heard and understood, we are peering into a nightmarish Salvador Dalí world, one that doesn't follow any of our logic, that doesn't make any sense, and that the depressed person will probably have difficulty describing for us. There is no easy way to get even partly into this alternate reality; we can only try to persevere through a leap of faith, through endless flexibility, and through a willingness to be humble before the fact that none of this makes any sense.

ELEVEN

The Art of Empathy

"Recognition is the first human quest," the journalist Andy Crouch writes in his book *The Life We're Looking For.* Babies come out of the womb looking for a face that will see them, a mother or a caretaker who will know them and attend to their needs. When they are not seen, they are traumatized. Psychologists sometimes conduct "still face" experiments in which they tell mothers not to respond to their babies. When the babies send out bids for attention and love, the mothers are supposed to just sit there, expressionless: with a still face. At first the babies squirm and are uncomfortable, then they cry in frustration, and then they collapse in misery. It is an existential crisis. If a baby goes unseen by their caretakers for long periods of time it can leave lasting emotional and spiritual damage. "The development of the soul in the child," the philosopher Martin Buber wrote, "is inextricably bound up with that of the longing for the Thou, with the satisfaction and disappointment of this longing."

This is the first education. Every child, even from birth, is looking for answers to the basic questions of life: Am I safe? How does love work? Am I worthy? Will I be cared for? Even in infancy, we internalize answers to those questions based on what we see around us and how we are treated. This education happens even though later, as adults, we have no conscious memory of this period at all.

When, in adulthood, you get to know someone really well, you often develop a sense for how they were raised. You see in some people's current insecurities how as children they must have been diminished and criticized. You see, in their terror over being abandoned, how they must have felt left behind when young. On the other hand, when you meet people who assume that the world is safe and trustworthy, that others will naturally smile upon them, you sense how as children they must have felt illuminated by love.

It should be so simple. We all want children to feel safe, to know that love is constant and unconditional, that they are worthy. The problem is that we as parents still carry, often unconsciously, the wounds and terrors of our *own* early years, which were, in turn, caused by the wounds and terrors of our parents' early years, and so on and so on. The wounds and traumas get passed down from generation to generation.

In his book *Deep Human Connection,* the psychotherapist Stephen Cope writes that his mother liked the idea of a baby more than actual babies and, as a result, didn't shower much attention and unconditional love on her children: "My twin sister and I readily agree, chewing over these issues as we have for the past many decades, that, alas, we were destined to be anxiously and ambiva-

lently attached little beings. . . . We had all the hallmarks: Insecure. Anxious. Hungry for more. Quickly seduced by the promise
of love. Never quite sure we could count on it."

The actress Demi Moore grew up with parents who were his-
trionic, unstable, self-sabotaging, and melodramatic. Her parents
moved the family around so much that she and her brother attended, on average, two schools a year. Her father committed suicide at thirty-six. After her mother attempted suicide, the young
Moore had to try to dig the pills out of her mouth. "They loved me
the way they loved each other," Moore wrote, "the only way they
knew how: inconsistently and conditionally. From them, I learned
that love was something you had to scramble to keep. It could be
revoked at any minute for reasons that you couldn't understand,
that you couldn't control. The kind of love I grew up with was
scary to need, and painful to feel. If I didn't have that uneasy ache,
that prickly anxiety around someone, how would I know it was
love?"

The famous Grant Study followed 268 Harvard men from
their days as college students in the 1940s until their deaths many
decades later, in an attempt to discover the patterns of human
development and achievement. The study found—and this was a
surprise decades ago—that the quality of your relationships determines the quality of your life. But relationships in childhood
had a special power. At one point the directors of the study wondered why some of the men in the study were promoted to officers during World War II and others weren't. They found that
the number one factor that correlated with success in wartime
was not IQ, physical endurance, or socioeconomic background.
The number one factor was the overall warmth of the man's

family home. The men who had been well loved and seen deeply by their parents could offer love and care to the men under their command.

The men in the study with warm relationships with their fathers enjoyed their vacations more through life, were better able to use humor as a coping mechanism, and were more content in their retirements. A warm childhood environment was also a better predictor of adult social mobility than intelligence.

On the other hand, men with a poor relationship with their mothers were more likely to suffer from dementia in old age. Those who grew up in cold homes took more prescription drugs of all kinds, and spent five times as much time in psychiatric hospitals. As the study's longtime director George Vaillant put it, "Whereas a warm childhood, like a rich father, tends to inoculate a man against future pain, a bleak childhood is like poverty; it cannot cushion the difficulties of life. Yes, difficulties may sometimes lead to post-traumatic growth, and some men's lives did improve over time. But there is always a high cost in pain and lost opportunities, and for many men with bleak childhoods the outlook remained bleak until they died, sometimes young and sometimes by their own hands."

Children respond to harsh circumstances the only way they know how. They construct defenses to protect against further wounding. They draw lessons—adaptive or maladaptive—about what they can expect from life and what they need to do to survive. These defenses and lessons are often unconscious. If you hope to know someone well, you have to know something about the struggles and blessings of their childhoods and the defensive architecture they carry through life.

Here are a few of the defenses that many people carry inside, sometimes for the rest of their lives:

AVOIDANCE. Avoidance is usually about fear. *Emotions and relationships have hurt me, so I will minimize emotions and relationships.* People who are avoidant feel most comfortable when the conversation stays superficial. They often overintellectualize life. They retreat to work. They try to be self-sufficient and pretend they don't have needs. Often, they have not had close relationships as kids and have lowered their expectations about future relationships. A person who fears intimacy in this way may be always on the move, preferring not to be rooted or pinned down; they are sometimes relentlessly positive so as not to display vulnerability; they engineer things so they are the strong one others turn to but never the one who turns to others.

DEPRIVATION. Some children are raised around people so self-centered that the needs of the child are ignored. The child naturally learns the lesson "My needs won't be met." It is a short step from that to "I'm not worthy." A person haunted by a deprivation schema can experience feelings of worthlessness throughout life no matter how many amazing successes they achieve. They often carry the idea that there is some flaw deep within themselves, that if other people knew it, it would cause them to run away. When they are treated badly, they are likely to blame themselves. (*Of course he had an affair; I'm a pathetic wife.*) They sometimes grapple with a fierce inner critic.

OVERREACTIVITY. Children who are abused and threatened grow up in a dangerous world. The person afflicted in this way often has, deep in their nervous system, a hyperactive threat-detection system. Such people interpret ambivalent situations as menacing situations, neutral faces as angry faces. They are trapped in a hyperactive mind theater in which the world is dangerous. They overreact to things and fail to understand why they did so.

PASSIVE AGGRESSION. Passive aggression is the indirect expression of anger. It is a way to sidestep direct communication by a person who fears conflict, who has trouble dealing with negative emotions. It's possible such a person grew up in a home where anger was terrifying, where emotions were not addressed, or where love was conditional and the lesson was that direct communication would lead to the withdrawal of affection. Passive aggression is thus a form of emotional manipulation, a subtle power play to extract guilt and affection. A husband with passive-aggressive tendencies may encourage his wife to go on a weekend outing with her friends, feeling himself to be a selfless martyr, but then get angry with her in the days before the outing and through the weekend. He'll let her know by various acts of withdrawal and self-pity that she's a selfish person and he's an innocent victim.

These defenses are not entirely bad. I once read a great phrase in a book by the British writer Will Storr that captures the dual nature of our defenses. He proposed that most great fictional characters—and, by implication, most great people—have a "sacred flaw." His point was that each of us goes around with certain models in our head that shape how we see the world. You build these models, starting early in life, and they work for you. They help you defend yourself from neglect or abuse. They help you anticipate how people are going to behave. They steer you to act in ways that get you affirmed and loved. The big thing your models do is help you see your life as a story in which you are the hero. We seek out the people, the articles, and the books that confirm our models.

Storr says you can get a sense for somebody's models, especially the defensive ones, by asking them to complete sentences like "The most important thing in life is . . ." or "I'm only safe when . . ." For example, I know plenty of people in politics who have built up overreactive defensive models. For them the most important thing is to struggle against injustice. They feel safe only when they are on the attack, fighting righteously against their foes. They learned in childhood that life is combat.

For a time these models—these defenses—worked for them. The models induced them to see the world as divided between the children of light and the children of darkness. As they waged their righteous battles against their political enemies, they rose in status, power, and esteem. Meanwhile, they grew tough and resilient. I once toured a vineyard where the guy giving the tour explained that they don't plant their vines in the kind of soil that is gentlest on the vines. They plant their vines in clay soil because clay resists the vines, and the vines grow strong by fighting against their environment. I feel like I know a lot of people like that, especially in politics. They've grown strong by resisting what is wrong with their environment.

Often, their anger is fully justified. But a sacred flaw is still a flaw. The first problem with, say, an overreactive defense architecture is that it causes people to lash out at everything. When somebody criticizes a defensive person's internal models, it doesn't feel like they are attacking her mere opinion. It feels like they are attacking her identity. The psychologist Jonathan Haidt says that if you find what is sacred to a person, there you will find "rampant irrationality." A person with an overreactive defense architecture is thinking, *My critics or opponents are not just wrong, they are evil.* Suddenly, such a person perceives apocalyptic threats coming from all directions and seizes on conspiracy theories that explain the malevolent forces she sees all around her. This person is perpetually on a war footing, dawn to dusk. She has to get her retaliation in first.

The second problem with such a defensive architecture is that you don't control it; it controls you. One problem with anger, for example, is that it has to find things to attach itself to. Angry people are always in search of others they can be angry at. Anger is unattractive. Anger is stupid. A person who is perpetually angry is always mishearing and misreading others. He misperceives what the other person said so he can have a pretext to go on the vicious attack. Worst of all, anger escalates. People are always talking about venting anger or controlling anger or directing anger. In fact, the anger is always in control, ratcheting up higher and higher, consuming the host.

In his 1949 book, *Jesus and the Disinherited,* the great Black theologian Howard Thurman, who had a lot to be angry about, wrote that "Jesus rejected hatred because he saw that hatred meant death to the mind, death to the spirit, and death to communion with his Father. He affirmed life; and hatred was the great denial."

The third problem with our defensive models—any defensive model—is that they tend to get outdated. The lessons we learned about how to survive childhood are often obsolete by the time we hit adulthood. But we continue to see the world through these old models; our actions are still guided by our old models. This is called "conceptual blindness" and explains why very smart people can sometimes do phenomenally stupid things. Think, for example, of those generals in World War I. They were educated as cadets in the age of the cavalry charges, and they built up models of war that were appropriate in the era of horses and rifles. But decades later, after they had become generals, they found themselves leading troops in the age of machine guns. Only they hadn't updated their models. Year after year, they sent millions of men charging directly into machine gun nests, and to their deaths, because they couldn't see that their models were obsolete. It was mass slaughter. Conceptual blindness can happen to anyone.

———

At some point in their lives, most people come to realize that some of their models are no longer working. The defenses they built up in childhood are limiting them in adulthood. The avoidant person wants to become more attached. The person with a deprivation schema wants to feel her full worth. The overreactive person realizes that a life of constant strife only brings ruin on herself and those she loves. This moment usually arises as a crisis. A person, because of their own stupid behavior, has broken a marriage, been fired from a job, lost a friend, hurt their children, suffered a public humiliation. Their world has crumbled.

In theory, it should be possible to repair yourself alone. In theory, it should be possible to understand yourself, especially the deep broken parts of yourself, through introspection. But the research clearly shows that introspection is overrated.

That's in part because what's going on in your mind is not only more complicated than you understand, it is more complicated than you can understand. Your mind hides most of your thinking so you can get on with life. Furthermore, you're too close to yourself. You can't see the models you use to perceive the world because you're seeing with them. Finally, when people are trying to see themselves by themselves, they tend to bend off in one of two unhelpful directions. Sometimes they settle for the easy insight. They tell themselves they've just had a great epiphany. In actuality, they've done nothing more than come up with a make-believe story that will help them feel good about themselves. Or else they spiral into rumination. They revisit the same flaws and traumatic experiences over and over again, reinforcing their bad mental habits, making themselves miserable.

Introspection isn't the best way to repair your models; communication is. People trying to grapple with the adult legacies of their childhood wounds need friends who will prod them to see their situation accurately. They need friends who can provide the outside view of them, the one they can't see from within. They need friends who will remind them, "The most important part of your life is ahead of you, not behind you. I'm proud to know you and proud of everything you've accomplished and will accomplish." They need people who will practice empathy.

That's where you and I come in. Empathy is involved in every stage of the process of getting to know a person. But it is especially necessary when we are accompanying someone who is wrestling with their wounds. The problem is that a lot of people don't know what empathy really is. They think it's an easy emotion: You open up your heart and you experience this gush of fellow feeling with another person. By this definition, empathy feels simple, natural, and automatic: I feel for you.

But that's not quite right. Empathy is a set of social and emotional skills. These skills are a bit like athletic skills: Some people are more naturally talented at empathy than others; everybody improves with training.

Empathy consists of at least three related skills. First, there is the skill of *mirroring*. This is the act of accurately catching the emotion of the person in front of you.

Every waking second, the people around you are experiencing emotions, which are sometimes subtle and sometimes overwhelming. Our emotions come in a continuous flow, not as discrete events. We encounter something—perhaps the aroma of a croissant or the sound of a door slamming—and we coat that encounter with a feeling, some evaluation that is positive or negative in some way. Every experience gets coated with an emotion.

This process of creating emotion starts deep in the body. As the people around you go about life, their heart, lungs, hormones, endocrine glands, pancreas, immune system, muscles, and gut are all in constant motion, depending on the situation they happen to be in. Though most of the attention recently has been spent on the neurons in the skull, the neurons in our bodies are contributing to some of the most important thinking we do. Information about these basic body states is sent up to the brain through the autonomic nervous system, which runs through the body up to the head.

The brain, which is in charge of regulating the body budget—how much energy different parts of your body need at any given second—monitors the body and recognizes different physical states. Let's say the brain perceives a faster heart rate, pupils dilating, muscles tightening, breath quickening, blood pressure rising, stress hormones releasing. Your mind observes all this and tries to discern which emotional concept to apply to this bodily state. "Is this sadness?" No. "Is this anger?" Not quite. "Oh, this is fear!"

Historically, emotions have had a bad reputation. They have been thought to be these primitive forces that sweep you up and lead you astray. Over the centuries many philosophers assumed that reason is separate from emotions—reason is the cool, prudential charioteer, and emotions are the hard-to-control stallions.

None of that is true. Emotions contain information. Unless they are out of control, emotions are supple mental faculties that help you steer through life. Emotions assign value to things; they tell you what you want and don't want. I feel love for this person and want to approach him; I feel contempt for that person and want to avoid her. Emotions help you adjust to different situations. You find yourself in a threatening situation and you feel anxiety. This emotional state alters your thinking so you are quick to look for danger. Emotions also tell you whether you are moving toward your goals or away from them. If I want to know you, it's moderately important that I know what you think, but it's very important that I have some sense of the flow of what you feel.

The body is the origin point of emotions, and the body communicates emotions. The face has more than forty muscles, especially around the mouth and eyes. The lips can produce the cruel smile that sadists wear, the grin-and-bear-it smile that polite people adopt when another commits a faux pas, the delighted-to-see-you smile that lights up another person's whole day. When you look someone in the eyes, you can see flirting eyes, glazed eyes, mad eyes, frenzied eyes, faraway eyes, sad eyes, and so much more. The body also tells the story of the heart—the drooping posture of hurt feelings, freezing to show fear, twisting with anxiety, turning red with anger.

A person who is good at mirroring is quick to experience the emotions of the person in front of them, is quick to reenact in his own body the emotions the other person is holding in hers. A person who is good at mirroring smiles at smiles, yawns at yawns, and frowns at frowns. He unconsciously attunes his breathing patterns, heart rate, speaking speed, posture, and gestures and even his vocabulary levels. He does this because a good way to understand what another person is feeling in their body is to live it out yourself in your own body, at least to some extent. People who have Botox injections and can't furrow their brow are less able to perceive another person's worry because they can't physically reenact it.

People who are good at mirroring also have what the Northeastern University neuroscientist Lisa Feldman Barrett calls high "emotional granularity," the ability to finely distinguish between different emotional states.

Some people are not good at recognizing emotions. They have low emotional granularity. Such people have just a few emotional concepts in their head. Many young children use the words "sad," "mad," and "scared" interchangeably because they haven't yet learned to distinguish between these states. They scream, "I hate you" to their mothers because they haven't learned to differentiate anger from hate. Many of Barrett's adult research subjects are unable to distinguish between "anxious" and "depressed." To be anxious is to be jittery, while being depressed means feeling sluggish, but these subjects lacked the conceptual granularity to be able to distinguish between these two very different states.

People who are good at mirroring, by contrast, have high emotional granularity and experience the world in rich, supple ways. They can distinguish between similar emotions, such as anger, frustration, pressure, stress, anxiety, angst, and irritation. These people have educated their emotions by reading literature, listening to music, reflecting on their relationships. They are attuned to their body and have become expert at reading it, and so they have a wide emotional repertoire to draw on as life happens. They have become emotion experts. It's like being a painter with more colors on your palate.

The second empathy skill is not mirroring but *mentalizing*. Most primates can mirror another primate's emotions at least to some degree. Only humans can figure out *why* they are experiencing what they are experiencing. We do this by relying on our own experience and memory. As with all modes of perception, we ask, "What is this similar to?" When I see what a friend is experiencing, I go back to a time in my life when I experienced something like that. I make predictions about what my friend is going through based on what I had to go through. This is what the eighteenth-century philosopher and economist Adam Smith presciently called "projective" empathy: the act of projecting my memories onto your situation. As we do this, we rise to a higher level of empathy. We don't see "woman crying." We see "woman who has suffered a professional setback and a public humiliation." I've been through a version of that, and I can project some of what I felt onto her.

When practiced well, this mentalizing skill helps us see emotional states in all their complexity. People generally have multiple emotions at once. If I see you on your first day on the job, I may notice your excitement about starting this new chapter in your life, your timidity in front of all these new people, your anxiety that maybe you're not yet up to the tasks in front of you. I remember my own first days on a new job, so I can predict the contradictory emotions flowing through you.

Mentalizing also helps us simultaneously sympathize with a person while also detaching to make judgments about them. I may feel genuinely bad that you are miserable because somebody scratched your Mercedes. I may also think you are reacting childishly because too much of your identity is wrapped up in your car.

The third empathy skill is *caring*. Con artists are very good at reading people's emotions, but we don't call them empathetic, because they don't have genuine concern for the people they are reading. Children are very good at empathetic distress—feeling what you are feeling—but are not as good at empathetic concern: knowing what to do about it. You're crying because you had a bad day at work, so they hand you a Band-Aid—which is sweet but not what you'd want a grown-up to do.

If mentalizing is me projecting my experiences onto you, caring involves getting out of my experiences and understanding that what you need may be very different from what I would need in that situation. This is hard. The world is full of people who are nice; there are many fewer who are effectively kind.

Let's say I'm with somebody who is having an anxiety attack. Caring is not necessarily offering what I would want in that situation: a glass of wine. Caring begins with the awareness that the other person has a consciousness that is different from my own. They might want me to hold their hand while they do some breathing exercises. I'm going to find that completely awkward, but I'm going to do it because I want to practice effective empathy.

Similarly, when writing a thank-you note, my egotistical instinct is to write a note about all the ways I'm going to use the gift you just gave me. But if I'm going to be an empathetic person, I need to get outside of my perspective and get inside yours. I'm going to write about *your intentions*—the impulses that led *you* to think that this gift is right for me and the thinking process that impelled *you* to buy it.

When you meet someone with cancer, it feels empathetic to tell the person how sorry you are, but my friend Kate Bowler, who actually has cancer, says that the people who show empathy best are those "who hug you and give you impressive compliments that don't feel like a eulogy. People who give you non-cancer-thematic gifts. People who just want to delight you, not try to fix you, and who make you realize that it is just another beautiful day and there is usually something fun to do." That is what caring looks like.

———

People vary widely in their ability to project empathy. The psychologist Simon Baron-Cohen, one of the leading scholars in this field, argues that there's an empathy spectrum and that people tend to fall within one of seven categories on it, depending on their genetic inheritance, the way life has treated them, and how hard they've worked to become empathetic. At level zero, people can hurt or even kill others without feeling anything at all. At level one, people can show a degree of empathy, but not enough to brake their cruel behavior. They blow up at others and cause emotional damage without restraint. At level two people are simply clueless. They say rude and hurtful things without awareness. They invade other people's personal space and miss social cues in ways that make others feel uncomfortable. At level three people avoid social encounters when possible because it is so hard for them. Small talk is exhausting and unpredictable. At level four people can interact easily with others but they do not like it when the conversation shifts to emotional or personal topics. People at level five have many intimate friendships and are comfortable expressing support and compassion. At level six we have people who are wonderful listeners, are intuitive about other's needs, and are comfortable and effective at offering comfort and support.

I've learned a lot from Baron-Cohen's work, but I think his empathy bell curve is off-kilter. He puts a lot of emphasis on people with empathy deficits, maybe because those are the people he studies. But I find that the vast majority of the people I encounter are empathetic to some significant degree and would rank as fours, fives, or even sixes on his scale. In most social encounters, even just checking out of the grocery store with the cashier, empathy is in the room.

You can measure how dispositionally empathetic you are by noting how much you agree or disagree with the following statements:

I find it hard to know what to do in social situations.
It doesn't bother me too much if I'm late meeting a friend.
People often tell me that I went too far in driving my point
home in a discussion.

Interpersonal conflict, even when it doesn't involve me, is
   physically painful to me.
I often mimic mannerisms, accents, and body language
   without meaning to.
When I make a social blunder, I feel extremely disturbed.

Agreement with the first three of these statements, taken from
Baron-Cohen, are signs that you have low empathy skills. Agree-
ment with the last three, taken from *The Art of Empathy* by Karla
McLaren, are signs of high empathy.

Low empaths can be cruel and pitiable creatures. Carol was a
thirty-nine-year-old woman Baron-Cohen met at his diagnostic
center. Carol had so much defensive architecture, she was like a
medieval fortress in human form. She harbored a vast reservoir of
hatred toward her parents, who she felt had mistreated her. She
also blew up at anybody she believed was disrespecting her. If her
children didn't immediately do what she wanted, she'd explode
with rage: "How dare you treat me with such disrespect? You can
just fuck off! I hate you! I never want to see you again. . . . You're
evil, selfish bastards. I hate you! I'm going to kill myself! And I
hope you're happy knowing you made me do it!"

After this kind of tirade, she would storm out of the house, in-
stantly feel better, and have a perfectly pleasant evening with her
friends while her kids were left to deal with the emotional wreckage back at home. Carol was simply incapable of understanding
the effect she had on others. In her mental universe, Baron-Cohen
observes, her own needs were paramount and other people's needs
were simply not on her radar. She was also bad at interpreting
other people's facial expressions or gestures. If someone in the same

room with her remained silent for a few minutes, preoccupied with something, she interpreted this silence as aggression and she would go viciously on the attack. She had few friends but treated the ones she did have in the same hot/cold manner.

Carol has borderline personality disorder. Borderlines make up about 2 percent of the general population and 15 percent of those in therapy. Borderlines rage against those they love. They have a constant fear of abandonment and are impulsive and self-destructive. Somewhere between 40 and 70 percent of borderlines report a history of sexual abuse while they were children. Carol herself had a cold mother who stopped breastfeeding after one week, abstained from anything that might be called maternal care, and beat her when she misbehaved. Carol started having sexual relationships at fourteen, in an effort to find love, and began cutting herself at eighteen. Even as a mother and an adult, she left her family many nights to go out clubbing. As Baron-Cohen puts it, "She doesn't want to hear about other people's problems. All she cares about is herself." There's a sad and tragic greediness about such people; they are trapped in a desperate vortex of want.

Highly empathic people, on the other hand, enjoy deeper relationships, exhibit more charitable behavior toward those around them, and, according to some studies, show higher degrees of nonconformity and social self-confidence. High empaths can perform world-class social skills, such as knowing which child needs kindness when she misbehaves and which child needs sternness, understanding which co-workers need to be told directly what they are doing wrong and which ones need help in coming to that awareness themselves.

High empaths are unusually aware of the subtleties in any situation—scents, tastes, emotional tremors. The novelist Pearl Buck argued that artists are people who tend to be extremely sensitive to any emotional input:

> The truly creative mind in any field is no more than this: A human creature born abnormally, inhumanely sensitive. To them, a touch is a blow, a sound is a noise, a misfortune is a tragedy, a joy is an ecstasy, a friend is a lover, a lover is a god, and failure is death. Add to this cruelly delicate organism the overpowering necessity to create, create, create. . . . By some strange unknown inward urgency, he is not really alive unless he is creating.

I confess that this sounds a little exhausting, and also a bit inspiring. I have a friend who is a high empath in just this way. She feels everything. Often she has to take a few days off from people just so she can rest and restore. But she is also one of the most effectively caring people I know. She can sense the subtle emotional tremors reverberating through a room, can locate the person who is feeling upset and left out. She identifies with that person in a way that is compelling and beautiful. She makes people feel seen.

As I said, we are all born with innate empathetic dispositions, the way we are born with innate athletic talents. But we can also get better with training. Here are some practices that can help you develop your empathy skills:

CONTACT THEORY. Decades ago, the psychologist Gordon All-port built on the obvious point that it's hard to hate people close up. He found that bringing hostile groups together really does increase empathy in each group. But the group dynamics have to be structured just right. It helps, for example, to put people in a circle to demonstrate that everybody in the group is equal to everybody else. It helps to give the group a shared focus and a common goal, so that from the start they are working to build something together. A community is a group of people with a common project.

DRAW IT WITH YOUR EYES CLOSED. People become more empathetic when they take the time to closely observe the people around them. I've found that actors are particularly good at this. Interviewed about how she prepares for a role, Viola Davis once replied:

> Actors walk through life so different because we have to be an observer. I always say you are an observer and a thief—that you're constantly seeing the minutiae of everything. The way someone puts their head down if you say a certain word. And you think, "Why did they do that? Is it something in their past? Were they traumatized? Do they not like me?" He's just sitting at the bus stop but look what he's eating and how he's eating it. Do you see how he smiled? Did you see how he didn't?

The actor Paul Giamatti has described how he got into the role of John Adams for the 2008 HBO miniseries. During his research, he came across a list of Adams's health complaints. He realized that Adams was plagued by real and hypochondriacal illnesses. He began to see him as a man perpetually dyspeptic because of digestive problems, toothaches, headaches, and more. He carried himself through the role in that manner.

The actor Matthew McConaughey once told me that he looks for some small gesture in a character that can offer a glimpse of the whole personality. One character might be a "hands in his front pockets" kind of guy. He goes through life hunched over, closed in. When he takes his hands out of his pockets and tries to assert himself, he's going to be unnatural, insecure, overly aggressive. McConaughey also tries to see how each situation looks to his character. A killer is not thinking, "I'm a killer." He's thinking, "I'm here to restore order." A good actor, like a good empath, has to understand the stories the character is telling himself.

If you really want your children to be more empathetic, get them involved in their school's drama program. Playing another character is a powerful way to widen your repertoire of perspectives.

LITERATURE. Researchers have found that people who read are more empathetic. Plot-driven genre books—thrillers and detective stories—do not seem to increase empathy skills. But reading biographies or complex, character-driven novels and plays like *Beloved* or *Macbeth,* in which the reader gets enmeshed in the changing emotional life of the characters, does.

EMOTION SPOTTING. The emotion scholar Marc Brackett has developed a tool to improve a person's emotional granularity, something he calls the "mood meter." It is based on the idea that emotions have two core dimensions, energy and pleasantness. So he constructed a chart with four quadrants. The top right quadrant contains emotions that are high in pleasantness and high-energy: happiness, joy, exhilaration. The bottom right quadrant contains emotions that are high in pleasantness but low-energy: contentment, serenity, ease. The top left contains emotions that are low in pleasantness but high-energy: anger, frustration, fear. The bottom left contains emotions that are low-energy and low in pleasantness: sadness, apathy.

The mood meter is a map of human emotions. At any given moment you can pause, figure out where your mood is on the map, and attempt to assign it a label. This exercise, Brackett notes, gives people "permission to feel"—permission to choose not to bottle up their emotions but to acknowledge and investigate them. Brackett reports that when you ask people in public where they are on the mood meter, almost everybody will say they are having positive emotions. When you ask people in confidential surveys where they are, 60 to 70 percent will put themselves on the negative-emotion side of the mood meter. That result is haunting, because it suggests that many of the people you meet, who seem fine on the surface, are actually suffering within.

Simply by pausing from time to time to track your emotional state with the mood meter, you can learn, for example, to discern the difference between anxiety (worrying about future uncertainty) and pressure (worrying about your performance at some task). Brackett has taken his technique to schools and run people through his RULER curriculum, in when he teaches people a set of emotional skills: how to Recognize, Understand, Label, Express, and Regulate their emotions. Brackett's technique is a very powerful way to improve the emotional awareness and emotional regulation of both children and adults. Recently, for example, Brackett and his team developed ways to measure the emotional intelligence of supervisors at various workplaces. They found that employees whose supervisors score low on emotional intelligence say they feel inspired about 25 percent of the time, whereas employees whose supervisors score high on emotional intelligence feel inspired about 75 percent of the time. In other words, people who are good at recognizing and expressing emotions have a huge effect on those around them.

SUFFERING. As Montaigne once observed, you can be knowledgeable with other men's knowledge, but you can't be wise with other men's wisdom. There are certain things you simply have to live through in order to understand. And so another way we grow more empathic is simply by living and enduring the slings and arrows that life generally brings. People who have survived natural disasters, for example, are more likely to help homeless people. People who have survived civil wars give more to charity. Those who use life's hard chapters well come out different.

Most of the truly empathetic people I know have been through hard times but were not broken by them. They did not harden their defensive architecture to protect themselves from life. Instead, paradoxically and heroically, they shed their defensive architecture. They made themselves more vulnerable and more open to life. They are able to use their own moments of suffering to understand and connect with others. There's a story Rabbi Elliot Kukla once told that illustrates how highly empathic people accompany others. Kukla knew a woman who, because of a brain injury, would sometimes fall to the floor. People would rush to immediately get her back on her feet. She told Kukla, "I think people rush to help me up because they are so uncomfortable with seeing an adult lying on the floor. But what I really need is for someone to get down on the ground with me." Sometimes you just need to get down on the floor with someone.

Throughout this chapter I've been trying to emphasize how physical emotions are, that becoming more empathetic is not some intellectual enterprise; it is training your body to respond in open and interactive ways. To recover from painful traumas, people need to live through experiences that contradict what happened to them earlier in their lives. Someone who has been abused has to experience intimacy that is safe. Someone who has been abandoned has to experience others who stayed. This is the kind of knowledge and learning that is held at the cellular level. The rational brain is incapable of talking the emotional body out of its own reality, so the body has to experience a different reality firsthand.

Empathetic people are able to provide that kind of physical presence. In our conversations the Columbia University physician and researcher Martha Welch has emphasized the power of "co-regulation." When two people are close to each other and trust each other, they may be just talking over coffee or they may be hugging, but something is communicated from body to body. They physically calm each other's viscera, they co-modulate each other's heart rates to produce "cardiac calming," and they produce what she calls "higher vagal tone"—which is a comprehensive state that occurs when your gut and innards feel secure and serene.

Over time, a person who enjoys a higher vagal tone will begin to see and construct the world differently. I mean this literally, too. As the neuroscientist Lisa Feldman Barrett writes in her book *How Emotions Are Made,* "You may think that in everyday life, the things you see and hear influence what you feel, but it's mostly the other way around: What you feel alters your sight and hearing." People who are scared take in a scene differently. Our ears, for example, immediately adjust to focus on high and low frequencies—a scream or a growl—rather than midrange frequencies, which include normal human speech. Anxiety narrows our attention and diminishes our peripheral vision. A feeling of happiness, by contrast, widens our peripheral vision. A person who feels safe because of the reliable and empathetic presence of others will see the world as a wider, more open, and happier place.

The people who practice effective empathy have suffered in ways that give them understanding and credibility. The playwright Thornton Wilder once described the compelling presence such a person brings to the world: "Without your wound where would your power be? It is your very remorse that makes your low voice tremble into the hearts of men. The very angels themselves cannot persuade the wretched and blundering children on earth as can one human being broken on the wheels of living. In love's service only the wounded soldiers can serve."

TWELVE

How Were You Shaped by Your Sufferings?

Barbara Lazear Ascher's husband, Bob, delivered the news in the most straightforward way possible. "Looks like pancreatic cancer," he told her matter-of-factly after his test results came back. The doctors said he had three months to live.

She and their friends gave him a wonderful leave-taking. They had theme-party nights—a Russian night with caviar and vodka, a Hawaiian night with grass skirts and leis scented with jasmine. They read poetry and had long conversations. "Having a gun pointed at our heads inspired us to become our best, most open hearted, honest and bravest selves," Lazear Ascher writes in her memoir *Ghosting*. At the end, their life together was stripped down to the essentials. "There were many times when we felt blessed. It was as though certain death had granted us an extra life."

When Bob got really sick, Barbara brought him home from the hospital so his final days would be more humane. She showered him with love and attention. "Dying was intimate, and I drew close," Ascher writes. "We were single-minded, welded together in the process of this long leave-taking."

Death was hard, but then grieving after he died was harder. After the memorial service and the wake, she was alone within the yawning silence of her apartment. She describes feeling that "a wind began to blow through the emptiness of my hollowed self." One day a neighbor whose husband had died five years before called out to her as they were crossing the street in opposite directions: "You'll think you're sane, but you're not." Before long she was screaming at CVS employees because "I'll Be Home for Christmas" was playing on the sound system . . . and her husband wouldn't be. She began to fear bathing and music and Saturday nights. She started giving her stuff away—and later regretted it. She had visions of seeing Bob on the street.

C. S. Lewis once observed that grief is not a state but a process. It's a river that runs through a long valley, and at every turn a new landscape is revealed, and yet somehow it repeats and repeats. Periods of grief and suffering often shatter our basic assumptions about who we are and how life works. We tend to assume that the world is benevolent, that life is controllable, that things are supposed to make sense, that we are basically good people who deserve good things. Suffering and loss can blast all that to smithereens.

"Trauma challenges our global meaning system," Stephen Joseph writes in *What Doesn't Kill Us.* "It confronts us with existential truths about life that clash with this system. The more we try to hold on to our assumptive world, the more mired we are in denial of such truths."

People who are permanently damaged by trauma seek to *assimilate* what happened into their existing models. People who grow try to *accommodate* what happened in order to create *new* models. The person who assimilates says, I survived brain cancer and I'm going to keep on chugging. The person who accommodates says, No, this changes who I am . . . I'm a cancer survivor. . . . This changes how I want to spend my days. The act of remaking our models involves reconsidering the fundamentals: In what ways is the world safe and unsafe? Do things sometimes happen to me that I don't deserve? Who am I? What is my place in the world? What's my story? Where do I really want to go? What kind of God allows this to happen?

The act of remaking your models is hard. Not everyone does it successfully. When Joseph surveyed people who had experienced train bombings and other terrorist attacks, he found that 46 percent reported that their view of life had changed for the worse, and 43 percent said their view of life had changed for the better. The journey of reconsideration and re-formation often involves taking what Stephen Cope, learning from Carl Jung, calls "the night sea journey," heading off into the parts of yourself that are "split off, disavowed, unknown, unwanted, cast out."

To know a person well, you have to know who they were before they suffered their losses and how they remade their whole outlook after them. If a subtext of this book is that experience is not what happens to you, it's what you do with what happens to you, then one of the subsequent lessons is that to know someone who has grieved, you have to know how they have processed their loss—did they emerge wiser, kinder, and stronger, or broken, stuck, and scared? To be a good friend and a good person you have to know how to accompany someone through this process.

———

In 1936, when Frederick Buechner was ten, he woke up one fall day at sunrise. He and his brother, who was eight, were excited because their parents were going to take them to a football game. The game was not what excited them; it was the thought of the whole family, grandmother included, going on an outing, with treats and fun and adventures. It was still too early to get up, so the boys lay in bed. At one point, their door opened, and their father looked in on them. Years later, neither brother could remember if their father said anything to them. It seemed like just a casual check any parent might make to ensure that everybody was safe.

A little while later, they heard a scream and the sounds of doors opening and closing. They looked out their window and saw their father lying on the gravel driveway, with their mother and grandmother, barefoot and still in their nightgowns, leaning over him. Each woman had one of his legs in her hands. They were lifting his legs up and down as if they were operating two handles of a pump. Nearby, the garage door was open and blue smoke was billowing out.

A car screeched to a halt at the foot of the driveway and a doctor scrambled out, crouched over their dad, and gave a small shake of his head. Their father had gassed himself to death. It took them a few days to find the suicide note, which their dad had scratched in pencil on the last page of *Gone with the Wind*. It was addressed to their mom: "I adore you and love you, and am no good. . . . Give Freddy my watch. Give Jamie my pearl pin. I give you all my love."

A month or two later, their mom moved them to Bermuda. Their grandmother was against their going, telling them to "stay and face reality." Decades later, Buechner thought that she had been both right and not right. He wrote, "Reality can be harsh and that you shut your eyes to it only at your peril because if you do not face up to the enemy in all his dark power, then the enemy will come up from behind some dark day and destroy you while you are facing the other way." On the other hand, they loved Bermuda, and some sort of healing did happen there.

"We all create our own realities as we go along," he would later write. "Reality for me was this. Out of my father's death there came, for me, a new and, in many ways, happier life. . . . I cannot say the grief faded because, in a sense, I had not yet, unlike my brother, really felt that grief. That was not to happen for thirty years or more. But the grief was postponed."

It was a time of sealing up. One day, about a year after the suicide, Buechner saw his brother crying and asked him what was wrong. When he realized he was crying for their father, he was astonished. He had gotten over that pain long ago—so he thought. His mother had closed down, too. Buechner didn't see her cry after the suicide, and they rarely spoke of his father afterward. She could be a warm person, and sometimes generous, but she kept her heart closed to other people's suffering as well as her own. "The sadness of other people's lives," Buechner recalled, "even the people she loved, never seemed to touch her where she lived."

Decades later, Buechner came to the following realization: "The trouble with steeling yourself against the harshness of reality is that the same steel that secures your life against being destroyed secures your life also against being opened up and transformed by the holy power that life itself comes from."

Buechner could not stay sealed up permanently. He became a teacher and a novelist. One evening early in his adulthood Buechner visited his mother at her apartment in New York. They were about to sit down to dinner when the phone rang. It was for him. A friend of his was weeping. He had just learned that his parents and pregnant sister had been in a car crash, and it was unclear if any of them would survive. Would Buechner be willing to come to the airport to sit with him until his plane departed? Buechner told his mother that he would have to leave at once. She found the whole situation absurd. Why was a grown man asking somebody to come sit with him? What good could it possibly do? Why ruin an evening they had both been looking forward to?

His mother was articulating the exact thoughts that had just run through his own head. But when he heard his mother saying them, he reacted with revulsion. How could anybody be so unfeeling, so cut off from the suffering of a friend? A few minutes later, his friend called back and said another friend had just agreed to come to the airport, so he was no longer needed. But that episode shocked Buechner and launched a journey. It was as if time, which had stopped the day his father killed himself, restarted.

What followed can best be described as a decades-long journey Buechner took down into the depths of what it means to be human. "What I was suddenly most drawn to now was the dimension of what lay beneath the surface and behind the face. What was going on inside myself, behind my own face, was the subject I started trying to turn to in my half-baked way." He realized that most of us are on a journey in search of a self to be. He saw that this journey inevitably involved facing your pain and using your experience to help others face their own.

Naturally, he went off in search of his father, too. Buechner wanted to know what it had been like for his father to grow up in a family that, as it turned out, produced two suicides and three alcoholics. When Buechner met people who had known his dad, he'd ask them questions about what he was like, but their answers failed to satisfy: He was charming, handsome, a good athlete. Nobody could solve the elemental mystery: What demons lurked within him that drove him to that ending?

By middle age, Buechner could weep real tears for his father. In his old age he wrote that not a single day went by without him thinking of his dad. He had grown up to be a novelist and writer of great compassion, faith, and humanity. He had come to realize that excavation is not a solitary activity. It's by sharing our griefs with others, and thinking together about what they mean, that we learn to overcome fear and know each other at the deepest level. "What we hunger for perhaps more than anything else is to be known in our full humanness, and yet that is often just what we also fear more than anything else," he wrote in his book *Telling Secrets*. "It is important to tell at least from time to time the secret of who we truly and fully are . . . because otherwise we run the risk of losing track of who we truly and fully are and little by little come to accept instead the highly edited version which we put forth in hope that the world will find it more acceptable than the real thing. It is important to tell our secrets too because it makes it easier . . . for other people to tell us a secret or two of their own."

The Buechner pattern is a familiar one. A person is hit by a blow. There is a period when the shock of the loss is too great to be faced. Emotions are packed away. The person's inner life is held "in suspension," as the psychologists say. But then, when the time is right, the person realizes that he has to deal with his past. He has to excavate all that was packed away. He has to share his experience with friends, readers, or some audience. Only then can he go on to a bigger, deeper life.

The writer David Lodge once noted that 90 percent of what we call writing is actually reading. It's going back over your work so you can change and improve it. The excavation task is like that. It's going back and back over events. The goal is to try to create mental flexibility, the ability to have multiple perspectives on a single event. To find other ways to see what happened. To put the tragedy in the context of a larger story. As Maya Angelou once put it, "The more you know of your history, the more liberated you are."

How does this process of excavation work? How do we help each other go back into the past and reinvent the story of our lives? There are certain exercises that friends can do together.

First, friends can ask each other the kinds of questions that help people see more deeply into their own childhoods. Psychologists recommend that you ask your friend to fill in the blanks to these two statements: "In our family, the one thing you must never do is

_____" and "In our family, the one thing you must do above all else is _____." That's a way to help a person see more clearly the deep values that were embedded in the way they were raised.

Second, you can try "This Is Your Life." This is a game some couples play at the end of each year. They write out a summary of the year from their partner's point of view. That is, they write, in the first person, about what challenges their partner faced and how he or she overcame them. Reading over these first-person accounts of your life can be an exhilarating experience. You see yourself through the eyes of one who loves you. People who have been hurt need somebody they trust to narrate their life, stand up to their own self-contempt, and believe the best of them.

The third exercise is called "Filling in the Calendar." This involves walking through periods of the other person's life, year by year. What was your life like in second grade? In third grade?

The fourth is story sampling. For decades, James Pennebaker of the University of Texas at Austin has had people do free-form expressive-writing exercises. He says: Open your notebook. Set a timer for twenty minutes. Write about your emotional experiences. Don't worry about punctuation or sloppiness. Go wherever your mind takes you. Write just for yourself. Throw it out at the end. In the beginning, people who take part in expressive-writing exercises sometimes use different voices and even different handwriting styles. Their stories are raw and disjointed. But then unconscious thoughts surface. They try on different perspectives. Their narratives grow more coherent and self-aware as the days go by. They turn from victims to writers. Some studies show that people who go through this process emerge with lower blood pressure and healthier immune systems. "I write," Susan Sontag once remarked, "to define myself—an act of self-creation—part of the process of becoming."

The fifth exercise is my favorite. Put aside all the self-conscious exercises and just have serious conversations with friends. If you've lost someone dear to you, tell each other stories about that person. Reflect on the strange journey that is grief; tell new stories about what life will look like in the years ahead.

———

By sharing their stories and reinterpreting what they mean, people create new mental models they can use to construct a new reality and a new future. They are able to stand in the rubble of the life they thought they would live and construct from those stones a radically different life. As a young woman who had been assaulted told Stephen Joseph, "If someone had said to me the day after I was attacked that I would be able to do what I'm doing now, or that I would see the attack as a turning point in my life, I would have wanted to strangle them, but it *was* a turning point. I like who I am now and I'm doing things I never would have thought I was capable of. If I was to erase the past then I wouldn't be who I am today."

Rabbi Harold Kushner's son, Aaron, died of a rare aging disease at fourteen. He's spent the years since reflecting on how the tragedy has shaped him, and studying how other people are remade by their sufferings. "I am a more sensitive person, a more effective pastor, a more sympathetic counselor because of Aaron's life and death than I would ever have been without it. And I would give up all those gains in a second if I could have my son back. If I could choose, I would forgo all the spiritual growth and depth which has come my way because of our experiences. . . . But I cannot choose."

Human beings, John Stuart Mill wrote, "are under a moral obligation to seek the improvement of our moral character." But what exactly does a good person look like? How can we make ourselves morally better? How can we cultivate good character?

One tradition has come down to us through the centuries; we might call it the warrior/statesman model of good character. According to this model, a person of character—or at least a *man* of character—looks like one of the ancient heroes, such as Pericles or Alexander the Great, or one of the more modern ones, like George Washington, Charles de Gaulle, or George C. Marshall.

This moral tradition, like all moral traditions, begins with a model of human nature. We humans are divided creatures. We have these primitive, powerful forces within us—passions such as lust, rage, fear, greed, and ambition. But people also possess reason, which they can use to control, tame, and regulate those passions. The essential moral act in this model of character formation is self-mastery. It is exercising willpower so that you are the master of your passions and not their slave. Developing your character is like going to the gym—working through exercise and habit to strengthen a set of universal virtues: honesty, courage, determination, and humility. In this model, character building is something you can do on your own.

This book has been built around a different ideal and a different theory of how to build good character. This book has been built around the Illuminator ideal. The Illuminator ideal begins with a different understanding of human nature. People are social animals. People need recognition from others if they are to thrive. People long for someone to look into their eyes with loving acceptance.

Therefore, morality is mostly about the small, daily acts of building connection—the gaze that says "I respect you," the question that says "I'm curious about you," the conversation that says, "We're in this together."

In the Illuminator model, character building is not something you can do alone. Morality is a social practice. It is trying to be generous and considerate toward a specific other person, who is enmeshed in a specific context. A person of character is trying to be generous and just to the person who is criticizing him. He is trying to just be present and faithful to the person suffering from depression. He is trying to be a deep and caring friend to the person who is trying to overcome the wounds left by childhood. He is a helpful sounding board to the person who is rebuilding her models after losing a spouse or child. Character building happens as we get better at these kinds of tasks.

What matters most is not the strength of an individual's willpower, but how skillfull she is in her social interactions. In the Illuminator model, we develop good character as we get more experienced in being present with others, as we learn to get outside our self-serving ways of perceiving. As Iris Murdoch wrote, "virtue is the attempt to pierce the veil of selfish consciousness and join the world as it really is."

The Illuminator model of character development is not austere, and its exemplars are not best captured by marble sculptures of men on horseback. The Illuminator model is social, humble, understanding, and warm. The man of character is not removed and strong; he's right there next to you on the bench as you work through the kinds of hard times I've tried to describe in this middle section. But the Illuminator is not just there to see the depths of your pain, she's there to see your strength, to celebrate with you in your triumphs. How do you see and recognize the gifts other people bring to the world? That is the subject of the final section of this book.

Part 3

I

SEE

YOU

WITH

YOUR

STRENGTHS

THIRTEEN

Personality: What Energy Do You Bring into the Room?

George W. Bush is an extremely extroverted person. From the time he was a boy, it was obvious how much little Georgie loved being around people. "Whenever I come home he greets me and talks a blue streak, sentences disjointed, of course, by enthusiasm and spirit boundless," George H. W. Bush wrote about his son when he was a toddler.

At school he was the class clown, the popular kid. Everybody else greeted their Sunday school teacher politely and respectfully. Bush blurted out, "Hiya, little lady. Lookin' sexy!"

When Bush was the Republican governor of Texas, the most powerful Democrat in the state was a man named Bob Bullock. Bush and Bullock got along famously, but from time to time, partisan divides still got in the way. Once, in 1997, Bush, Bullock, and the leading officials from both parties were attending a breakfast to talk about a piece of legislation the Republicans had proposed.

The Democrats had decided they couldn't support it. "I'm sorry, Governor," Bullock said at one point, "but I'm going to have to fuck you on this one." The room fell silent, the atmosphere tense and awkward. Bush stood up, walked over to Bullock, grabbed him by the shoulders, and kissed him on the lips. "What the hell did you do that for," Bullock asked, wiping off his lips. "If you're going to fuck me," Bush replied, "you'll have to kiss me first." The room erupted in laughter.

One biographer wrote that Bush's particular genius was the ability to eliminate, in milliseconds, any distance between him and another person. He wrapped his arms around people, gave them nicknames, treated them with instant familiarity. I've certainly found that being in a small room with Bush is a very different experience from watching him on TV. In person he's an electric, boisterous presence. People, even those who might detest him politically, are happy to be around the guy.

If Bush would score phenomenally high on any measure of extroversion, the psychologist Dan McAdams argues, he would not score high on a measure of curiosity. As a young man, he didn't pay much attention to the historic world events unfolding around him. He didn't distinguish himself as a student. When he was president, even his allies noticed his lack of intellectual curiosity. The occasional meetings he had with us newspaper columnists were different, in my experience, from those hosted by other presidents. Usually, the meetings are like a free-flowing conversation. We randomly pepper the president with questions, and the president talks. But Bush controlled the room quite rigidly. He went around the table in order, and we each got to ask one question per session. His answers were unambiguous. He had read one book on any topic or absorbed one point of view, and he rarely tried on alternate perspectives.

This mixture of high extroversion (take bold action) and low curiosity (don't try on other perspectives), McAdams argues, con-tributed to Bush's catastrophic decision to start the Iraq War. In other words, Bush's personality traits shaped his destiny as a leader in good and bad ways. If you want to understand George W. Bush, you have to know something about his personality. And that goes for every person you meet. If you want to understand another per-son, you have to be able to describe the particular energy they bring into a room.

———

A healthy society depends on a wide variety of human types. Such a society has outgoing people to serve as leaders, organized people to make companies and schools run smoothly, curious people to invent new products and try on new ideas, nervous people to warn of danger, and kind people to care for the sick and ill. Fortunately, evolution has helped us out here. Human beings come into this world with a wide variety of personalities, which prepare them to serve a wide variety of social roles. As Rabbi Abraham Kook put it, God "dealt kindly with his world by not putting all the talents in one place."

Personality traits are dispositional signatures. A personality trait is a habitual way of seeing, interpreting, and reacting to a situ-ation. Every personality trait is a gift—it enables its bearer to serve the community in some valuable way.

Unfortunately, our public conversation about personality is all messed up. For example, sometimes when I'm giving a public talk, I ask people to raise their hands if they are familiar with the Myers-Briggs personality assessment. Usually, 80 to 100 percent of the people raise their hands. Then I ask them if they are familiar with the Big Five personality traits. Somewhere between 0 and 20 percent of the audience members raise their hands. This strikes me as a ridiculous situation.

The Myers-Briggs test has no scientific validity. About half the people who take it twice end up in entirely different categories the second time around. That's because human beings just don't fit consistently into the categories the Myers-Briggs people imagine are real. The test has almost no power to predict how happy you'll be in a given situation, how you'll perform at your job, or how satisfied you'll be in your marriage. Myers-Briggs relies on false binaries. For example, it divides people into those who are good at thinking and those who are good at feeling. But in real life, the research shows, people who are good at thinking are also more likely to be good at feeling. As Adam Grant, who writes about organizational psychology, once put it, the Myers-Briggs questionnaire is like asking someone, "What do you like more, shoelaces or earrings?" and expecting that question to produce a revealing answer.

On the other hand, over the past decades, psychologists have cohered around a different way to map the human personality. This method has a ton of rigorous research behind it. This method helps people measure five core personality traits. Psychologists refer to these as the Big Five.

The Big Five traits are extroversion, conscientiousness, neuroticism, agreeableness, and openness. Psychologists have devised a series of questionnaires to help you discover how high or low you score on each of these traits—whether, for example, you are extremely extroverted (like George W. Bush), or not so extroverted, or, like most of us, somewhere near the middle.

Let's delve into these Big Five traits. If you understand the essence of each trait, you'll be able to look at people with more educated eyes. Just as geologists can see a rocky outcropping more subtly because they can distinguish between igneous, sedimentary, and metamorphic rocks, or just as a sommelier can judge a wine more subtly because they have a feel for characteristics like minerality or qualities like "well structured" or "strong finish," we'll be able to see people more clearly if we have a better understanding of the traits that make up a person's personality. We'll be sommeliers of people.

EXTROVERSION. We often think of extroverts as people who derive energy from other people. In fact, people who score high in extroversion are highly drawn to all positive emotions. They are excited by any chance to experience pleasure, to seek thrills, to win social approval. They are motivated more by the lure of rewards than the fear of punishment. They tend to dive into most situations looking for what goodies can be had. If you follow extroverts on social media, you'll see that their posts teem with comments like "Can't wait!" "So excited!!" and "Love my life!!!"

People who score high in extroversion are warm, gregarious, excitement seekers. People who score high on extroversion are more sociable than retiring, more fun-loving than sober, more affectionate than reserved, more spontaneous than inhibited, and more talkative than quiet.

In his book *Personality,* the British behavioral scientist Daniel Nettle describes a highly extroverted woman named Erica who, like all high extroverts, has spent her life energetically pursuing pleasure, intensity, and excitement. She joined a band, built a following, and lived a life of ceaseless activity—walking, riding horses, sailing, cycling, and dancing. Her desire for excitement in public was matched by an intense desire for excitement in private. "I also spent my entire life, from puberty onwards, utterly driven and ruled by my high sexual appetite," Erica confessed. "Until I met my husband, I was compulsively promiscuous. Being with him took care of that; we had a wonderful sexual relationship for some years, but as he aged his drive slowed. . . . When we moved to Italy I began having lovers, married Italian men; there were two with whom I remained close for many years." As she aged, her desire for sex waned but her desire for other kinds of positive experiences didn't. She just hungered for a different set of positive rewards. As she told Nettle, "I LOVE to stay in bed, reading, drinking coffee, taking a nap." Extroverts don't have to be out with people all the time. They just are driven to powerfully pursue some sort of pleasure, some sort of positive reward. Erica is a classic high extrovert.

Extroversion is generally a good trait to have, since high extroverts are often so much fun to be around. But all traits have their advantages and disadvantages. As studies over the years have shown, people who score high in extroversion can be quick to anger. They take more risks and are more likely to die in traffic accidents. They are more likely to abuse alcohol in adolescence and less likely to save for retirement. Extroverts live their lives as a high-reward/high-risk exercise.

People who score low on extroversion just seem more chill. Such people have slower and less volatile emotional responses to things. They are often creative, thoughtful, and intentional. They like having deeper relationships with fewer people. Their way of experiencing the world is not lesser than that of high-extroversion people, just different.

CONSCIENTIOUSNESS. If extroverts are the people you want livening up your party, those who score high in conscientiousness are often the ones you want managing your organization. People who score high on this trait have excellent impulse control. They are disciplined, persevering, organized, self-regulating. They have the ability to focus on long-term goals and not get distracted.

People high in conscientiousness are less likely to procrastinate, tend to be a bit perfectionist, and have high achievement motivation. They are likely to avoid drugs and to stick to fitness routines. As you'd expect, high conscientiousness predicts all sorts of good outcomes: higher grades in school, more career success, longer life spans. Nevertheless, it's not as if people who score high in conscientiousness are all enjoying fantastic careers and living to age ninety. The world is complicated, and many factors influence the outcomes of a life. But more conscientious people do tend to display more competence and grit.

Just as this trait has its upsides, like all traits, it also has its downsides too. People high in conscientiousness experience more guilt. They are well suited to predictable environments but less

well suited to unpredictable situations that require fluid adapta-
tion. They are sometimes workaholics. There can be an obsessive
or compulsive quality to them. Nettle describes a man, named
Ronald. Each night before going to bed, "He must spray his si-
nuses, take two aspirin, straighten up the apartment, do thirty-five
sit-ups and read two pages of the dictionary. The sheets must be of
just the right crispness and the room must be noiseless. Obviously,
a woman sleeping over interferes with his inner sanctum." After
sex, Ronald asks his female visitors to either leave or sleep in the
living room. As you'd expect, they don't put up with this for very
long. I think we'd say Ronald is rigidly conscientious. He has an
obsessive need to control the minute details of life—and, apparently, of other people's lives. He has a wonderful gift, conscientiousness, but he ruins it by taking it to the extreme.

NEUROTICISM. If extroverts are drawn to positive emotions, people who score high in neuroticism respond powerfully to negative
emotions. They feel fear, anxiety, shame, disgust, and sadness very
quickly and very acutely. They are sensitive to potential threats.
They are more likely to worry than to be calm, more highly strung
than laid-back, more vulnerable than resilient. If there is an angry
face in a crowd, they will fixate on it and have trouble drawing
their attention away.

People who score high in neuroticism have more emotional ups
and downs over the course of the day. They can fall into a particular kind of emotional spiral: They are quick to see threats and negative emotions; they interpret ambiguous events more negatively;
they are therefore exposed to more negative experiences; this expo-
sure causes them to believe even more strongly that the world is a

dangerous place; and thus they grow even more likely to see threats; and so on and so on. They often feel uncomfortable with uncertainty; they prefer the devil they know to the devil they don't know.

People who score high in neuroticism often struggle. Neuroticism is linked to higher rates of depression, eating disorders, and stress disorders. Such people go to the doctor more often. They are quick to make unrealistic plans for themselves and quick to abandon them. Even though they are always ready to perceive danger, neurotics often enter into relationships with precisely those people who will threaten them. They also have a lot of negative emotions toward themselves, and think they deserve what they get.

High neuroticism in adolescence predicts lower career attainment and worse relationships in adulthood. But, like all traits, neuroticism has its upsides as well. It prepares people for certain social roles. If your community is in danger, it helps to have a prophet who can spot it early on. If there is a lot of emotional pain in your community, it's good to have a person who scores high in neuroticism, like Sigmund Freud, around to study and understand it. If there's a need for social change, it's useful to have indignant people who are calling for it. In a world in which most people are overconfident about their abilities and overly optimistic about the outcomes of their behavior, there's a benefit in having some people who lean the other way.

AGREEABLENESS. Those who score high on agreeableness are good at getting along with people. They are compassionate, considerate, helpful, and accommodating toward others. Such people tend to be trusting, cooperative, and kind—good-natured rather than foul-tempered, softhearted rather than hard-edged, polite more than rude, forgiving more than vengeful.

Those who score high in agreeableness are naturally prone to paying attention to what's going on in other people's minds. If you read high-agreeable people complex stories, they have so much emotional intelligence that they will be able to recall many facts about each character. They are able to keep in mind how different people are feeling about one another. In one experiment that Daniel Nettle describes, high agreeables could keep track of four levels of social belief: "Tom hoped that Jim would believe that Susan thought that Edward wanted to marry Jenny." Some can even handle more social complexity than that: "John thought that Penny thought that Tom wanted Penny to find out whether Sheila believed that John knew what Susan wanted to do." I think I'm a bit above average in agreeableness, but asking me to follow that last sentence is like asking me to flap my arms and fly to the moon.

If you're going to marry someone, you should understand their personality traits so you can prepare to love them in the right way. Agreeableness, which is basically being kind, doesn't seem like a very romantic or sexy trait, but high agreeables have lower divorce rates and in some studies are found to be better in bed. In his book *The Science of Happily Ever After,* Ty Tashiro advises that when picking a marriage partner, it's best to go with agreeableness and avoid neuroticism. I once gave this advice to a friend and he responded, "What do you do if you're the neurotic one?" I told him, "Marry another neurotic; that way you'll make two people miserable and not four." I was just kidding. Any kind of person can be a good spouse; you just have to know how to live with each trait.

In the workplace, agreeableness is a mixed trait. Those high in agreeableness do not always get the big promotions or earn the most money. People sometimes think, rightly or wrongly, that high agreeables are not tough enough, that they won't make the unpopular decisions. Often it's the people who score lower on agreeableness who get appointed to CEO jobs and make the big bucks.

OPENNESS. If agreeableness describes a person's relationship to other people, openness describes their relationship to information. People who score high on this trait are powerfully motivated to have new experiences and to try on new ideas. They tend to be innovative more than conventional, imaginative and associative rather than linear, curious more than closed-minded. They tend not to impose a predetermined ideology on the world and to really enjoy cognitive exploration, just wandering around in a subject.

Artists and poets are the quintessential practitioners of openness. Picasso spent his life constantly experimenting with new forms. David Bowie spent his trying on a variety of new personas. People high in openness are good at divergent thinking. If you ask them to name a four-legged animal, they won't just default to cat or dog; they'll say antelope or armadillo. Reality is a little more fluid for such people. They report having more transcendent spiritual experiences and more paranormal beliefs. When they wake up in the morning, they are sometimes not sure if they experienced something the previous day or merely dreamed it the night before. One study showed that having a mystical experience while consuming mushrooms led to a sharp increase in openness even a year later.

Such people are able to appreciate a wide array of artistic forms. When we approach a painting or a song, we want it to be familiar but also a bit surprising. That's known as the fluency sweet spot. People low in openness feel comfortable when the artwork feels familiar. People high in openness find anything moderately familiar to be boring.

The great journalist Nancy Dickerson once described John F. Kennedy in a way that makes me think he was high in openness: "To Jack, the cardinal sin was boredom; it was his biggest enemy, and he didn't know how to handle it. When he was bored, a hood would come down over his eyes and his nervous system would start churning. You could do anything to him—steal his wallet, insult him, argue with him—but to bore him was unpardonable."

As with all traits, people's openness ratings vary a bit as they proceed through different stages of life. People tend to get more open as they enter young adulthood and different life opportunities become available. Those who are able to retire often become more open to new experiences, especially if they try their hand at new activities like gardening or carpentry, or go to more museums and concerts.

––––––––

If you want to understand how you rate on these Big Five traits, you can go online and find any number of questionnaires to help you do it. But, when you walk into a party, or sit down with someone at a meeting, you're probably not going to hand them a personality test. You really don't need to. A person's personality isn't buried deep down inside them. It's right there on the surface. It's their way of being in the world. If you are well informed about the nature of each trait, and you observe people closely, you'll be able to make a pretty good guess about whether an individual person scores high on agreeableness, low on extroversion, and so on. And then, of course, if the time is right, you can ask them how they assess their own traits. Just don't expect them to have a completely accurate understanding of their own personality. On matters like this, our friends often know us better than we know ourselves.

Personality traits certainly don't tell you everything you might want to know about a person. You can be a conscientious nurse or a conscientious Nazi. But personality traits are a very important part of a person's makeup. In a paper called "The Power of Personality," the psychologist Brent Roberts and his colleagues calculated that personality traits predict certain life outcomes about as well as a person's IQ or socioeconomic status does. This means that if you understand someone's traits, you understand a lot about them.

Furthermore, understanding a person's personality traits is one key to knowing how to treat them appropriately. The geneticist and psychiatrist Danielle Dick argues that it's very important for parents to have a sense of their kid's personality traits. That's because there is no such thing as the right way to parent. There's only the right way to parent that brings together the particular personality of the parent and the particular personality of the child. If Dad is low in agreeableness and thus quick to criticize and his daughter is high on neuroticism and sensitive to negative emotion, she will hear even his mild critiques as a brutal attack. What seems gentle to him seems violent to her. Dad has to modulate his tone and approach if he wants his daughter to hear what he is saying, and if he wants to preserve a loving relationship. Danielle Dick adds that a lot of parenting is pushing gently against your kid's traits: encouraging your timid child to try new experiences or teaching your extroverted child to slow down and have some quiet time. Punishing children so they won't repeat bad behavior doesn't work, she argues. Focusing on the "positive opposite" does. Instead of calling attention to the behavior you want your child to stop, call attention to the behavior you want them to do.

———

Personality psychology has always struck me as one of the happier neighborhoods in academia. Maybe that's because it's about receiving gifts and using gifts. The general vibe is that each of us has been given the gift of a unique personality. Of course, there are things about each of our personalities that we may regret, but we should all be grateful for what we have. Each set of traits can be used to build a marvelous life.

Charlotte and Emily Brontë had the same two parents, spent most of their lives in the same small Yorkshire town, and received practically identical educations, and both of them became novelists. Yet, as the Columbia University literary critic Edward Mendelson has observed, the two sisters saw the world and enjoyed the world in starkly different ways. One of them savored interior delights, and the other preferred the delights found among friends. "Emily Brontë wanted privacy in which to experience sublimity and vision," Mendelson writes. "Charlotte Brontë wanted company with whom to seek justice and love." Both sisters wrote great novels, but their writing reflects their differing temperaments. Emily's classic novel, *Wuthering Heights,* is more inward. It takes place in the realm of private life, and in that realm the characters find it hard to communicate with one another. Charlotte's best-known book, *Jane Eyre,* is more outward. The story crosses over into the public worlds of religion and politics. In Charlotte's novel, human communication is not difficult—talking, writing, teaching, and drawing are pretty much what her characters do all day.

Is it better to be more like Emily or Charlotte? Well, it would be great to be as perceptive as either. It would be great to put one's traits to such good effects. And it would be great to live in a family in which people have such radically different ways of construing the world.

Personality traits are not only gifts, they are gifts you can build over your lifetime. As Brent Roberts and Hee J. Yoon wrote in a 2022 review on personality psychology, "Although it is still widely thought that personality is not changeable, recent research has roundly contradicted that notion. In a review of over 200 intervention studies, personality traits, and especially neuroticism, were found to be modifiable through clinical intervention, with changes being on average half of a standard deviation over periods as short as 6 weeks." In general, people get better as they age. They become more agreeable, conscientious, and emotionally stable versions of themselves. If you have that sommelier's expertise in the human personality, you can see people more clearly as, like wine, they improve with age.

FOURTEEN

Life Tasks

As I mentioned earlier, babies come out of the womb hungry for recognition. Their first life task, at the moment of birth, is to bond with the person who will feed and care for them. Their minds at this age are perfectly adapted to that imperative. In their book *How Babies Think,* Alison Gopnik, Andrew Meltzoff, and Patricia Kuhl point out that newborns are nearsighted. An object a foot away—like the face of a nursing mother—is in sharp focus, but everything farther away is blurred. To a newborn, the world looks like a bunch of Rembrandt portraits: brightly lit faces, full of meaning and expression, popping out from a blurry background.

Then as they get older, a new task enters the picture: to learn about how the world works. Their field of vision expands. They notice keys, teddy bears, doors, rattles, and balls. Babies develop a powerful explanatory drive, a desire to know about the world. The baby's perspective adapts to effectively perform this task. Adults, Gopnik argues, have a spotlight consciousness. We tend to focus on one thing at a time. Babies develop a very different kind of consciousness, a lantern consciousness. In this phase of maximum learning, they attend to the whole room. They pay attention to anything that is unexpected or interesting. To put it another way, they are bad at not paying attention, so their attention shifts from one thing to another. The lantern shines in all directions, and the baby learns at a rapid clip.

A couple years down the road, yet another life task emerges. The toddler is gripped by an intense desire to establish herself as a separate person. Before, the baby was embedded in her caretaking system, embedded in Mom and Dad. But around age two, the child realizes, "Oh, I am not my mother. I have a mother, but I am my own person." And so begins the terrible twos—driven by the child's desire to say, "No! No! No!" This is a developmental crisis, for both child and parents. As Gopnik, Meltzoff, and Kuhl put it, it's not just that your child does something you don't want her to; she does it *because* you don't want her to.

The life tasks continue to roll, throughout one's life. The theme of this chapter is that if you want to understand someone well, you have to understand what life task they are in the middle of and how their mind has evolved to complete this task.

The people who think most carefully about this procession of life challenges are called developmental psychologists. This field has been led by people like Jean Piaget, Erik Erikson, Robert

Kegan, Jane Loevinger, and Bernice Neugarten. For over a century, developmental psychologists have been trying to understand how people change and grow over their lifetimes.

Developmental psychology is a bit out of fashion now, mostly because the field got associated with a couple of ideas that are now widely considered to be false. First, most of human development happens in childhood: People go through a series of developmental stages until about age twenty-one, and then they're done. That seems to be wrong. People develop across the life span. Second, some developmental psychologists argued that life is a march through a series of distinct "stages," and you can't enter one stage of life unless you've completed the previous stage. You have to take Algebra I before you can take Algebra II. That turned out to be wrong too. Human lives aren't so formulaic; they can't be reduced to a series of neat stages.

But I've found the insights of developmental psychology to be tremendously helpful in understanding other people. Their wisdom is unfairly neglected. We don't want to fall back into the old concept of "stages," but we do want to see life as a succession of common life tasks. Not everybody does the tasks in the same order, and not everybody performs all the tasks, but when we look at someone we want to see them engaged in the heroic activity of their life, tackling this or that task.

Over the next few pages, I'd like to sketch out this theory of life tasks, which I've adapted from the developmental psychologists, especially from scholars like Erik Erikson, the author of "Life Cycle Completed," and Robert Kegan, author of "The Evolving Self." As I lay them out for you, I should make it clear once again that these are just templates, not photographs. It's not like every person goes through the same life tasks in the same way. The templates simply name some common patterns of human behavior. They help us step back and recognize ways in which you or I might be like the template and ways in which you or I might be different from the template. The templates also remind us that each person you meet is involved in a struggle. Here are a few common life tasks, along with the states of consciousness that arise to help us meet each one.

THE IMPERIAL TASK

Pretty early in life, sometime in boyhood or girlhood, each of us has to try to establish a sense of our own agency. We have to demonstrate to ourselves and others that we can take control, work hard, be good at things. In the middle of this task, Erikson argues, a person has to either display industry or succumb to inferiority. If children can show themselves and the world that they are competent, they will develop a sense of self-confidence. If they can't, they will experience feelings of inferiority.

To establish a sense of agency, people develop what Kegan calls an imperial consciousness. People with this mindset can be quite self-centered. Their own desires and interests are paramount. *The world is a message about me, about how I am valued.* People can also be quite competitive at this stage. They want to win praise, achieve glory. Whether it's in sports or schoolwork or music or something else, they crave other people's positive judgments about their own value. In John Knowles's novel *A Separate Peace,* set in a boys' prep school, the narrator notes, "There were few relationships among us at Devon not based on rivalry."

We tolerate this somewhat self-centered consciousness in kids and teenagers, but sometimes the imperial consciousness carries on into adulthood. An adult who has never left this mindset behind experiences his days as a series of disjointed contests he wants to win. Whether in business, pickup basketball, or politics, he has an intense desire to see himself as a winner, and a touchy pride that causes him to react strongly against any sign of disrespect.

For people with this consciousness, relationships tend to be instrumental. The person is always angling, manipulating the situation to get what he wants. He is emotionally sealed up, hiding any vulnerabilities, even from himself. His message is: *I get something out of my friendships. My hot girlfriend is a sign of my status as a winner.* A guy I know goes into every party scanning the room for high-status people he can make contact with. Every time you meet him he has some agenda, something he wants from you.

If you try to become intimate with such a person, they will complain that you are not giving them enough space. They can form alliances with people (working with others to get what they want), but they can't form collaborations (working with others to serve shared wants). They just can't see the world from the perspective of another person. They can't internalize another person's affection for them, so they need constant reminders in the form of other people's affirmation and praise.

A person embedded in this task, and the imperial consciousness that emerges to help people complete it, probably doesn't have a rich internal life. He's not going for self-knowledge; he's trying to make his presence impressive to the world. Donald Trump and Vladimir Putin strike me as men who experienced an imperial consciousness in childhood, and then never moved beyond it.

THE INTERPERSONAL TASK

There's a rough rhythm to life. Periods that are dominated by an intense desire to stand out and be superior are often followed by periods dominated by an intense desire to fit in. For many of us there's a moment in life, often in adolescence, when the life task is to establish your social identity. Friendships and social status become the central obsessions in our lives. At this point, Erikson notes, the person will either achieve intimacy or suffer isolation. The person who succeeds at this life task develops the ability to be an intimate partner, a devoted lover, and a faithful friend. Those who can't fall into isolation.

The mind adjusts to meet the challenge. A person with an interpersonal consciousness has the ability to think psychologically. If you asked somebody embedded in an imperial consciousness who she is, she might talk about her actions and external traits: "I'm a sister. I'm blond. I play soccer." A person with an interpersonal consciousness is more likely to describe herself according to her psychological traits: "I'm outgoing. I'm growing more confident. I'm kind to others but sometimes afraid people won't like me."

A person with this consciousness has a greater capacity to experience another person's experience. In his book *The Discerning Heart,* Philip M. Lewis tells the story of a married woman who, while away at a business conference, faltered and spent the night with another man. A person with an imperial consciousness would be *worried* as she flies home—worried that her transgression might be discovered and that it might have negative consequences for her personally. But a person with an interpersonal consciousness feels *guilty*. Her sense of herself is defined by the shared love she has with her husband. She has potentially hurt her husband and betrayed that shared love.

People in the midst of the interpersonal task often become idealistic. The person with an interpersonal consciousness can not only experience other people's experiences, she can experience the experience of humanity as a whole. She can feel the pain of the community and be driven to heal that pain. Kegan writes that at this moment the person goes from being physical to being metaphysical. She sees not only what is but also the ideal of what might be. Teenage idealism can be intense but also dogmatic and unforgiving. The purpose of idealism, at this moment of consciousness, is not only to seek the common good; it's also to help you bond more tightly with some group. *I fight injustice because it makes me cool, helps me belong; that's what superior people like us do.*

During this task, people are quick to form cliques and think a lot about social status. The interpersonal person's ultimate question is: Do you like me? At this point, her own self-appraisal is not yet the arbiter of her sense of self-worth. The opinions of others are still the ultimate arbiters. That is a voracious master to try to please. As Seneca put it, "Nature's wants are small, while those of opinion are limitless." This also leads to a lot of conformism. You'll see cliques of adolescents—and even adults—at the mall all wearing the same types of clothes, speaking with the same vocal tones.

A person in this consciousness tends to be conflict averse, tends to be a pleaser. She has trouble saying no to people and is afraid of hurting their feelings. She suppresses her moments of anger. Anger would be a declaration that she has a self that is separate from the social context. She doesn't yet possess that separate independent self. So instead of feeling angry when she is affronted, she feels sad or wounded or incomplete. Part of the problem is that her conception of self is not sturdy enough to stand up to people.

A person with an interpersonal consciousness will sometimes be in a relationship with someone with an imperial consciousness. She'll wonder why he doesn't open himself up emotionally and share the way she does. But he can't do these things because he doesn't possess the consciousness that she has access to.

Breakups, when we're in the interpersonal phase, can feel particularly devastating. To lose a friend, a boyfriend, a girlfriend, or a spouse is to lose your very self—the source of your approval and value. When a person with an interpersonal consciousness loses the external structure of the relationship, she may find there is no internal structure to keep her together. Thrown back onto herself by a breakup, she becomes aware of the limitations of this level of consciousness. She realizes that while she treasures relationships, she can't be embedded and controlled by them. She has to embark on another life task. Along the way, as Kegan puts it, she is changing not just what she knows but the way she knows. Each new life task requires a different level of consciousness.

CAREER CONSOLIDATION

Lori Gottlieb worked as a TV scriptwriter, entered and then left med school, gave birth to a child, and got a job as a journalist, but she was dissatisfied. She wanted to make a difference in people's lives, not just write about them. She thought of becoming a psychiatrist. But that's mostly prescribing medication, she worried. One day, her former med school dean told her, "You should go to graduate school and get a degree in clinical psychology." If you do that, the dean continued, you'll be able to get to know your patients better. The work will be deeper and leave lasting benefits.

"I got chills," Gottlieb would later write. "People often use that expression loosely, but I actually did get chills, goose bumps and all. It was shocking how right this felt, as if my life's plan had finally been revealed."

At a certain point in life, we have to find the career that we will devote ourselves to, the way we will make a difference in the world—whether it's a job or parenting or something else entirely. While confronting this task, Erikson argues, a person must achieve career consolidation or experience drift.

Most of us figure out what to do through a process of experimentation and fit. Some people bounce around among different jobs and try new projects. The psychologist Brian Little argues that people generally have on average fifteen "personal projects" going at any one time. These can be small, like learning to surf, or larger, like serving as an apprentice to a plumber.

During these periods of experimentation, life can feel scattered. But eventually, many of us become passionate about one vocation in particular. Robert Caro has spent much of his life studying and writing about Lyndon Johnson. In his book *Working,* about the craft of being a biographer, he describes the furnaces of desire that gripped Johnson while he was a young congressional aide. Johnson would leave his basement room in the shabby hotel where he was staying and walk toward the U.S. Capitol Building. After a few blocks, the building would loom on the hill before him. He was so eager, so ambitious, that his pace would quicken and he would start running, winter or summer, up the hill and across the plaza to get to his office. People gawked at this awkward rushing figure, his long skinny arms and legs flapping all over the place. Running. The running was Johnson's ambition in physical form.

Johnson was propelled by a dream to do something monumental in government. He was also propelled to get as far away as possible from the poverty he'd grown up amid in Texas. And he was running to get away from his father and his failures. Caro writes, "You can't get very deep into Johnson's life without realizing that the central fact of his life was his relationship with his father. His brother, Sam Houston, once said to me, 'The most important thing for Lyndon was not to be like Daddy.'" Johnson and his father bore many similarities. They looked uncannily alike, they both went into politics, and they both had the habit of persuading people by grabbing their lapels and leaning in close to their face as they talked. But Johnson's father was an idealist and a romantic. In the 1870s, his family had owned a ranch along the Pedernales River, but they had lost it because the soil just wasn't good enough to make it profitable. In 1918, the ranch came on the market, and Johnson's father was determined to buy it. He overpaid for the ranch, found that once again his family couldn't make a living on it, and four years later, when Lyndon was fourteen, he went broke and lost the ranch all over again. Lyndon lost respect for his father and became, by consequence, a man who was hostile to romanticism, hostile to trust and believing in the good of others. He became an astoundingly accurate vote counter in the Senate because he looked, cynically, to people's interests and not what they said.

People gripped by the career consolidation task are often driven by a desire for mastery—the intrinsic pleasure of becoming quite good at something. They get up in the morning and work their rut. There's a big field to be farmed out there, the great project of their vocation, but each day they can only work their rut. When they do that, they have a sense of progress being made.

As usual, the consciousness changes to meet the task. People in the midst of career consolidation often develop a more individual-istic mindset: *I am the captain of my own ship, the master of my own destiny.* They become better at self-control, at governing their emo-tions. They possess a greater ability to go against the crowd. They are able to say no to things that might distract them from their core mission. During this phase, people can appear a bit selfish and ego-tistical, but as George Vaillant of the Grant Study argued, "only when developmental 'self-ishness' has been achieved are we reli-ably capable of giving the self away."

During this life task, intimacy motivation takes a step back and achievement motivation takes a step forward. A person who is pri-marily interested in consolidating his career has a tendency, Kegan observes, to "seal up," to become less open to deep relationships. Such a person also has a tendency to detach from his or her emo-tions. Later in life he may wonder how he managed to suppress so many feelings.

You can begin to see why most people eventually rebel against this consciousness. Career success fails to satisfy. The sense of self, which once seemed so exciting to build, now feels a little claustro-phobic. People tire of following the formulas the world uses to define "success." Sébastien Bras is the owner of Le Suquet, a res-taurant in Laguiole, France, that earned three Michelin stars, the world's highest culinary distinction, for eighteen consecutive years. Then one year he asked the Michelin folks to stop coming to his restaurant and never come back again. He'd realized that his desire to please the Michelin system had imposed tremendous pressure, crushing his creativity.

Carl Jung once wrote, "The achievements which society rewards are won at the cost of a diminution of personality." Eventually the costs become too high. The person at the end of this task realizes that there is a spiritual hunger that's been unmet, a desire to selflessly serve some cause, to leave some legacy for others.

This crisis sometimes comes as a sense that you simply no longer want what you used to want. Cristina Peri Rossi wrote a short story called "Breaking the Speed Record," about a runner who has devoted himself to beating a record at his distance. He trained rigorously for the climactic race and by that race's seventeenth lap he is far ahead of all the other runners, on pace to realize his dream. "It was then that he felt an enormous desire to stop," she writes. "Not that he was tired; he had trained for a long time and all the experts felt that he would succeed; in fact, he was only running in order to establish a new record. But now, this irresistible desire to stop. To lie on the side of the track and never get up again." His compulsion to break the record simply dries up. At the end of the story, he longs to stop and does stop. "And he raised his eyes to the sky."

It's not that all desire is quenched at the end of this task. It's just that one set of desires has been satisfied. People in this moment of crisis can suddenly get gripped by thicker and bigger desires. At the end of the career consolidation task, they realize they have overly differentiated themselves from others and the world around them. It's time to come in from the cold.

THE GENERATIVE TASK

The Grant Study, as I've mentioned, is a famous longitudinal study that followed the lives of hundreds of men from the time they enrolled at Harvard in the 1940s to their deaths, decades later. Adam Newman (a pseudonym) was one of the men tracked by the Grant researchers. When the researchers first encountered Newman, he was one of saddest and most hapless men in the study. He came from a loveless home. His mother, his sister reported, "could make anyone feel small." When, as a boy, he would throw temper tantrums, she would tie him to his bed, using his father's suspenders. He never spoke about his father's death, which happened when he was seventeen.

He earned excellent grades in high school, became an Eagle Scout, and was ferociously ambitious in college—to prove himself to his domineering mother. He had few close friends. Most of the Grant Study interviewers found him aloof, rigid, self-centered, selfish, and repellent. He was quite religious, but in a legalistic sort of way, attending Mass four times a week and being harshly judgmental toward anybody who didn't meet his impossible standards.

He went on to med school at the University of Pennsylvania, married during his second year there, and wound up running a fifty-person biostatistics department at NASA. His career progressed nicely, and his marriage was both devoted and unusual. Both he and his wife regarded each other as best friends and both said they had no other friends at all.

At forty-five, he had become a stern father, dealing with two rebellious daughters. He pressured them to achieve excellence, just as he had. While he was in his forties, one daughter called him an "extreme achievement perfectionist." She later told the researchers that he had permanently destroyed her self-esteem.

As he aged, though, he began to grow more emotionally open and self-aware. In college he had insisted that his relationship with his mother was outstanding. In middle age he confessed that when he thought of his mother, he wanted to vomit. "All my life I have had Mother's dominance to battle against," he now admitted.

His life took a radical turn in middle age. He came to realize, as he put it, that "the world's poor are the responsibility of the world's rich." He quit his job, moved to Sudan, and used his facility with statistics to help local farmers solve agricultural problems. At this point in his life, he wrote, his daughters had taught him that "there was more to life than numbers, thought and logic."

Then he returned to the United States and began teaching psychology and sociology at a local college, mentoring the next generation. From age fifty-five to sixty-eight he worked in city planning—which had been his childhood interest—helping cities in Texas manage their growth. By the end of his life he had become gentle and kind. When he was seventy-two, research director George Vaillant came to visit him, and Newman spoke cheerfully with him for two hours. When Vaillant stood up to leave, Newman said, "Let me give you a Texas good-bye!" and engulfed him in a bear hug. Vaillant concluded his interview and wrote in his notes, "I was entranced."

Most of the action in Newman's life happened during the second half. The later Newman didn't even realize how much he had changed. When he was fifty-five, Vaillant sent him the transcript of an interview he had given while in college. Newman wrote back: "George, you must have sent this to the wrong person."

There was absolutely no way that the guy in those transcripts could have been him. But it was. He simply didn't recognize any of the stories and facts he had related three decades before. He had reinvented his own consciousness and reinvented his past to fit the person he now was.

During the generative life task, people try to find some way to be of service to the world. One either achieves generativity, Erikson argues, or one falls into stagnation. Vaillant defines generativity as "the capacity to foster and guide the next generations." I like that definition because it emphasizes that people commonly tackle the generativity task at two different points in their lives. First, when they become parents. Parenthood often teaches people how to love in a giving way. And later, when they are middle-aged or older and become mentors. They adopt a gift logic—how can I give back to the world—that replaces the meritocratic logic of the career consolidation years.

Many people adopt the generative mindset when they get promoted to a leadership position. A person moves from being a teacher in the classroom to being an administrator in the front office, from being a reporter to being an editor, from working in a small department in an organization to managing a large division.

Often these promotions take people away from the core task that caused them to fall in love with their profession in the first place. Teachers go into education, for instance, because they love direct interaction with students. But people generally accept these promotions because they believe in their organization's mission, because they feel a responsibility to steward the organization, because they sense that in order to grow in life, they need to keep moving toward larger and larger states of consciousness—and, of course, because the leadership jobs usually pay more.

Sometimes it takes a while for people who move into these leadership jobs to switch consciousness. In their book *Immunity to Change,* Robert Kegan and Lisa Laskow Lahey describe a business executive, Peter, who was supposed to be managing a team but was stuck within that me-centered career consolidation consciousness. His values were these: I want to do things my way; I want to feel pride of ownership in our projects; I want to preserve my sense of myself as the super problem solver here. He couldn't even see that he was being dismissive and domineering toward those around him, and making them miserable.

Eventually the people around him delivered the hard news: He needed to change, to become more open to new ideas, to listen better, to delegate authority. He had to rise above his loyalty to his self-image as a solitary hero and develop a higher loyalty to the organization. A generative leader serves the people under him, lifts other people's vision to higher sights, and helps other people become better versions of themselves.

The generative person often assumes the role of guardian. A person with this consciousness is often leading or serving some institution, whether it is a company, a community organization, a school, or a family. A guardian has an in-depth respect for the institution she has inherited. She sees herself as someone who has been entrusted with something, has taken delivery of something precious and thus has a responsibility to steward it, and to pass it along in better shape than she found it. A person with this mindset is defined not by what she takes out of the institution but by what she pours into it.

At this moment in maturity, such a person fully appreciates that she didn't create her own life. The family she grew up in, the school she went to, and the mentors and friends and organizations who helped her all implanted certain values, standards of excellence, a way of being. She is seized with a fervent desire to pass it on.

Philip M. Lewis writes that as a younger professor, he felt bad about himself when his students looked bored. Their approval or disapproval defined his experience of teaching. Later, functioning at a more generative level, he realized that there are simply pieces of information in any domain that have to be taught, even if they are dry, if one is going to honor the subject. He became willing to bore his students in order to meet the standards of good teaching, to honor the subject and serve the institution.

A generative person gives others the gift of admiration—seeing them for the precious creatures they are. She gives the gift of patience—understanding that people are always developing. He gives them the gift of presence. I know a man who suffered a public disgrace. In the aftermath, one of his friends took him out to dinner every Sunday night for two years—the definition of a generative act.

There can be a kind of loneliness to a person in this consciousness. As a co-founder of Weave: The Social Fabric Project, I interviewed hundreds of community builders—people who led youth programs, food banks, homeless shelters, and the like. They were deeply satisfied by having the chance to help others, but they often noted that no one was actually there to serve them, to minister to them in their weak and exhausted moments. The person who seems strongest in any family or organization can also feel alone.

I would also say that these people were as ambitious, or even more ambitious, than the young adults who were just starting out on their careers. *The needs of the world are so many,* they often told me. *I can't let people down.* In my experience, selfless people are as prone to burnout as selfish ones—maybe more so.

INTEGRITY VERSUS DESPAIR

The final task Erik Erikson wrote about was the struggle to achieve integrity or endure despair. Integrity is the ability to come to terms with your life in the face of death. It's a feeling of peace that you have used and are using your time well. You have a sense of accomplishment and acceptance. Despair, by contrast, is marked by a sense of regret. You didn't lead your life as you believe you should have. Despair involves bitterness, ruminating over past mistakes, feeling unproductive. People often evade and externalize their regret. They become mad at the world, intent on displacing their disappointment about themselves into anger about how everything is going to hell.

People in this stage often have a strong desire to learn. The lecture halls of the world are filled with senior citizens who seek greater knowledge and wisdom. The explanatory drive that was there when they were babies is still there now.

Wisdom at this phase of life is the ability to see the connections between things. It's the ability to hold opposite truths—contradictions and paradoxes—in the mind at the same time, without wrestling to impose some linear order. It's the ability to see things from multiple perspectives. The psychoanalyst Philip M. Bromberg wrote, "Health is the ability to stand in the spaces between realities without losing any of them. This is what I believe self-acceptance means and what creativity is really all about—the capacity to feel like one self while being many."

When I interview people engaged in this life task, I often find that they derive great satisfaction from everyday actions—tending a garden, sharing breakfast with friends at a diner, visiting familiar vacation spots, the contemplation of everyday beauty. A dying man told me that he had never before so much enjoyed walks in nature.

You would think this phase would be a solitary phase, sitting alone in a room and reviewing your life. But it is an incredibly social phase. The psychologist Laura Carstensen finds that as people get older, emotion often takes the place of rational thinking. People feel free to cry more, are more adept at pulling differentiated emotions into consciousness. The awareness of death tends to make life's trivialities seem . . . trivial. "Cancer cures psychoneuroses," one of Irvin Yalom's therapy patients told him. "What a pity I had to wait till now, till my body was riddled with cancer, to learn how to live."

The historian Wilfred McClay's mother was a brilliant mathematician, lively, highly verbal, a reader, a teacher, a conversationalist. She was hit by a stroke that rendered her unable to talk. At first, she thought a life like this was not worth living, and wept bitterly. But gradually a change overtook her. As McClay remembers it, "An inner development took place that made her a far deeper, warmer, more affectionate, more grateful, more generous person than I had ever known her to be." She and her family devised ways to communicate, through gestures, intonations, and the few words she still possessed. She clapped and sang. "Most surpris-

ingly," McClay notes, "my mother proved to be a superb grandmother to my two children, whom she loved without reservation,
and who loved her the same way in return." Her grandkids saw
past her disability into who she was, and could not have known
how they made life worth living for her. Being around her was a
joy.

––––––

My hope is that this focus on life tasks can help remind that each
person you meet is at one spot on their lifelong process of growth.
We are often blind to how much we are changing. The psychologist Daniel Gilbert has a famous saying about this: "Human beings
are works in progress that mistakenly think they are finished." We
are also often blind to the fact that a change in life circumstance
often requires a renovation of our entire consciousness. As Carl
Jung put it: "We cannot live the afternoon of life according to the
program of life's morning, for what was great in the morning will
be little at evening, and what in the morning was true will at evening have become a lie."

Like all templates, the theory of life tasks is useful in prompting
you to pay attention to your life, to see where your life fits the pattern and where it doesn't. But overall, I have to say I recognize
myself in this evolution. When I was in high school, I was in that
interpersonal phase. Senior year I fell deeply in love with a woman,
but it was a desperate, need-based love. When she dumped me, it
was crushing. By midlife I was certainly involved in that career
consolidation life task, and became familiar with how it seals you
up. Today, I wish I were purely in a giving, generative phase, but
if I'm honest, I think I'm sort of in between career consolidation

and generativity. I do seek to serve, but I still pay too much attention to the metrics of success. A few years ago, I wrote a book on how to live your life for others, then spent the weeks after publication checking my Amazon rankings! I go into a dinner party determined to listen deeply, but then I have a glass of wine and start telling stories about myself. I have a civil war going on inside, evidently, between my generative consciousness I aspire to and that little Imperial ego that I can't quite leave behind. I suspect I'm not alone in this.

Periods of transition between tasks can be rough. When you're locked in a task, you're embedded in a certain mindset. When that mindset stops working for you, you have to let it crumble inside you. "All growth is costly," Kegan writes. "It involves leaving behind an old way of being in the world."

It's a process of disembedding from one mindset and then re-embedding in another. An infant believes, *I am my parents,* but then around age two realizes: *I am not my parents. I have parents.* A teenager may be so embedded in the interpersonal consciousness that she believes, *I am my friendships.* But later she realizes: *No, I am not my friendships. I am a person who has friendships.* It's not that friendships suddenly become unimportant, but what was once ultimate becomes relative. *I treasure my friendships, but my entire existence today is not riding on whether this or that person likes me.*

I have friends in their fifties who suffered severe life crises when their kids left home for college or work. Their vision of themselves was as active parents; parenting structured their day-to-day; and then, suddenly, all that was gone. They floundered for a bit until they found the next task. I have friends facing retirement who are terrified that without their work, they will lose their identity. They're not quite ready for the fact that at some point they will have to leave their résumé behind. It's not going to be who they are anymore. That requires a new construction of reality. As the saying goes, they are not going to solve their problem at the same level of consciousness at which they created it.

FIFTEEN

Life Stories

A couple of years ago I was talking with Dan McAdams, the Northwestern psychology professor who wrote the book on George W. Bush I quoted from in the personality chapter. He and I were discussing another aspect of his work. He also studies how people construct their personal narratives—how they tell the story of their lives. To find out, he invites research subjects onto campus, offers them some money for their time, and then over four hours or so, asks them questions that elicit their life stories. He asks people, for example, to tell him about the high points of their lives, the low points, and the turning points. Half the people he interviews end up crying at some point, recalling some hard event in their lives. At the end of the session, most of them are elated. They tell him that no one has ever asked them about their life story before. Some of them want to give the research fee back.

"I don't want to take money for this," they say. "This has been the best afternoon I've had in a long time." Apparently we live in a society in which people don't get to tell their stories. We work and live around people for years without ever knowing their tales. How did it come to be this way?

Part of it must be the normal busyness of life: Who has time to ask another human about their story, when we have kids to pick up and groceries to shop for and TikTok videos to watch? Part of it must also be fear of the rejection that may come if I make a social advance toward you and am rebuffed. Social anxiety is real. But perhaps there's a simpler and much more fixable reason for why people don't ask each other about their life stories or talk about their own.

One day, about a decade ago, Nicholas Epley was commuting by train to his office at the University of Chicago. As a behavioral psychologist, he was well aware that social connection is the number one source of happiness, success, good health, and much of the sweetness of life. Human beings are social animals who love to communicate with each other. Yet on this commuter train that day, he looked around and it hit him: Nobody was talking to anyone. It was just headphones and screens. And he wondered: Why aren't these people doing the thing that makes them the happiest? He later conducted some experiments in which he induced people to talk with other commuters during their rides downtown. When the ride was over and they arrived at their destination, researchers were there to ask them how much they enjoyed the trip. The comments were overwhelmingly positive. People, introverts as well as extroverts, reported that a commute spent talking with someone was much more fun than a commute spent locked into your screen.

So why don't people talk more? Epley continued his research and came up with an answer to the mystery: We don't start conversations because we're bad at predicting how much we'll enjoy them. We underestimate how much others want to talk; we underestimate how much we will learn; we underestimate how quickly other people will want to go deep and get personal. If you give people a little nudge, they will share their life stories with enthusiasm. As I hope I've made clear by now, people are eager, often desperate, to be seen, heard, and understood. And yet we have built a culture, and a set of manners, in which that doesn't happen. The way you fix that is simple, easy, and fun: Ask people to tell you their stories.

———

Since Epley told me about his research, I've become more likely to talk to strangers on a plane or train or at a bar. And as a result, I've had many more memorable experiences than I would have had if I had just been ensconced with my headphones. A few days before writing these words, I was on a plane from JFK airport in New York to Reagan airport in D.C. I was seated next to an elderly gentleman, and instead of burying myself in my book, I asked him where he was coming from, and then I asked him about his life. It turned out he had been born in Russia and had immigrated to the United States alone at age seventeen. To earn a living, he started by sweeping floors at a factory and then wound up exporting T-shirts and other articles of clothing from the States to the developing world. He told me about how much he used to love Donald Trump and why he had begun to sour on him. Then he pulled out his phone and showed me photos from the vacation in Italy he had just completed—cruising around on big yachts, surrounded by glamorous-looking people, hoisting bottles of champagne. This guy was still running around like a playboy at age eighty! He ended up telling me the whole story of his life, which involved more twists and turns—and more divorces—than I could keep track of. He's not the type of person who would be in my inner circle of friendship, but it was really fun to peek into his world.

Since learning about Epley's and McAdams's research, I've also tried to make my conversations storytelling conversations and not just comment-making conversations. The psychologist Jerome Bruner distinguished between two different modes of thinking, which he called the paradigmatic mode and the narrative mode. The paradigmatic mode is analytical. It's making an argument. It's a mental state that involves amassing data, collecting evidence, and offering hypotheses. A lot of us live our professional lives in the paradigmatic mode: making PowerPoint presentations, writing legal briefs, issuing orders, or even, in my case, cobbling together opinion columns. Paradigmatic thinking is great for understanding data, making the case for a proposition, and analyzing trends across populations. It is not great for seeing an individual person.

Narrative thinking, on the other hand, is necessary for understanding the unique individual in front of you. Stories capture the unique presence of a person's character and how he or she changes over time. Stories capture how a thousand little influences come together to shape a life, how people struggle and strive, how their lives are knocked about by lucky and unlucky breaks. When someone is telling you their story, you get a much more personal, complicated, and attractive image of the person. You get to experience their experience.

We live in a culture that is paradigmatic rich and narrative poor. In Washington, for example, we have these political talk shows that avoid anything personal. A senator or some newsmaker comes on to offer talking points on behalf of this or that partisan position. The host asks gotcha questions, scripted in advance, to challenge this or that position. The guests spit out a bunch of canned talking-point answers. The whole thing is set up as gladiatorial verbal combat. Just once I'd love to have a host put aside the questions and say, "Just tell me who you are." It would be so much more interesting, and it would lead to a healthier political atmosphere. But we don't live in a culture that encourages that.

What you do for a living shapes who you become. If you spend most of your day in paradigmatic mode, you're likely to slip into depersonalized habits of thought; you may begin to regard storytelling as non-rigorous or childish, and if you do that, you will constantly misunderstand people. So when I'm in a conversation with someone now, I'm trying to push against that and get us into narrative mode. I'm no longer content to ask, "What do you think about X?" Instead, I ask, "How did you come to believe X?" This is a framing that invites people to tell a story about what events led them to think the way they do. Similarly, I don't ask people to tell me about their values; I say, "Tell me about the person who shaped your values most." That prompts a story.

Then there is the habit of taking people back in time: Where'd you grow up? When did you know that you wanted to spend your life this way? I'm not shy about asking people about their childhoods: What did you want to be when you were a kid? What did your parents want you to be? Finally, I try to ask about intentions and goals. When people are talking to you about their intentions, they are implicitly telling you about where they have been and where they hope to go. Recently, for example, my wife and I were sitting around with a brilliant woman who had retired from a job she'd held for many years. We asked her a simple question: How do you hope to spend the years ahead? All sorts of stuff spilled out: How she was coping with losing the identity that her job had given her. How, for so long, people came to her asking for things, but now she was forced to humble herself and approach others for favors. She told us she had already come to realize that she was a poor predictor of what made her happy. Her original ideas about what retirement would look like weren't working; now she found it was best just to open herself up to unexpected possibilities and let things in. The story she told us about her previous few years was fascinating, but the best part was that her narrative was so open-ended; her posture toward the future was one of readiness, acceptance, and delight.

The ability to craft an accurate and coherent life story is yet another vital skill we don't teach people in school. But coming up with a personal story is centrally important to leading a meaningful life. You can't know who you are unless you know how to tell your story. You can't have a stable identity unless you take the inchoate events of your life and give your life meaning by turning the events into a coherent story. You can know what to do next only if you know what story you are a part of. And you can endure present pains only if you can see them as part of a story that will yield future benefits. "All sorrows can be borne if you put them into a story," as the Danish writer Isak Dinesen said.

Thus I now work hard to push against the paradigmatic pressures of our culture, and to "storify" life. "This is what fools people," the philosopher Jean-Paul Sartre once observed. "A man is always a teller of stories. He lives surrounded by his stories and the stories of others, he sees everything that happens to him through them; and tries to live his life as if he were recounting them."

———

As people are telling me their stories, I'm listening hard for a few specific things. First, I'm listening for the person's characteristic *tone of voice*. Just as every piece of writing has an implied narrator—the person the writer wants you to think he is—every person has a characteristic narrative tone: sassy or sarcastic, ironic or earnest, cheerful or grave. The narrative tone reflects the person's basic attitude toward the world—is it safe or threatening, welcoming, disappointing, or absurd? A person's narrative tone often reveals their sense of "self-efficacy," their overall confidence in their own abilities.

That inner voice is one of the greatest miracles in all nature. Life itself can often seem like a blizzard of random events: illnesses, accidents, betrayals, strokes of good and bad luck. Yet inside each person there is this little voice trying to make sense of it all. This little voice is trying to take the seemingly scattershot events of a life and organize them into a story that has coherence, meaning, and purpose.

Think about it: You have a three-pound hunk of neural tissue in your skull, and from this, somehow, conscious thoughts emerge. *You* emerge. No one understands how this happens! No one understands how the brain and body create the mind, so at the center of the study of every person there is just a giant mystery before which we all stand in awe.

The odd thing about this little voice, this storyteller, is that it comes and goes. When researchers study the inner voice, they find that for some people, the inner voice is chattering away almost every second. Other people experience long periods of inner silence. Russell T. Hurlburt and his colleagues at the University of Nevada, Las Vegas, found that, on average, people have an experience of inner speech about 23 percent of the time. The rest of the time the voice there may be a sense of mood, or a song bouncing around, but the sense of an inner narrator is absent. This is what I try to tell my wife when she asks me what I'm thinking about: "Honestly, honey, it's just a big crate of nothing up there a lot of the time."

Sometimes the voice sounds like normal speech, and sometimes it's a torrent of idea fragments and half-formed thoughts. In his book *Chatter,* the University of Michigan psychologist Ethan Kross reports on one study suggesting that we talk to ourselves at a rate equivalent to speaking four thousand words a minute out loud. About a quarter of all people hear the sounds of other people's voices in their heads. About half of all people address themselves in the second person as "you" often or all the time. Some people use their own name when talking to themselves. By the way, the people who address themselves in the second or even the third person have less anxiety, give better speeches, complete tasks more efficiently, and communicate more effectively. If you're able to self-distance in this way, you should.

Charles Fernyhough, a professor at Durham University, in the United Kingdom, and one of our leading scholars on inner speech, points out that sometimes it feels like we're not saying our inner speech, we're hearing it. That is, sometimes it feels like we are not in charge of the voice; we are its audience. The voice tortures us with embarrassing memories we'd rather not relive, cruel thoughts we'd rather not have. Sometimes it seems we're no more in charge of our voice than we are of our dreams. Or as William James put it, "Thoughts themselves are the thinkers."

Fernyhough observes that our inner speech is often made up of different characters in the mind having a conversation. The Polish researcher Małgorzata Puchalska-Wasyl asked people to describe the characters they heard in their head. She found that people commonly named four types of inner voices: the Faithful Friend (who tells you about your personal strengths), the Ambivalent Parent (who offers caring criticism), the Proud Rival (who badgers you to be more successful), and the Helpless Child (who has a lot of self-pity).

So when I'm listening to someone tell their story, I'm also asking myself, What characters does this person have in his head? Is this a confident voice or a tired voice, a regretful voice or an anticipating voice? For some reason, I like novels where the narrator has an elegiac voice. In F. Scott Fitzgerald's *The Great Gatsby,* Robert Penn Warren's *All the King's Men,* and Ford Madox Ford's *The Good Soldier,* the narrators have a world-weary tone. It's like they're looking back on glorious past events when dreams were fresh and the world seemed new and the disappointments of life had not yet settled in. That voice sounds to me like writing done in the minor key, and I find it tremendously moving. But I guess I wouldn't like to be around people with that voice in real life. In real life I'd prefer to be around my friend Kate Bowler's voice. As I mentioned, Kate got cancer a few years ago, when she was a young mother, and her voice is filled with vulnerability and invites vulnerability, but mostly it says: Life can suck, but we're going to be funny about it. She has a voice that pulls you into friendship and inspires humor; in her voice, laughter is never very far away.

The next question I'm asking myself as people tell me their stories is: Who is the hero here?

By our late twenties or early thirties, most of us have what McAdams calls an *imago,* an archetype or idealized image of oneself that captures the role that person hopes to play in society. One person, he finds, might cast himself as the Healer. Another might be the Caregiver. Others maybe be the Warrior, the Sage, the Maker, the Counselor, the Survivor, the Arbiter, or the Juggler. When someone is telling me their story, I find that it's often useful to ask myself, What imago are they inhabiting? As McAdams writes, "Imagoes express our most cherished desires and goals."

One day, on the set of the movie *Suicide Squad*, the actor Will Smith went up to Viola Davis and asked her who she was. She didn't quite get the question, so Smith clarified: "Look, I'm always going to be that fifteen-year-old boy whose girlfriend broke up with him. That's always going to be me. So, who are you?" Davis replied, "I'm the little girl who would run after school every day in third grade because these boys hated me because I was . . . not pretty. Because I was . . . Black."

In her book *Finding Me,* Davis depicts a very clear imago. She is someone who grew up amid desperate poverty, with an angry alcoholic father, always feeling like the outsider and the condemned. But her identity is built around her heroic resistance to those circumstances, even as a girl. "When I won spelling contests," she writes, "I would flaunt my gold star to everyone I saw. It was my way of reminding you of who the hell I was." Davis presents herself in the imago of the Fighter: "My sisters became my platoon. We were all in a war, fighting for significance. Each of us was a soldier fighting for our value, our worth."

In Davis's book, you know who the hero is and what she is like. Not everyone has established such a clear heroic identity. The psychologist James Marcia argues that there are four levels of identity creation. The healthiest people have arrived at what he calls "identity achievement." They've explored different identities, told different stories about themselves, and finally settled on a heroic identity that works. Less-evolved people may be in a state of "foreclosure." They came up with an identity very early in their life— *I'm the child who caused my parents to divorce,* for instance, or *I'm the jock who was a star in high school*. They rigidly cling to that identity and never update it. Others may find themselves caught in "identity diffusion." These are immature people who have never explored their identity. They go through life without a clear identity, never knowing what to do. Then there is "moratorium." People at this level are perpetually exploring new identities, shape-shifting and trying on one or another, but they never settle on one. They never find that stable imago.

The third thing I'm asking myself as people tell me their stories is: What's the plot here? We tend to craft our life stories gradually, over a lifetime. Children don't really have life stories. But around adolescence most people begin imposing a narrative on their lives. At first there's a lot of experimentation. In one study, for example, McAdams asked a group of college students to list the ten key scenes in their life. When he asked the same students the same question three years later, only 22 percent of the scenes were repeated on the second list. The students were in the early process of understanding the plot of their lives, so they had come up with a different list of episodes that really mattered.

By adulthood most of us have settled on the overarching plot-lines of our lives, and we have often selected those plotlines from stories that are common in our culture. In *The Seven Basic Plots,* Christopher Booker describes the relatively few plotlines that show up in our culture again and again, and how we apply them to tell our own life stories. Some people, for example, see their lives as "Overcoming the Monster," in which the hero defeats some central threat, like alcoholism, through friendship and courage. Other people view their lives as "Rags to Riches," in which the hero starts out impoverished and obscure and rises to prominence. Or they see their lives as a "Quest," a story in which the hero undertakes a voyage in pursuit of some goal and is transformed by the journey. There must be more than seven plots, but it's probably true that every mentally healthy person has one overriding self-defining myth, even if they are only semi-aware of it.

Many Americans, McAdams has found, tell redemption stories. That is to say, they see their lives within a plotline in which bad things happened, but they emerged from them stronger and wiser. For example: *I had some early blessing. I saw the suffering of others. I realized my moral purpose. I endured periods of suffering. I grew from my pain. I'm looking toward a beautiful future.* If you're talking with an American and you want to get a sense of who they are, find out if their life story falls into this pattern, and if not, why not.

In *Composing a Life,* the cultural anthropologist Mary Catherine Bateson argued that we often shoehorn our lives into neat, linear stories of decision and then commitment: *I decided to become a doctor and pursued my dream.* She argues that many lives are not like that. They are nonlinear. They have breaks, discontinuities, and false starts. Young people, she wrote, need to hear that the first job they take at twenty-two is not necessarily going to lead in a linear way to what they are going to be doing at forty. I'm always intrigued by people who see their lives as a surfing story: *I caught a wave and rode it, then I caught another wave. Then another.* That's a relaxed acceptance of life few of us can muster.

The next question I ask myself when hearing stories is: How reliable is this narrator? I guess all of our stories are false and self-flattering to some degree. The seventeenth-century French moralist François de La Rochefoucauld issued the crucial warning here: "We are so used to disguising ourselves from others that we often end up by disguising ourselves from ourselves." Some people, however, take fabulation to the extreme. They are beset by such deep insecurities and self-doubts that when you ask them to tell their story, what you end up getting is not an account but a performance. The novelist William Faulkner returned home from World War I in a pilot's uniform, overflowing with tales of his heroic exploits gunning down German planes. In reality, he never saw combat. The great conductor Leonard Bernstein once told an interviewer, "My childhood was one of complete poverty." He said his high school offered "absolutely no music at all." In fact, Bernstein grew up wealthy, with maids, at times a chauffeur and a second home. He was the piano soloist in his school's orchestra and sang in the glee club.

Some people tell evasive stories. Stephen Cope writes that his mother often told stories of her life but "here was the rub: she left out almost all the hard parts. So actually her narrative was woven from *pieces* of the truth, but when it was all put together, it turned out to be a kind of elaborate cover story. It was a wish. The shadow side was left out." Because she felt that it's shameful to admit you're in pain, she left the moments of pain out of her story. Since confronting pain wasn't in her story, she wasn't able to confront it in real life. One day Cope called her, sobbing, after his best friend had died suddenly. "She barely knew what to say or how to comfort me," he recalls. "After all, who had comforted her? She couldn't wait to get off the phone."

Some people tell you life stories that are just too perfect. There are never any random events; each episode of their life was, supposedly, masterfully planned in advance. Such people describe one triumph after another, one achievement after another in a way that's just not real. "The only way you can describe a human being is by describing his imperfections," the mythologist Joseph Campbell wrote. That goes for self-description, too.

Finally, when I'm hearing life stories, I'm looking for narrative flexibility. Life is a constant struggle to refine and update our stories. Most of us endure narrative crises from time to time—periods in which something happened so that your old life story no longer makes sense. Perhaps you dreamed all your life of becoming an architect. When people asked you about your childhood, you would talk about how even as a kid you were fascinated by buildings and homes. But let's say you didn't get into architecture school or got there and found it boring. You ended up doing something else. You have to go back and rewrite the history of your childhood so that it coherently leads to the life you are now living.

Therapists are essentially story editors. People come to therapy because their stories are not working, often because they get causation wrong. They blame themselves for things that are not their fault, or they blame others for things that are. By going over life stories again and again, therapists can help people climb out of the deceptive rumination spirals they have been using to narrate themselves. They can help patients begin the imaginative reconstruction of their lives. Frequently the goal of therapy is to help the patient tell a more accurate story, a story in which the patient is seen to have power over their own life. They craft a new story in which they can see themselves exercising control.

I find that most of us construct more accurate and compelling stories as we age. We learn to spot our strengths and weaknesses, the recurring patterns of our behavior, the core desire line that will always propel our life forward. We go back and reinterpret the past, becoming more forgiving and more appreciative. "Calm is a function of retrospective clarification," the Swarthmore literature professor Philip Weinstein writes, "a selective ordering after the fact."

———

These days, as I hear people tell me their stories, I try to listen the way I listen to music. I try to flow along with the melodies, feeling the rises and dips along with them. Like music, stories flow; they are about rhythm and melody. I'm aware that telling a life story can be a form of seduction. So I'm asking myself, Are they giving me a full story?

I recently visited a friend in the hospital who, it turned out, was a week away from dying of cancer. I didn't have to pull stories out of him. He was actively reviewing the story of his life. He focused mostly on stories in which people had done him acts of kindness he didn't deserve. He told me he was surprised by how often he woke up in the middle of the night thinking about his mother. "It's such a powerful bond," he said, with wonder. He talked regretfully about a time when he had held an important job and how it had made him crueler to the people around him. He went back and back into the past and found gratitude at every turn. When we go back and tell our life story with honesty and compassion, the theologian H. Richard Niebuhr wrote, "we understand what we remember, remember what we forgot, and make familiar what had before seemed alien."

There's one more thing that happens as I listen to life stories. I realize I'm not just listening to other people's stories; I'm helping them create their stories. Very few of us sit down one day and write out the story of our lives and then go out and recite it when somebody asks. For most of us it's only when somebody asks us to tell a story about ourselves that we have to step back and organize the events and turn them into a coherent narrative. When you ask somebody to tell part of their story, you're giving them an occasion to take that step back. You're giving them an opportunity to construct an account of themselves and maybe see themselves in a new way. None of us can have an identity unless it is affirmed and acknowledged by others. So as you are telling me your story, you're seeing the ways I affirm you and the ways I do not. You're sensing the parts of the story that work and those that do not. If you feed me empty slogans about yourself, I withdraw. But if you stand more transparently before me, showing both your warts and your gifts, you feel my respectful and friendly gaze upon you, and that brings forth growth. In every life there is a pattern, a story line running through it all. We find that story when somebody gives an opportunity to tell it.

SIXTEEN

How Do Your Ancestors Show Up
in Your Life?

Zora Neale Hurston was born in Alabama in 1891. Her family moved to Eatonville, Florida, when she was three. Eatonville, just outside Orlando, was an all-Black town, with a Black mayor, a Black town marshal, and Black city council.

Hurston was in a hurry from the start. She emerged from her mother's womb prematurely, while the midwife was away, and was delivered by a white passerby who heard her mother's screams, cut the umbilical cord with his Barlow knife, and swaddled her as best he could. Her father, a big, powerful man—a carpenter and, later, a preacher who was known as "God's Battle Axe"—never forgave Zora for being born a girl and never warmed to her. Her mother was small, caring, and ambitious. She refused to quench Zora's spirit, no matter how troublesome it could be. "I was Mama's child," Hurston recalled years later.

The family lived by a road, and when she was a young girl, Zora used to approach carriages that passed by. "Don't you want me to go a piece of the way with you?" she'd ask daringly, not caring whether the drivers were white or Black. Charmed by her self-assurance, they'd invariably lift her up into the carriage, drive for a bit while she peppered them with questions, and then let her out so she could walk home.

One year her father asked what she wanted for Christmas. Zora burst out: "A fine black riding horse with white leather saddle."

In her outstanding biography *Wrapped in Rainbows,* Valerie Boyd writes that Zora's father exploded. "A saddle horse! It's a sin and a shame! Lemme tell you something right now, my young lady; you ain't white. Riding horse!! Always trying to wear de big hat. I don't know how you got in this family nohow. You ain't like none of de rest of my young'uns."

Her parents fought over her assertiveness. Her mother often told her, "Jump at the sun. We may not land on the sun, but at least we would get off the ground." Her father, meanwhile, was trying to prevent her from getting into trouble with the wider world. "He predicted dire things for me," she would later recall. "The white folks were not going to stand for it. I was going to be hung before I got grown."

In those days the social center of town was the front porch of Joe Clarke's store. The men would hang out there through the afternoons and evenings—boasting, trading gossip, exchanging passing opinions on the world. "For me, the store porch was the most interesting place I could think of," she recalled in her memoir *Dust Tracks on a Road.*

As a young girl, Zora wasn't allowed to hang around on the porch, but she did drag her feet every time she walked by, and she kept her ears open. She overheard conversations about the forbidden adult world—men bragging about their sexual exploits, lurid stories about the scandals this or that neighbor had fallen into. "There were no discreet nuances of life on Joe Clarke's porch," she wrote. "There was open kindnesses, anger, hate, love, envy and its kinfolks, but all emotions were naked, and nakedly arrived at."

She picked up glints and bits of language. There was the way the men played with each other with mock insults. They called each other mullet-headed, mule-eared, wall-eyed, hog-nosed, gator-faced, goat-bellied, shovel-footed, and every other name in the book. They also told each other stories, the folklore of the Black South—Brer Rabbit, Brer Fox, stories about God and the Devil, animal stories about the Fox, the Lion, the Tiger, and the Buzzard. The men called these storytelling marathons "lying sessions."

This language and these stories formed the raw material for Hurston's later career as a writer. As Valerie Boyd notes, "Essentially everything that Zora Hurston would grow up to write, and to believe, had its genesis in Eatonville. The setting of her earliest childhood memories and the site of her coming of age, Eatonville was where Hurston received her first lessons in individualism and her first immersion in community."

It's like this for many of us. There's a certain spot on this earth that is somehow sacred, the place where you come from, the place you never quite leave. When you think back to your hometown or home neighborhood, sometimes it's the very soil and mountains that you remember, the way a certain wind would blow through a certain kind of crop, perhaps the way a certain factory would scent the town. Always it's the people, the characters in the small dramatic panorama that was, when you were a child, your whole life.

I grew up in Manhattan. If you start around Fourteenth Street on the East Side and walk south for a mile or so, you'll pass where my great-grandfather had his butcher shop, where my grandfather worked at a law firm, where my father, on the other side of my family, grew up, where I went to elementary school, and where my son, for a time, went to college. Five generations in one spot, and that spot is thus coated with memory and emotion—the playground where I was attacked by a dog, the deli counter where I'd go for cream soda, the spot on Lafayette Street where the hippies used to hang out, the place on Second Avenue where my grandfather took me for pancakes and let me go wild with the syrup. I may never live in New York again, but I'll never be able to completely live anywhere else. First I inhabited New York, and forever after it inhabits me, and I live with this semiconscious prejudice that if you're not living in New York, you're not really trying.

We live our childhoods at least twice. First, we live through them with eyes of wonderment, and then later in life we have to revisit them to understand what it all meant. As adults, artists often return to their childhood homes as a source of spiritual nourishment and in search of explanations for why they are as they are. Toni Morrison put it this way: "All water has a perfect memory and is forever trying to get back to where it was. Writers are like that: remembering where we were, what valley we ran through, what the banks were like, the light that was there and the route back to our original place. It is emotional memory—what the nerves and skin remember as well as how it appeared."

As a girl, Hurston had visions. One day, she fell into a strange sleep. She dreamed of scenes from her future life. They didn't form a story. They were just a series of disjointed images, like a slide show: scenes of wandering, scenes of love betrayed, an image of two women, one old, one young, in a big house, rearranging strange flowers while waiting for her.

"I had knowledge before its time. I knew my fate," she wrote. "I knew that I would be an orphan and homeless. I knew that while I was still helpless, that the comforting circle of my family would be broken, and that I would have to wander cold and friendless until I had served my time."

Sure enough, her mother, Lucy, soon grew gravely ill. In those days in the South there were certain superstitions about how to behave in the presence of the dying: remove the pillow from beneath the dying person's head to ease their trip into the afterlife; cover the faces of any clocks in the room, because a clock would never work again if the dying person looked at it; drape all the mirrors. Lucy wanted none of these superstitions observed as she lay dying and asked Zora to make sure they wouldn't be. As her mother was rasping her last breaths, the other family members took the pillow away and covered the clocks and mirrors. Zora protested, but her father held her down. Her mother was heaving, trying to say something, but no one could tell what. Then she died. That failure to heed her mother's final wishes tortured Hurston for the rest of her life. "In the midst of play, in wakeful moments after midnight, on the way home from parties, and even in the classroom during lectures. My thoughts would escape occasionally from their confines and stare me down." She would never know what her dying mother wanted to tell her.

After her mother's death the family broke apart and Hurston began her wanderings. As if an orphan, as prophesied, she moved about: Jacksonville, Nashville, Baltimore, Washington, Harlem. She worked as an assistant in a traveling theater troupe. When she was twenty-six, she lied and said she was sixteen, so she could qualify for free high school. From then on, she passed as a decade younger than she really was. She had her own grand ambitions, her sense of her own epic quest. "Oh, if you knew my dreams! My vaulting ambition!" she wrote to a friend. She studied at Howard University, Columbia, and Barnard (where she was the only Black student). She was at the center of the Harlem Renaissance with her friend Langston Hughes. She published a series of short stories, many of them set in Eatonville, using the dialect of the people she'd grown up among. She made a name for herself as a writer in New York, but never quite felt at home there.

At Columbia she studied anthropology under the German émigré Franz Boas, then the leading anthropologist in the nation. When he asked her where she would like to go to pursue her work, she replied immediately: Florida. So she returned home to Eatonville and began collecting information about the folklore, dances, and customs she had grown up with. She began recording the stories and voices. "I'm getting inside Negro art and lore. I am beginning to *see* really," she wrote to Langston Hughes. "This is going to be *big*. Most gorgeous possibilities are showing themselves constantly."

Hurston determined that she would bring these old stories of Black culture to the wider world. In 1932, for example, she introduced the songs and the jumping dance of the freed slaves in the Bahamas to an audience at the John Golden Theatre in New

York—long before "Negro spirituals" got cleaned up and made palatable for Broadway. Hurston used this cultural legacy to fight back against those who would diminish Black life and southern Black culture. "Memory, history, were their weapons of resistance," the contemporary writer Danté Stewart wrote in *Comment* magazine.

———

Zora Neal Hurston was an ambitious woman who was always climbing upward, always exploring, always on the move. She had the strength to do that because she knew where she came from, and she knew the legacy her ancestors had left to her, the many ways the long dead showed up in her life. Edmund Burke once wrote that "people will not look forward to posterity who never look back to their ancestors." Each person's consciousness is formed by all the choices of her ancestors, going back centuries: who they married, where they settled, whether they joined this church or that one. In other words, a person is part of a long movement, a transmission from one generation to another, and can only be seen rightly as part of that movement. For Hurston, it was the neighbors in Eatonville, her ancestors who had been enslaved, her more ancient ancestors back in Africa, and the lessons and the culture they had passed down century after century.

Hurston had a visceral connection with that long cultural procession, which penetrated not just her mind but her bones. Sitting in a Harlem nightclub while listening to jazz could arouse something primeval in her. "I dance wildly inside myself; I yell within, I whoop. . . . My face is painted red and yellow and my body is painted blue. My pulse is throbbing like a war drum."

But her stories were not about stock characters, or representative types, or the Black experience in general. They were about unique individuals. "My interest lies in what makes a man or a woman do such and so, regardless of his color," she wrote. Her own people, she felt, were so varied. A Black woman could be wise or foolish, compassionate or callous, considerate or cruel. "If you have received no clear cut impression of what the Negro in America is like, then you are in the same place with me. There is no *The Negro* here. Our lives are so diversified, internal attitudes so varied, appearances and capabilities so different, that there is no possible classification so catholic that it will cover us all, except, My people! My people!"

Hurston defied the lazy way people today classify others according to their group. Today, in our identity politics world, we are constantly reducing people to their categories: Black/white, gay/straight, Republican/Democrat. It's a first-class way to dehumanize others and not see individuals. But Hurston, through her example, shows us what the true task of opening your eyes to others involves: How do I see a person as part of their group? And how, at the same time, do I see them as a never-to-be-repeated unique individual, bringing their own unique mind and viewpoint?

If I tried to see a person like Zora Neal Hurston without seeing Black culture, that would be ridiculous. But if I saw her only as a Black person, that would also be ridiculous. When people tell me about times when they have felt mis-seen, it is often because somebody saw them not as an individual but just as someone in a category. Two years ago, a brilliant young Ugandan student told me about the time a middle-aged white woman saw him approaching down a New Haven street in the evening. She crossed the street to get away from him. She hid behind a tree. The tree was skinny, so it didn't conceal even a quarter of her. But still she cowered there, feigning invisibility, having reduced my student to an idiotic category, one defined by fears and stereotypes. In a tone of bemused amazement, my student said that since he'd arrived in America, this had happened all the time. People saw only his alleged group and affixed all sorts of stereotypes to that.

The challenge in seeing a person, therefore, is to adopt the kind of double vision I mentioned in the chapter on hard conversations. It means stepping back to appreciate the power of group culture and how it is formed over generations and then poured into a person. But it also means stepping close and perceiving each individual person in the midst of their lifelong project of crafting their *own* life and their *own* point of view, often in defiance of their group's consciousness. The trick is to hold these two perspectives together at the same time.

And you have to manage both these things at a level of high complexity. One of the great fallacies of life is to think culture is everything; another great fallacy is to think culture is nothing. I've found it helpful to start with the idea that each of us exists in a state of givenness. Each of us can say, "I am the receiver of gifts. I am part of a long procession of humanity and I have received much from those who came before." But people are not passive vessels into which culture is poured; each person is a cultural co-creator, embracing some bits of their culture, rejecting others— taking the stories of the past and transforming them with their own lives. To see a person well, you have to see them as culture inheritors and as culture creators.

What is culture? It's a shared symbolic landscape that we use to construct our reality. People who grow up in different cultures see the world differently—sometimes on the most elemental level. Let me give you some examples. Between 1997 and 2002, diplomats to the United Nations didn't have to pay fines on any tickets they might acquire by parking illegally on New York City streets. Basically, they got free "park where you want" permission. People from low-corruption cultures, however, still refused to break the rules. Diplomats from the United Kingdom, Sweden, Canada, Australia, and a few other similar nations got a total of zero parking tickets during these five years. Meanwhile, diplomats from countries that had higher tolerance for corruption and rule breaking (*You got to do what you got to do to feed your family*) took full advantage of the regulation. Diplomats from Kuwait, Albania, Chad, and Bulgaria accumulated more than one hundred tickets *per diplomat.* They saw the situation differently, and it's important to emphasize that it's not because some individual diplomats were more honest or less honest than others. It's because some were descended from people who'd grown up in places where it made sense to follow the establishment's rules. Other diplomats' ancestors grew up in places where perhaps there was colonialism or oppression or autocracy, and the establishment's rules were illogical or even immoral, and so it made sense to break the rules when you could. Each person saw the world in a way that made sense according to their ancestors' circumstances.

The cultural psychologist Michele Gelfand studies what she calls tight and loose cultures. Some groups settled in places where infectious diseases and foreign invasions were common. They developed cultures that emphasized social discipline, conformity, and the ability to pull together in times of crisis. Other groups settled in places that had been spared from frequent foreign invasion and frequent epidemics. Those people developed loose cultures. They tended to be individualistic and creative, but civically uncoordinated, divided, and reckless. The United States, she shows, is a classic loose culture.

The evolutionary biologist Joseph Henrich wrote a book called *The WEIRDest People in the World*. In it, he makes the point that those of us in our Western, Educated, Industrialized, Rich, and Democratic culture are complete outliers when compared to most other cultures in world history. For example, when people in our WEIRD culture get married, they tend to go off and set up their own separate household. But that is the dominant pattern in only 5 percent of the twelve hundred societies that have been studied. We often live in nuclear families. That's the dominant family mode in only 8 percent of human societies. We have monogamous marriages. That's predominant in only 15 percent of societies. And so on and so on.

People who grew up in WEIRD cultures, Henrich finds, are much less conformist than people in most other cultures. They are more loyal to universal ideals and maybe a little less loyal to friends. For example, while most people in Nepal, Venezuela, or South Korea would lie under oath to help a friend, 90 percent of Americans and Canadians do not think their friends have a right to expect such a thing. That's weird! One of Henrich's core points is that if we conduct all our experiments using only WEIRD research subjects at Western universities, we shouldn't use that data to draw wide conclusions about human nature in general.

Richard Nisbett is one of America's most prominent psychologists. He has spent long stretches of his career studying the cultural differences between the East and the West. He traces these differences in part to the values that were emphasized by early Eastern and Western thinkers and philosophers. The classical Greeks, at the source of Western culture, emphasized individual agency and competition. Westerners thus tend to explain a person's behavior by what's going on inside their individual mind—the person's traits, emotions, and intentions. Early Confucianism, meanwhile, emphasized social harmony. In *The Geography of Thought,* Nisbett quotes Henry Rosemont, an authority on Chinese philosophy: "For the early Confucians, there can be no me in isolation . . . I am the totality of roles I live in relation to specific others." Thus Easterners, he argues, are quicker to explain a person's behavior by looking at the context outside the individual's mind. What is the situation that person found him- or herself in?

These ancient differences still shape behavior today. A study asked fifteen thousand people around the world if they'd prefer a job in which individual initiative is encouraged or one in which no one is singled out for honor but everybody works as a team. More than 90 percent of American, British, Dutch, and Swedish respondents chose the individual initiative job. But fewer than 50 percent of Japanese and Singaporean respondents did.

In a classic 1972 study, students from Indiana and Taiwan were given groups of three things and asked which two of the three go together. When shown pictures of a man, woman, and child, the

American kids tended to put the man and woman together, because they are both adults. The Taiwanese kids tended to put the
woman and child together because the mother takes care of the
baby. When shown pictures of a chicken, a cow, and grass,
the American kids put the chicken and cow together because
they are both animals. The Taiwanese kids put the cow and the
grass together because a cow eats grass. In these and many other
cases, the Americans tended to sort by categories and the Taiwanese tended to sort by relationships.

One has to be very careful with these kinds of generalizations.
It's not as if you can dump all people from the West in a box called
"individualism" and all people from the East in a box called "col-
lectivism," but the averages of behavior in each community are different. You have to look for the generalization but then see through
the generalization; if this person grew up in an individualistic culture but is very communal, what does it say about him?

I'm trying to emphasize the presence of the past, how the dead
live in us. Research by Alberto Alesina, Paola Giuliano, and Nathan Nunn found that people who are descended from those who
practiced plow-heavy agriculture tend to live in cultures that have
strongly defined gender roles, because it was mostly men who
drove the plow. On the other hand, people who are descended
from those who did non-plow farming tend to have less defined
gender roles. People descended from sheepherding cultures tend
to be individualistic, because a shepherd's job requires him to go
off on his own. People descended from rice-farming cultures tend
to be very interdependent, because everybody has to work together
to raise and harvest rice. One researcher in China found that the
divorce rate for people in historic wheat-farming regions was

50 percent higher than the divorce rate for those from historic rice-farming regions.

In his brilliant book *Albion's Seed,* the historian David Hackett Fischer shows us the long continuities that mark the different streams of white Anglo-Saxon Protestant culture in the United States. When the English settled in America, he notes, they settled in clumps. People from eastern England tended to settle in New England, people from southern England went to Virginia, people from the English Midlands went to Pennsylvania, and people from northern England went to Appalachia. This was all roughly 350 years ago.

They carried their cultures with them—a way of speaking, a way of building a home, a way of raising children, playing sports, cooking food, as well as attitudes about time, attitudes about social order, power, and freedom.

The eastern English who settled New England, Fischer writes, were highly moralistic, had an acute awareness of social sin, strongly valued education, were very industrious, were highly time conscious, were emotionally buttoned up, valued town halls, and were active in civic life. That sounds a lot like New England today.

Those from southern England who went to Virginia were more aristocratic. They built, when they could afford it, palatial homes, and had extended patriarchal families. They liked showy and frilly clothing, were more comfortable with class differences, and were less obsessed about staying on the clock.

Those who moved from northern England to Appalachia favored a more militant Christianity and ascribed to an honor culture. They were more violent and put a greater emphasis on clan and kin. Their child-rearing techniques fostered a fierce pride that celebrated courage and independence. They cultivated a strong warrior ethic. Sure enough, even today people from Appalachia make up a disproportionate share of the U.S. military.

A lot has changed over the past three centuries, but the effects of these early settlement patterns were still evident when Fischer was writing in the 1980s. The murder rate in Massachusetts was much lower than the murder rate in Appalachia. In 1980, the high school graduation rate was 90 percent in New England but 74 percent in Virginia. New Englanders tolerated much higher tax rates than people in the mid-Atlantic or Appalachian states. New England remains more communal and statist and Appalachia and the South more clannish and combative, with a culture of "we take care of ourselves."

Throughout American history, the New England states have tended to vote one way and the Appalachian states have tended to vote the opposite way. The electoral map of 1896 looks very much like the electoral map of 2020. The populist candidates did very well in the southern and midwestern states in both elections. The only difference was that in 1896 William Jennings Bryan was a Democrat and in 2020 Donald Trump was a Republican. The parties had switched places, but the combative populist ethos stayed the same. The seeds of this behavior were planted over three centuries ago, and many of the people who live them out today are not even aware of where they come from.

———

When I'm looking at you, and trying to know you, I'm going to want to ask you how your ancestors show up in your life. And if you are looking at me, you'll want to ask how the past lives in me. I recently attended a great dinner party during which everybody talked about how their ancestors have influenced their lives. Some people at the dinner were Dutch, some were Black, and some were something else, and we all developed interesting and revealing theories about how we were shaped by those long dead.

I recently came across a passage from the twentieth-century psychoanalyst therapist Theodor Reik that I could relate to: "I am an infidel Jew. I can scarcely read Hebrew any longer; I have only a smattering of Jewish history, literature, and religion. Yet I know that I am a Jew in every fiber of my personality. It is as silly and as useless to emphasize it as it is to disavow it. The only possible attitude toward it is to acknowledge it as a fact."

I, too, am an infidel Jew, maybe even more so than Reik. My faith journey has taken me in unexpected directions. I don't go to synagogue anymore; I go to church. I don't speak Hebrew, and I no longer keep kosher. Yet I, too, am a Jew down to the very fiber of my being. There's no escape. It shows up in the obvious ways Jewish culture is often described. I have a deep reverence for the written word. For Jews, argument is a form of prayer, and I went into the disputation business. Jews put intense focus on education and achievement, and so did my family.

But there are subtler ways my ancestors show up in me. One is reverence for the past, this sense that we are living in the legacies of Abraham, Joshua, and Jacob, Sarah, Rachel, and Naomi. Jews have tended to congregate in verges, in places like Jerusalem and New York and Istanbul where different civilizations come together. Jews have been commanded to be a creative minority in those places, culturally distinct, yet serving the whole. And yet

Jewish life has always been insecure. Through the long centuries of exile Jews developed an awareness that everybody needs some place in the world they can call home. I think that insecurity never goes away. You're always, to some small degree, a stranger in a strange land, with an affinity for all the other strangers.

I've always found it interesting that three of the most influential modern Jewish thinkers—Marx, Freud, and Einstein—all focused their attention on the forces that drive history from under the surface. For Marx they were economic forces, for Freud the unconscious, for Einstein the invisible forces of the physical world, but they each wanted to probe beneath the surface, into the deep causes that drive people and events.

But do you want to know the biggest way I think my ancestors show up in my life? Thousands of years ago Jews were a small, insignificant people living in a marginal part of the world. And yet they believed that God had centered history around them. It was an audacious conviction! And that notion has come down to us in the form of a related conviction: that life is an audacious moral journey. Life asks a moral question: Have you lived up to the covenant? This, in turn, raises further questions: Have you taken your Exodus journey? Are you striving to be good and repair the world? It's a pressure-packed demand to grow and be better, and it's one that lives in me.

———

So when I see you, I want to see back into the deep sources of your self. That means asking certain key questions: Where's home? What's the place you spiritually never leave? How do the dead show up in your life? How do I see you embracing or rejecting your culture? How do I see you creating and contributing to your culture? How do I see you transmitting your culture? How do I see you rebelling against your culture? How do I see you caught between cultures?

As we talk about this, we're going to get beyond the shallow stereotypes and the judgments people might lazily rely on. We're going to talk about how you were gifted by those who came before, and formed by them. And as we talk, I'll begin to see you whole. "You live through time, that little piece of time that is yours," the novelist Robert Penn Warren wrote, "but that piece of time is not only your own life, it is the summing-up of all the other lives that are simultaneous with yours. . . . What you are is an expression of History."

SEVENTEEN

What Is Wisdom?

These days my ears perk up whenever I come across a story in which one person deeply saw another. For example, recently a friend mentioned to me that his daughter had been struggling in second grade. She felt like she wasn't quite fitting in with her classmates. But then one day her teacher said to her, "You know, you're really good at thinking before you speak." That one comment, my friend said, helped turn his daughter's whole year around. Something that she might have perceived as a weakness— her quietness or social awkwardness—was now perceived as a strength. Her teacher saw her.

That story reminded me of a time when one of my teachers deeply saw me, though in a different way. I was in eleventh-grade English, making some kind of smart-ass observation in class, as I was prone to do. My teacher barked at me in front of the whole class, "David, you're trying to get by on glibness. Stop it." I felt humiliated . . . and strangely honored. I thought, "Wow—she really knows me!" I was indeed talking to show off in those days, not talking to contribute. I learned, thanks to her, that I had to fight against my facility with words; I had to slow down and metabolize what I was thinking, so the ideas would come from my inner depths and not just off the top of my head.

A woman told me about the time when she was thirteen and she went to her first party and had her first alcohol. She was dropped off at home so drunk that all she could do was lie on the front porch, barely able to move. Her father—a big, strict disciplinarian—came out and she thought he was going to scream at her the very thoughts she was thinking about herself: "I'm bad. I'm bad." Instead, he scooped her up in his arms and carried her inside and placed her on the living room couch and said, "There'll be no punishment here. You've had an experience." He knew what she was thinking; she felt seen.

Sometimes in history books I come across occasions in which one person sees into the core of another. For example, one day in the 1930s, Franklin Roosevelt was hosting a twenty-eight-year-old congressman named Lyndon Johnson in the White House. After Johnson left his office, FDR turned to his aide Harold Ickes and said, "You know, Harold, that's the kind of uninhibited young pro I might have been as a young man—if I hadn't gone to Harvard." FDR continued with a prediction: "In the next couple of generations the balance of power in this country is going to shift to the South and the West. And that kid Lyndon Johnson could well be the first Southern President."

I've also come to savor those moments when a novelist gives

you piercing insights into one of his or her characters. Guy de Maupassant captured one of the characters this way: "He was a gentleman with red whiskers who always went first through a doorway." With that one line, I felt a whole character was revealed—a guy who was pushy, competitive, full of himself.

I like to think of these little everyday insights as moments of wisdom. Wisdom isn't knowing about physics or geography. Wisdom is knowing about people. Wisdom is the ability to see deeply into who people are and how they should move in the complex situations of life. That's the great gift Illuminators share with those around them.

———

My view of what a wise person looks like has been transformed over the past couple of years, as I have been researching this book. I used to have a conventional view of wisdom. The wise person is that lofty sage who doles out life-altering advice in the manner of Yoda, Dumbledore, or Solomon. The wise person knows how to solve your problems, knows what job you should take, can tell you whether or not you should marry the person you're dating. We're all attracted to this version of wisdom because we all want easy answers delivered on a silver platter.

Yet when I think of the wise people in my own life now, I realize it's not the people capable of delivering a sparkling lecture or dropping a life-altering maxim that pop first to mind. Now I take the more or less opposite view of wisdom.

I've come to believe that wise people don't tell us what to do; they start by witnessing our story. They take the anecdotes, rationalizations, and episodes we tell, and see us in a noble struggle.

They see the way we're navigating the dialectics of life—intimacy versus independence, control versus uncertainty—and understand that our current self is just where we are right now, part of a long continuum of growth.

The really good confidants—the people we go to when we are troubled—are more like coaches than philosopher-kings. They take in your story, accept it, but push you to clarify what it is you really want, or to name the baggage you left out of your clean tale. They ask you to probe into what is really bothering you, to search for the deeper problem underneath the convenient surface problem you've come to them for help about. Wise people don't tell you what to do; they help you process your own thoughts and emotions. They enter with you into your process of meaning-making and then help you expand it, push it along. All choice involves loss: If you take this job, you don't take that one. Much of life involves reconciling opposites: I want to be attached, but I also want to be free. Wise people create a safe space where you can navigate the ambiguities and contradictions we all wrestle with. They prod and lure you along until your own obvious solution emerges into view.

Their essential gift is receptivity, the capacity to receive what you are sending. This is not a passive skill. The wise person is not just keeping her ears open. She is creating an atmosphere of hospitality, an atmosphere in which people are encouraged to set aside their fear of showing weakness, their fear of confronting themselves. She is creating an atmosphere in which people swap stories, trade confidences. In this atmosphere people are free to be themselves, encouraged to be honest with themselves.

The knowledge that results from your encounter with a wise person is personal and contextual, not a generalization that can be captured in a maxim that can be pinned to a bulletin board. It is particular to your unique self and your unique situation. Wise people help you come up with a different way of looking at yourself, your past, and the world around you. Very often they focus your attention on your relationships, the in-between spaces that are so easy to overlook. How can this friendship or this marriage be nourished and improved? The wise person sees your gifts and potential, even the ones you do not see. Being seen in this way has a tendency to turn down the pressure, offering you some distance from your immediate situation, offering hope.

We all know people who are smart. But that doesn't mean they are wise. Understanding and wisdom come from surviving the pitfalls of life, thriving in life, having wide and deep contact with other people. Out of your own moments of suffering, struggle, friendship, intimacy, and joy comes a compassionate awareness of how other people feel—their frailty, their confusion, and their courage. The wise are those who have lived full, varied lives, and reflected deeply on what they've been through.

This is a lofty ideal. None of us are going to be that perceptive about other people all of the time. But I believe in lofty ideals. I believe in holding up standards of excellence. As Hurston's mother put it, we should all try to jump at the sun. Even if we don't reach it, we'll still reach higher than before. And if we falter, at least it won't be because we had an inadequate ideal. Let me close this book with four more cases in which one human being saw deeply into another human being. I think we have a few more things to learn about this skill from these examples.

The first involves the writer Tracy Kidder, who was born in New York City in 1945. A couple of decades ago, Kidder met an African man named Deogratias who was three decades younger and had grown up in the rural hills of Burundi. He eventually wrote a book about Deo, called *Strength in What Remains*. This book is proof that it really is possible to know another person deeply, even a person very different from yourself.

As the book opens, Deo is twenty-two years old. We are inside his head as he boards an airplane for the first time in his life—traveling from Burundi to New York City. He has spent his life in a rural village with cows, his little school, and his family. The plane is the largest man-made object he has ever seen. Kidder has us feeling his wonder. Deo sees the interior of the plane with startled eyes. He sees chairs in perfect rows, and notices that they have white cloths draped over their tops. "This was the most nicely appointed room he'd ever seen," Kidder writes. As the plane takes off, Deo is terrified, but he finds the cushioned chair very comfortable, and he enjoys the feeling of flight: "How wonderful to travel in an easy chair instead of on foot." One thing that puzzles him is that the literature in the pouch in front of him is not in French. He'd been told since elementary school that French was the universal language, used all around the world.

He finally lands in New York with two hundred dollars, no English, and no friends or even contacts. Strangers help him survive, and before long he is working as a delivery boy for a grocery store and sleeping in Central Park. A former nun named Sharon adopts Deo as her project. She helps him find shelter, legal status, and a future. Kidder lets us see how uncomfortable Deo—a mature, independent man—feels to be on the receiving end of charity:

"She was like a mother, who couldn't stop worrying about you, who couldn't help reminding you that you still needed her help, which was infuriating because in fact you did." More strangers come along and help him. Deo shows one middle-aged American the books he has brought from Burundi. The American tells his wife, "This man loves books. He needs to go to school." They enroll him in an English as a Second Language course at Hunter College. They take him to visit colleges, and the second Deo walks through the gates of Columbia, he thinks, "This is a university!" He enrolls in Columbia's American Language Program. His new friends pay the tuition of six thousand dollars. He finally takes a group of entrance exams, including the SAT and a calculus test. He finishes the latter before the other test takers and brings it up to the proctor, who takes a look at his answers, smiles at him, and, beaming, says, "De-*oh*-Gratias! Well done!"

Just a couple years after arriving in New York with nothing, he is a student at an Ivy League college. He studies medicine and philosophy, because he wants to close "the gap between what he'd experienced and what he was able to say."

What he experienced before coming to New York is the core of his story. Years before, Deo had been working in a healthcare center in Burundi when a genocide broke out, Hutus massacring Tutsis. One day, Deo heard trucks, whistles, militia in the courtyard outside. He ran to his room and hid under his bed. He heard people pleading, "Don't kill me!" Then shots, the smell of burning flesh. Then it became quiet, except for the sounds of dogs fighting over the bodies of the dead. That night was dark, and when the killing subsided Deo started running. Over the next four days he walked forty-five miles, to get away from the genocide. He saw a dead mother slumped against a tree, with her baby still alive, but Deo could not take it with him. Kidder captures Deo's mind as he experiences all this: "It was as if the sights and sounds and smells of the past few days—screams, corpses, burning flesh—were all collecting into something like another version of himself, another skin growing over him."

The trip on foot out of Burundi was haunted by more bodies, more menace, the constant threat that every person he encountered might take a machete to his head.

Kidder met Deo more than a decade after that trek, after he had, by that point, moved to New York and graduated from Columbia. Kidder heard the outline of Deo's story, but decided that this was a tale he wanted to capture in a book only when Deo confided to him that in the days when he was sleeping in Central Park, he would always sneak into the park after dark, when no one would notice him. He didn't want strangers looking down on him, seeing him as a pathetic homeless man. There was much in Deo's life that Kidder couldn't relate to, but this fear of the judgmental eyes of strangers, this cringing under the disdain of people he would never know—that emotion Kidder was familiar with, and that emotion could be a bridge between their experiences.

Deo was a tough subject to interview. The culture of Burundi is stoical. "It's a language that has not one but two words for bringing up something from the past, and they are both negative," Kidder told me. But gradually, over two years of conversations, Deo's story came out. "I don't see any way of doing this without spending time with a person," Kidder said. "If you spend time, what you want to know will creep out." The key is to listen, to be attentive, to be patient and not interrupt. Kidder told me he likes the version of himself that comes out when he's trying to learn about another. He's humbler, not talking so much.

Kidder didn't merely interview Deo; he accompanied him to the places where his story played out. They went back and visited the spot where he slept in Central Park, the supermarket where he worked as a delivery boy. Their walks together were a way of planting themselves in the concrete details of Deo's experience. Eventually, they went to Burundi, to trace his journey through the genocide.

As they drove toward the hospital where Deo had hidden under the bed while his neighbors were massacred outside, Kidder felt a creeping sensation across his skin. There was some evil presence in this place. The trip was taking them too deep inside something that felt dark and menacing. "Maybe we should just go back," Kidder said to Deo from the backseat of the car as they approached the hospital. Deo replied, "You may not see the ocean but right now we are in the middle of the ocean and we have to keep swimming."

When they arrived at the hospital, Kidder told me, Deo slipped into a kind of angry trance, which manifested itself as a fierce and false smile for all who greeted him. The hospital was now an empty shell, a Potemkin facility with a doctor who wasn't really a doctor and no patients. They finally made it to the room where Deo had hidden. "Deo had tried to describe his nightmares to me," Kidder writes about that visit. "In the telling, they hadn't seemed unusual. Everyone has bad dreams. . . . Up until now I hadn't fully understood the difference: that even his most lurid dreams weren't weirder or more frightening than what inspired them. He didn't wake up from his nightmares thankful they weren't real."

The evil atmosphere was palpable. Kidder was now tasting Deo's experience in a more visceral way: "This was a place of unreason, and at that moment I had no faith in the power of reason against it. Part of the problem, I think, was that for a moment I didn't trust Deo. The smile he turned on 'the doctor' was radiant. I had never seen him so angry."

Periodically, while working on the book, Kidder felt guilty for bringing Deo back into the trauma of his past. Kidder could see the damage the genocide had done to Deo. There were times when he would suddenly erupt with anger. At other times he would disappear inside himself. A friend said it was like Deo had no protective shell; everything he touched penetrated him so deeply and was felt so powerfully.

I read *Strength in What Remains* with a kind of awe. Kidder not only created a rich, complex portrait of Deo; he enabled us to see the world through his eyes. When I called Kidder to talk about the book, Deo's brother was staying at his house, and had become a family friend. Deo himself had gone back to Burundi to open a health center for the kinds of people he grew up with, including members of the Hutu tribe that had tried to massacre him. Kidder's curiosity about Deo was still pulsating as we spoke, though it had been a decade since his book came out.

I've tried to learn from Kidder to be more patiently attentive. I've learned to try to accompany people through the concrete particulars of their lives, and not be content with the much-rehearsed stories. I've learned that it really is possible to see people whose experiences are radically different from your own. From Deo, I've learned something about trust. Deo found in Kidder a man he could gradually tell his story to. And when he found that man, and bore witness to what he'd been through, he gave a gift to the world.

———

The second case study involves Lori Gottlieb, the therapist we met in chapter 14. She once told me that "most people have their answers inside them, but they need a guide so they can hear themselves figure it out." In her book *Maybe You Should Talk to Someone,* she describes a journey she took with a man called John. John was your classic self-absorbed, narcissistic jerk. By day he worked as a writer on fabulously successful TV shows, winning Emmy after Emmy. But he was a monster to everyone around him, cruel, inattentive, impatient, demeaning. He came to therapy because he was having trouble sleeping, because his marriage was crumbling, because his daughters were acting out. At first, he treated Gottlieb the way he treated everyone else, like an idiot he had to tolerate. He pulled out his phone during therapy sessions and she had to text him from across the room to get his attention. He ordered lunch for himself so he could multitask while he talked to her. He called her his "hooker," because he paid her for her time. John's dominant narrative was that he was the alpha performer, the successful one, but that he was surrounded by mediocrities.

Gottlieb could have reduced John to a category: narcissistic personality disorder. But, she told me, "I didn't want to lose the person behind the diagnosis." She knew from prior experience that people who are demanding, critical, and angry tend to be intensely lonely. She intuited that there was some internal struggle inside John, that there were feelings he was hiding from, which he had built moats and fortresses to keep away. She kept telling herself, "Have compassion, have compassion, have compassion." She later explained to me that "behavior is how we speak the unspeakable. John couldn't speak something unspeakable, so he did it by being rude to others and by having this sense of himself as better than everybody else."

Her first task with John was to establish a relationship with him, to make him feel felt. Her method, as she describes it, is "In this room, I'm going to see you, and you'll try to hide, but I'll still see you, and it's going to be okay when I do."

Gottlieb showed enormous forbearance with John, overlooking the countless episodes when he was a jerk, waiting for a sign of what bigger trauma he was grieving. Successful friendship, like successful therapy, is a balance of deference and defiance. It involves showing positive regard, but also calling people on their self-deceptions. The Buddhists have a useful phrase for unconditional positive regard: "idiot compassion," which is the kind of empathy that never challenges people's stories or threatens to hurt their feelings. It consoles but also conceals. So Gottlieb challenged John, but not too aggressively. She realized she could only prod him at the pace he was comfortable with or he would flee. She was trying to make him curious about himself with her questions. "Typically therapists are several steps ahead of their patients," she writes, "not because we're smarter or wiser but because we have the vantage point of being outside their lives."

As Gottlieb accompanied him, John's story about himself got less distorted. Experiences that he had been hiding began to bubble out. One day, John mentioned, in a matter-of-fact tone, that his mother had died when he was six. A teacher, she was exiting the school when she saw a student in the street in the path of a speeding car. She ran into the street, pushed the student out of the way, but was killed herself. Gottlieb wondered if John was told to bury his emotions and expected to show "strength" after his mother's death.

One day John was venting about all the stresses in his life. He was talking about how his wife and daughters were ganging up on him and he blurted out, "And Gabe is getting so emotional." Gottlieb had often heard him talk about his daughters but asked, "Who is Gabe?" He flushed and evaded the question. Gottlieb persisted: "Who's Gabe?" A wash of emotions swept across his face. Finally, he said, "Gabe is my son." He picked up his phone and walked out of the office.

Weeks later, when he finally returned, he revealed that he had had a son. The sentence about Gabe being emotional must have hurtled out from somewhere in his unconscious because Gabe was dead. When Gabe was six, the whole family was driving to Legoland. John was at the wheel when his cellphone rang. John and his wife started arguing about the way the phone intruded into their lives. Eventually John looked down to see who had called him and at that instant an SUV hit them head-on. Gabe was killed. John never knew if his act of glancing at his phone was the crucial error. If he'd been looking at the road, could he have avoided the SUV? Would it have hit them anyway?

John was finally learning to tell a truer story about his life. As this happened, he found that he was able to spend an evening with his wife and have a wonderful time. He was able to accept that sometimes he would be happy and sometimes he would be sad. In letting Gottlieb see him, he had arrived at a new way to see himself. "I don't want your head to get too big or anything," he told

Gottlieb, "but I thought, you have a more complete picture of my total humanity than anyone else in my life."

Gottlieb writes of that moment, "I'm so moved I can't speak."

I like the Gottlieb-and-John story because it illuminates many of the gentle skills it takes to be truly receptive—particularly, the ability to be generous about human frailty, to be patient and let others emerge at their own pace—but it also illuminates the mental toughness that is sometimes required. The wise person is there not to be walked over but to stand up for the actual truth, to call the other person out when need be, if they are hiding from some hard reality. "Receptivity without confrontation leads to a bland neutrality that serves nobody," the theologian Henri Nouwen wrote. "Confrontation without receptivity leads to an oppressive aggression which hurts everybody."

———

The third case study is from a scene in a movie you've probably seen, *Good Will Hunting*. In the first section of the movie, Will Hunting, an orphan and a math prodigy, played by Matt Damon, goes from triumph to triumph, effortlessly solving math problems, deflating pompous grad students with his superior knowledge, leveling others with his wit. He gets into a fight with a gang member who used to bully him, winds up attacking a responding police officer, and is arrested. He can avoid jail time, as long as he is treated by a therapist, played by Robin Williams. Over the course of the movie, the therapist creates a zone of hospitality where Will can lay down his defenses. They bond over the Red Sox; they share each other's traumas. But at one point Will makes fun of the therapist, belittles him, criticizes a painting he has made—just as he's belittled and teased most other people in the movie. The therapist is devastated by Will Hunting's simplification of his life. He's tortured and sleepless for part of a night. Then a realization creeps across his mind. This kid doesn't actually know what he's talking about. Will Hunting may know math, may have information, but he doesn't know how to see people. The Robin Williams character invites Will to meet him on a park bench, in front of a pond, and tells him the truth:

> "You're a tough kid. I ask you about war, and you'll probably throw Shakespeare at me, right? 'Once more into the breach, dear friends.' But you've never been near one. You've never held your best friend's head in your lap and watched him gasp his last breath, looking to you for help. And if I asked you about love, you'd probably quote me a sonnet. But you've never looked at a woman and been totally vulnerable. Known someone who could level you with her eyes. Feeling like God put an angel on earth just for you, who could rescue you from the depths of hell. . . .
>
> "I look at you; I don't see an intelligent confident man; I see a cocky, scared-shitless kid. But you're a genius, Will. No one denies that. . . . Personally, I don't give a shit about all that, because you know what? I can't learn anything from you I can't read in some fuckin' book. Unless you wanna talk about you, who you are. And I'm fascinated. I'm in. But you don't wanna do that, do you, sport? You're terrified of what you might say."

The therapist gets up and leaves. As he was speaking, you could see an expression of self-recognition creep across Will Hunting's face. You could see that Will Hunting already knew this about himself but didn't trust himself to face these hard truths. He'd been hiding from himself. To me, this speech flows from great listening. The therapist has heard not only what Will said but what Will didn't say—about the fear and vulnerability that came from his life as an orphan. He's heard the deepest secret that Will wants to hide. He puts that shameful secret on the table and says, in effect, "I know this about you, and I care for you anyway."

The therapist is prodding Will toward a different way of knowing, the kind of knowing I've been reaching for and trying to push us toward in this book. He's moving Will beyond an impersonal way of knowing, a catalog of facts, which Will has mastered and uses as a defensive fortress. The therapist is prodding Will toward a personal way of knowing, the kind of knowledge that is earned only by those willing to take emotional risks, to open themselves up to people and experiences and fully feel what those people and experiences are about. This is the kind of knowledge held not only in the brain but in the heart and body. The therapist has bestowed a painful and important honor. He sees Will as he is, even in the ways he is stunted. The therapist sees what Will has the potential to become and points him toward the way to get there.

The *Good Will Hunting* story is an education in how to critique with care. It's about how to tell someone about their shortcomings in a way that offers maximal support. Let me give you a trivial, everyday example of why critiquing with care can be so effective. When I'm writing, I sometimes unconsciously know that a part of what I'm writing is not working. I have these vague vibrations that something is wrong, kind of like the vibrations you feel when you leave the house and you subtly sense you've left something important behind but you don't know what. I often suppress these vibrations because I'm lazy or I want to be finished with the work. Invariably a good editor will locate the exact spot I semiconsciously knew wasn't working. It's only when the editor has named it for me that I fully face the fact that I need to make some changes. Critiquing with care works best when someone names something we ourselves almost but did not quite know. Critiquing with care works best when that naming happens within a context of unconditional regard, that just and loving attention that conveys unshakable respect for another person's struggles.

This is what our friends do for us. They not only delight us and call forth our best; friends also hold up a mirror so we can see ourselves in ways that would not otherwise be accessible. When we see ourselves that way, we have the opportunity to improve, to become our fuller selves. "A man with few friends is only half-developed," the radical writer Randolph Bourne observed. "There are whole sides of his nature which are locked up and have never been expressed. He cannot unlock them himself, he cannot discover them; friends alone can stimulate him and open them."

———

Not long ago I was at a dinner party at which two very good novelists were present. Someone asked how they began the process of writing their novels. Did they start with a character and then build the story around that, or did they start with an idea for a plot and then create characters who operate within that story? They both said they didn't use either of these approaches. Instead, they said, they started with a relationship. They started with the kernel of an idea about how one sort of person might be in a relationship with another sort of person. They started to imagine how the people in that relationship would be alike and different, what tensions there would be, how the relationship would grow, falter, or flourish. Once they had a sense of that relationship, and how two such characters would bounce off and change each other, then the characters would flesh out in their minds. And then a plot tracing the course of that relationship would become evident.

Listening to them that night helped me read novels differently. Now when I'm reading a novel I ask, What is the relationship at the center of this book? With good novels there will generally be one such central relationship, or perhaps a few core relationships will drive everything else. But that conversation also helped me see something bigger: that wisdom is not mostly a trait possessed by an individual. Wisdom is a social skill practiced within a relationship or a system of relationships. Wisdom is practiced when people come together to form what Parker Palmer called a "community of truth."

A community of truth can be as simple as a classroom— a teacher and students investigating some problem together. It can be two people at a table in a coffee shop, noodling over some problem. It can be as grand as the scientific enterprise. Science moves forward as thousands of minds dispersed all across the world pool their separate imaginations to look together at some problem. Or it can be as intimate as one person alone reading a book. One author's mind and one reader's mind coming together, sparking insight. Toni Morrison once wrote, "Frederick Douglass talking about his grandmother, and James Baldwin talking about his father, and Simone de Beauvoir talking about her mother, these people are my access to me; they are my entrance into my own interior life."

A community of truth is created when people are genuinely interested in seeing and exploring together. They do not try to manipulate each other. They do not immediately judge, saying, "That's stupid" or "That's right." Instead, they pause to consider what the meaning of the statement is to the person who just uttered it.

When we are in a community of truth, we're trying on each other's perspectives. We're taking journeys into each other's minds. It gets you out of the egotistical mindset—*I am normal, what I see is objective, everyone else is odd*—and instead gives you the opportunity to take a journey with another person's eyes.

A funny thing happens to people in a community of truth. Somebody has a thought. The thought is like a little circuit in their brain. When someone shares a thought and others receive it, then suddenly the same circuit is in two brains. When a whole classroom is considering the thought, it's like the same circuit in twenty-five brains. Our minds are intermingling. The cognitive scientist Douglas Hofstadter calls these circuits loops. He argues that when we communicate, and loops are flowing through different brains, we are thinking as one shared organism, anticipating each other, finishing each other's sentences. "Empathy" is not a strong enough word to describe this intermingling. It is not one person, one body, one brain that marks this condition, Hofstadter argues, but the interpenetration of all minds in ceaseless conversation with each other.

Let's say you're in a book club. You've been meeting for years and years. Sometimes you can no longer remember which ideas were yours and which were someone else's. You come to see that all your conversations over the years have been woven together into one long conversation. It's almost as if the club has its own distinct voice, one greater than the individual voice of each member.

Two sorts of knowledge have been generated here. The first kind, of course, is a deeper understanding of the books. The second kind of knowledge is more subtle and important. It's knowledge about the club. It's each member's awareness of the dynamics of the group, what role each member tends to take in the conversations, what gifts each member brings.

Maybe it's misleading to use the word "knowledge" here. Maybe it's more accurate to call this second kind of knowledge an "awareness." It's the highly attuned sense each person has for how the conversation should be pushed along, for when to talk and when to hold back, when to call in a member who has been quiet. This is the kind of awareness that can be achieved only by a group of people practicing the skills we've explored in this book.

There are magical moments in a community of truth, when people deeply talk with crystalline honesty and respect. As I mentioned near the start, I don't try to teach by argument; I try to teach by example. I'll conclude the book with one final example of seeing and being seen. I came across it in Kathryn Schulz's recent memoir *Lost & Found*. Schulz's dad, Isaac, was one of the millions of Europeans whose lives were tossed about by the events of the twentieth century. During World War II and the years after, he bounced around from Palestine, to postwar Germany, and eventually to the United States. He grew to adulthood, became a lawyer, and offered his family the kind of happiness and stability he had not known as a child.

He was a cheerful, talkative man. He was curious about everything and had something to say about everything—the novels of

Edith Wharton, the infield fly rule in baseball, whether apple cobblers were better than apple crisps. When they were young, he read to his daughters each night, playacting the characters in the stories with dramatic voices and hilarious gestures. Some nights he just ditched the books entirely and crafted suspenseful stories out of his childhood—riling his daughters into a peak of excitement at the time of the day when his theoretical parental job was to soothe them before bed. Schulz's portrait is of a warm, curious, and gregarious guy, the anchor of his family—a man who turned his family into a community of truth.

His health gradually failed him during the last decade of his life, and then toward the end, he just stopped talking. His doctors could not explain it; nor could his family. Talking was his great delight.

One night, as he was fading toward death, the family gathered around him. "I had always regarded my family as close, so it was startling to realize how much closer we could get, how near we drew around his waning flame," Schulz wrote. That evening the members of the family went around the room and took turns talking to their father. They each said the things they didn't want to leave unsaid. They each told him what he had given them and how honorably he had lived his life.

Schulz described the scene:

My father, mute but seemingly alert, looked from one face to the next as we spoke, his brown eyes shining with tears. I had always hated to see him cry, and seldom did, but for once, I was grateful. It gave me hope that, for what may have been the last time in his life, and perhaps the most important, he understood. If nothing else, I knew that everywhere he looked that evening, he found himself where he had always been with his family: the center of the circle, the source and subject of our abiding love.

That was a guy who was truly seen.

———

By now you'd think I'd be a regular old Sigmund Freud. I've spent several years thinking about the problem of how to see others deeply and be deeply seen. You'd think that by now I'd be able to walk into a room and pierce into people's souls with my eyes. You'd think I had the ability to burst forth with earthshaking insights about who they really are. You'd think I'd glide through parties as a brilliant Illuminator, leaving all those Diminishers feeling inferior and ashamed. But if I were to honestly assess how much I've mastered the skills I've described in this book, I would have to say: A lot of progress has been made, but there's still a lot of work yet to be done.

For example, yesterday, the day before writing these final paragraphs, I had two long conversations. I had lunch with a young woman who is leaving her current job, moving across the country with her husband, and trying to figure out what to do with her life. Then I had dinner with a government official who is facing an enormous amount of partisan criticism. That these people even came to me for conversation and advice is a sign of progress, I suppose. People rarely approached the old David ready to display vulnerability and seeking accompaniment. But in each case, I now realize, I missed the moment. There was a crucial moment in each conversation, and I did not have the presence of mind to pause the flow of talk so we could linger and go deep on what was just said. At lunch the woman said she was going to spend the next four months soul-searching. I could have stopped the conversation and asked her what exactly she meant. How was she going to do this soul-searching? Had she ever done this kind of soul-searching before in her life? What did she hope to find? Similarly, my dinner partner mentioned that he was terrible at staying present with people. He'd be in the middle of an important meeting with someone and his mind was always going back to reconsider something that had already happened or leaping forward to think about something he had to do later in the day. That was an important confession! I should have stopped him to ask him how he had become aware that he had this weakness, had this flaw marred his relationships, how did he hope to address the problem? After this one day's encounters, I realized that I have to work on my ability to spot the crucial conservational moments in real time. I have to learn how to ask the questions that will keep us in them, probing for understanding.

At the end of this book, I'm going to try to assess myself honestly, in the hopes that the exercise will help you assess yourself honestly. My chief problem is that for all my earnest resolutions and all that I know about the skill of seeing others, in the hurly-burly of everyday life I still too often let my ego take control. I still spend too much social time telling you the smart things I know, the funny stories I know, putting on the kind of social performance that I hope will make me seem impressive or at least likable. I'm still too much of a topper. If you tell me about something that happened in your life, I'll too often tell you about something vaguely similar that happened in mine. What can I say? I spend my life as an opinion columnist; the habits of pontification are hard to shake.

My second problem is that I still possess a natural diffidence that, I suppose, I will never completely overcome. I know that being a loud listener is important, but my face and demeanor are still more calm than responsive, more tranquil than highly emotive. I know that every conversation is defined by its emotional volleys as much as what's actually said, but open emotion-sharing is still a challenge. The other day at a dinner party, I looked across the large table and saw my wife and a woman sitting next to her locked in conversation. They were looking directly into each other's eyes and talking with such rapt attention and delight that the other people in the room might as well have not existed. Then I glanced toward another part of the room and saw two acquaintances leaning into each other, their foreheads close, one with his hand on the other's shoulder, bonding with such palpable friendship that they were like a single dyad. For some of us reserved types, that kind of easy intimacy remains a challenge.

On the plus side, I think there's been a comprehensive shift in my posture. I think I'm much more vulnerable, open, approachable, and, I hope, kind. My gaze is warmer, and I see the world through a more personal lens. Even when we're talking about politics, or sports, or whatever, what I really want to know about is you. I'm more aware of your subjectivity—how you are experiencing your experience, constructing your point of view. I'm a lot better at taking average conversations and turning them into memorable conversations.

Plus, I've learned a lot more about humanity. I know about personality traits, how people are shaped by the life task they are in the middle of, how people are formed by their moments of suffering, how to talk with someone who is depressed, how to recognize the ways different cultures can shape a person's point of view. This knowledge not only gives me some expertise about people in general, it gives me more self-confidence as I approach a stranger or walk with a friend. When I'm talking with a person, I know what to look for. I'm much better at asking big questions, much better at sensing all the dynamics of conversations, much bolder when talking with someone whose life is radically different from my own. When somebody gets truly vulnerable, I don't freeze anymore; I'm having fun, honored by their trust.

The wisdom I've learned and tried to share in this book has given me a clear sense of moral purpose. Parker Palmer's words ring in my head: Every epistemology implies an ethic. The way I try to see you represents my moral way of being in the world, which will either be generous and considerate or judgmental and cruel. So I am trying to cast the "just and loving attention" that Iris Murdoch wrote about. Having written this book, I know, in some concrete detail, what kind of person I seek to be, and that's a very important kind of knowledge to have.

An Illuminator is a blessing to those around him. When he meets others he has a compassionate awareness of human frailty, because he knows the ways we are all frail. He is gracious toward human folly because he's aware of all the ways we are foolish. He accepts the unavoidability of conflict and greets disagreement with curiosity and respect.

She who only looks inward will find only chaos, and she who looks outward with the eyes of critical judgment will find only flaws. But she who looks with the eyes of compassion and understanding will see complex souls, suffering and soaring, navigating life as best they can. The person who masters the skills we've been describing here will have an acute perceptiveness. She'll notice this person's rigid posture and that person's anxious tremor. She'll envelop people in a loving gaze, a visual embrace that will not only help her feel what they are experiencing, but give those around her the sense that she is right there with them, that she is sharing what they are going through. And she will maintain this capacious loving attention even as the callousness of the world rises around her, following the advice in that sage W. H. Auden poem: "If equal affection cannot be / Let the more loving one be me." She's learned, finally, that it's not only the epic acts of heroism and altruism that define a person's character; it's the everyday acts of encounter. It is the simple capacity to make another person feel seen and understood—that hard but essential skill that makes a person a treasured co-worker, citizen, lover, spouse, and friend.

Acknowledgments

On one level writing is a solitary business. I wake up each morning and I write from about 7:30 to 1 P.M. I used to wear a Fitbit. It would tell me I was napping in the mornings. I wasn't napping; I was writing, but I guess my heart rate dropped. The gizmo thought I was asleep, but in reality I was doing what I'm wired to do.

But I've been lucky, and my writing life is also embedded in institutions, filled with people who guide, help, support, and share the ride. My former *New York Times* colleague Michal Leibowitz provided invaluable guidance as this book was coming together. She told me which parts were working and which parts weren't— the outside view, critiquing with care. Michal has a great career in writing and editing ahead of her. My *Times* editor Nick Fox always pushes me to clarify my arguments. When I wrote a piece for *The Times* about my friend Peter Marks, which I've adapted for this book, he pushed me to get more personal, to let my emotions show.

At *The Atlantic,* friends like Jeffrey Goldberg, Scott Stossel, and many others have pushed me to do the social analysis that led me to believe that this book is necessary—that helped me understand the social and relational crisis we are in the middle of, and what we can do about it.

I may be that rarest of creatures—an author who is entirely happy with his publisher. This is my fourth book with Penguin Random House and I've been well treated straight through. My editor, Andy Ward, and his team clarified my thinking on nearly every page and provided the kind of intellectual and emotional support that any writer needs to keep going. This is my fourth book with London King, who helps get my books out into the world. I tell London that I know almost nobody who is as good at their job as London is good at hers. This book has also benefitted from two exceptional editors, fact checkers, and all around smart readers, Bonnie Thompson and Hilary McClellan.

I had the chance to teach the subject of this book at Yale's Jackson School of Global Affairs, even though the topic is only tenuously related to global affairs. My students, who ranged from college students to Marines to environmental scientists to social entrepreneurs, deepened my thinking, warmed my heart, and reminded me again and again that it really is fun to get to know people.

Many of my friends read drafts of this book, and offered wise advice that, frankly, spared me from going seriously off course. In particular, I'd like to thank Pete Wehner, David Bradley, Gary Haugen, Francis Collins, Yuval Levin, Mark Labberton, Philip Yancy, Andrew Steer, James Forsyth, and Russell Moore. Two members of our merry band died as I was finishing this book, Michael Gerson and Tim Keller. I treasure the memories of our conversations and miss them terribly.

Books like this don't get written without experts. I'm grateful to all those who returned my calls, especially Nick Epley, Lisa Feldman Barrett, Dan McAdams, Lori Gottlieb, Tracy Kidder, Robert Kegan, and many others.

My two oldest friends in the world are Peter Marks and his wife, Jenifer McShane. We've known and loved each other practically all our lives. When Pete died in 2022, Jen and her boys, Owen and James, bravely let me tell Pete's story. I hope we've helped many people understand depression a little better, and how to walk with people who are enduring it. I lack the words to fully convey my admiration for Jen, Owen, and James.

My children, Joshua, Naomi, and Aaron, were once kids, playing and growing. Now they're adults—comrades through life, shaping my thoughts and hopes. This book wouldn't exist without my wife, Anne Snyder Brooks; in part because I wouldn't remotely be the kind of person capable of writing it. Anne is a writer too, and the editor of *Comment* magazine. You put two writers in a house, and you'd think things would be quiet and lonely. But thanks to her generous and transcendent nature, and a lot of hard work, our house is perpetually filled with friends and guests, with music, games, sports, and conversation. I seem to spend my years writing books Anne doesn't need. She is already loving, other-centered and perceptive, gifted at making others feel seen, truly a delight to all who know her, wise in ways that can't be learned from books, generous in ways you can't manufacture through some formula—but which emerge as fruits of the spirit.

Notes

CHAPTER 1: THE POWER OF BEING SEEN

10 In a 2021 study Aaron De Smet, Bonnie Dowling, Marino Mugayar-Baldocchi, and Bill Schaninger, "'Great Attrition' or 'Great Attraction'? The Choice Is Yours," *McKinsey Quarterly,* September 2021.

11 "The roots of resilience" Quoted in Bessel A. van der Kolk, *The Body Keeps the Score: Brain, Mind and Body in the Healing of Trauma* (New York: Penguin Books, 2014), 107.

13 "To speak to him" Wendy Moffat, *A Great Unrecorded History: A New Life of E. M. Forster* (New York: Farrar, Straus and Giroux, 2010), 11.

13 a story from Bell Labs Jon Gertner, *The Idea Factory: Bell Labs and the Great Age of American Innovation* (New York: Penguin Books, 2012), 135.

14 read each other accurately Nicholas Epley, *Mindwise: Why We Misunderstand What Others Think, Believe, Feel, and Want* (New York: Vintage, 2014), 9.

14 scale of "empathic accuracy" William Ickes, *Everyday Mind Reading: Understanding What Other People Think and Feel* (Amherst, N.Y.: Prometheus), 78.

14 But other people Ickes, *Everyday Mind Reading,* 164.

14 Ickes finds that the longer Ickes, *Everyday Mind Reading,* 109.

CHAPTER 2: HOW NOT TO SEE A PERSON

21 To demonstrate this phenomenon Epley, *Mindwise,* 55.

24 "Mourning Papa became her profession" Vivian Gornick, *Fierce Attachments: A Memoir* (New York: Farrar, Straus and Giroux, 1987), 76.

24 "My relationship with my mother" Gornick, *Fierce Attachments,* 6.

25 "The unhappiness is so *alive*" Gornick, *Fierce Attachments,* 32.

25 "She doesn't know" Gornick, *Fierce Attachments,* 104.

25 "I had only your father's love" Gornick, *Fierce Attachments,* 204.

CHAPTER 3: ILLUMINATION

30 "is a moral act" Iain McGilchrist, *The Master and His Emissary: The Divided Brain and the Making of the Western World* (New Haven: Yale University Press, 2009), 133.

33 "are so remarkably seen" Frederick Buechner, *The Remarkable Ordinary: How to Stop, Look, and Listen to Life* (Grand Rapids, Mich.: Zondervan, 2017), 24.

34 "I rarely entered a friend's home" Zadie Smith, "Fascinated to Presume: In Defense of Fiction," *New York Review of Books,* October 24, 2019.

34 In the biblical world Parker J. Palmer, *To Know as We Are Known: Education as a Spiritual Journey* (San Francisco: HarperCollins, 1993), 58.

36 "That's a lot of nonsense" Nigel Hamilton, *How to Do Biography: A Primer* (Cambridge, Mass.: Harvard University Press, 2008), 39.

36 "One of the commonest" Leo Tolstoy, *Resurrection,* trans. Aline P. Delano (New York: Grosset & Dunlap, 1911), 59.

37 "Every epistemology becomes" Palmer, *To Know as We Are Known,* 21.

38 Moral behavior happens Iris Murdoch, *The Sovereignty of Good* (Abingdon, U.K.: Routledge, 2014), 36.

38 essential immoral act Martha C. Nussbaum, introduction to *The Black Prince,* by Iris Murdoch (New York: Penguin Classics, 2003), xviii.

38 "just and loving attention" Murdoch, *The Sovereignty of Good,* 27.

39 "Nothing in life" Murdoch, *The Sovereignty of Good,* 85.

40 "grow by looking" Murdoch, *The Sovereignty of Good,* 30.

40 "a way of paying attention" Mary Pipher, *Letters to a Young Therapist: Stories of Hope and Healing* (New York: Basic Books, 2016), 180.

41 "In therapy, as in life" Pipher, *Letters to a Young Therapist,* xxv.

41 "All families are a little crazy" Pipher, *Letters to a Young Therapist,* 30.

41 "Inspiration is very polite" Pipher, *Letters to a Young Therapist,* 43.

42 "I'm thinking of the phrase" Pipher, *Letters to a Young Therapist,* 109.

CHAPTER 4: ACCOMPANIMENT

43 "I was going to float" Loren Eiseley, "The Flow of the River," in *The Immense Journey* (1946; repr., New York: Vintage Books, 1959), 15–27.

47 "Whoever wants life" D. H. Lawrence, *Lady Chatterley's Lover* (New York: Penguin Books, 2006), 323.

49 Laughter happens when Dacher Keltner, *Born to Be Good: The Science of a Meaningful Life* (New York: W. W. Norton, 2009), 134.

49 "If the two of us" Gail Caldwell, *Let's Take the Long Way Home: A Memoir of Friendship* (New York: Random House, 2010), 83.

49 "mutual caution" Caldwell, *Let's Take the Long Way Home,* 87.

52 "I'll be there" Margaret Guenther, *Holy Listening: The Art of Spiritual Direction* (Lanham, Md.: Rowman & Littlefield, 1992), 23.

53 "This is compassion" Daniel Goleman, *Social Intelligence: The New Science of Human Relationships* (New York: Bantam, 2006), 257.

CHAPTER 5: WHAT IS A PERSON?

55 "We were simply watching" Emmanuel Carrère, *Lives Other Than My Own,* trans. Linda Coverdale (New York: Metropolitan, 2011), 2.

57 "Delphine screamed" Carrère, *Lives Other Than My Own,* 11.

58 "Her determination is frightening" Carrère, *Lives Other Than My Own,* 31.

59 "I know that we loved them" Carrère, *Lives Other Than My Own,* 43.

60 "I looked at Hélène's" Carrère, *Lives Other Than My Own,* 51.

61 "Well-being depends" Marc Brackett, *Permission to Feel: Unlocking the Power of Emotions to Help Our Kids, Ourselves, and Our Society Thrive* (New York: Celadon, 2019), 63.

62 noticed the small personal acts Irvin D. Yalom, *The Gift of Therapy: An Open Letter to a New Generation of Therapists and Their Patients* (New York: Harper Perennial, 2009), 31.

65 "a generative, creative act" Anil Seth, *Being You: A New Science of Consciousness* (New York: Dutton, 2021), 97.

66 "action-oriented construction" Seth, *Being You,* 281

66 "Scientific evidence shows" Lisa Feldman Barrett, *How Emotions Are Made: The Secret Life of the Brain* (New York: Houghton Mifflin Harcourt, 2017), 27.

66 Researchers present subjects with Stanislas Dehaene, *How We Learn: Why Brains Learn Better Than Any Machine . . . for Now* (New York: Penguin Books, 2021), 155.

66 asks a student for directions Michael J. Spivey, *Who You Are: The Science of Connectedness* (Cambridge, Mass.: MIT Press, 2020), 19.

67 "The data here indicate" Quoted in Dennis Proffitt and Drake Baer, *Perception: How Our Bodies Shape Our Minds* (New York: St. Martin's, 2020), 170.

67 "The model we choose" McGilchrist, *The Master and His Emissary,* 97.

67 people often slur and mispronounce Barrett, *How Emotions Are Made,* 85.

CHAPTER 6: GOOD TALKS

72 "Unhesitatingly I should" John Buchan, *Pilgrim's Way: An Essay in Recollection* (Boston: Houghton Mifflin, 1940), 155.

74 the average person speaks Kate Murphy, *You're Not Listening: What You're Missing and Why It Matters* (New York: Celadon, 2020), 70.

77 "If a story" Murphy, *You're Not Listening,* 106.

77 around the elbow Proffitt and Baer, *Perception,* 123.

77 Japanese culture encourages Murphy, *You're Not Listening,* 186.

79 In the 1970s Murphy, *You're Not Listening,* 145.

81 "The experience of being *listened*" Mónica Guzmán, *I Never Thought of It*

That Way: How to Have Fearlessly Curious Conversations in Dangerously Divided Times (Dallas, Tex.: BenBella, 2020), 200.

CHAPTER 7: THE RIGHT QUESTIONS

84 The average child asks Will Storr, *The Science of Storytelling: Why Stories Make Us Human and How to Tell Them Better* (New York: Abrams, 2020), 17.

88 "Tell me about the last time" Murphy, *You're Not Listening,* 96.

91 "What is the no" Peter Block, *Community: The Structure of Belonging* (Oakland, Calif.: Berrett-Koehler, 2009), 135.

91 "Why you?" Guzmán, *I Never Thought of It That Way,* xxi.

92 "The human need" Ethan Kross, *Chatter: The Voice in Our Heads, Why It Matters, and How to Harness It* (New York: Crown, 2021), 35.

92 A 2012 study Kross, *Chatter,* 37.

92 found that people Kross, *Chatter,* 30.

CHAPTER 8: THE EPIDEMIC OF BLINDNESS

97 Depression rates Holly Hedegaard, Sally C. Curtin, and Margaret Warner, "Suicide Mortality in the United States, 1999–2019," Data Brief No. 398, National Center for Health Statistics, February 2021.

98 Between 2009 and 2019 Moriah Balingit, "'A Cry for Help': CDC Warns of a Steep Decline in Teen Mental Health," *Washington Post,* March 31, 2022.

98 By 2021, it had shot up Chris Jackson and Negar Ballard, "Over Half of Americans Report Feeling Like No One Knows Them Well," Ipsos, accessed April 12, 2023, https://www.ipsos.com/en-us/news-polls/us-loneliness-index-report.

98 number of American adults "Loneliness in America: How the Pandemic Has Deepened an Epidemic of Loneliness and What We Can Do About It," Making Caring Common, accessed April 12, 2023, https://mcc.gse.harvard.edu/reports/loneliness-in-america.

98 In 2013, Americans spent Bryce Ward, "Americans Are Choosing to Be Alone: Here's Why We Should Reverse That," *Washington Post,* November 23, 2022.

98 Between 1990 and 2018 David Brooks, "The Rising Tide of Global Sadness," *New York Times,* October 27, 2022.

99 When people feel unseen Johann Hari, *Lost Connections: Why You're Depressed and How to Find Hope* (New York: Bloomsbury, 2018), 82.

99 "It becomes a deceiving filter" Giovanni Frazzetto, *Together, Closer: The Art and Science of Intimacy in Friendship, Love, and Family* (New York: Penguin Books, 2017), 12.

100 "Knowing that we are seen" Van der Kolk, *The Body Keeps the Score,* 80.

100 In 2021, hate-crime reports Joe Hernandez, "Hate Crimes Reach the Highest Level in More Than a Decade," NPR, August 31, 2021.

100 roughly two-thirds "Only Half of U.S. Households Donated to Charity, Worst Rate in Decades," CBS News, July 27, 2021.

100 only 30.3 percent did David Brooks, "America Is Having a Moral Convulsion," *Atlantic,* October 5, 2020.

101 lonely people are seven times Ryan Streeter and David Wilde, "The Lonely (Political) Crowd," American Enterprise Institute, accessed April 14, 2023, https://www.aei.org/articles/the-lonely-political-crowd/.

103 "I wanted attention" Tom Junod, "Why Mass Shootings Keep Happening," *Esquire,* October 2, 2017.

103 "At that fatal instant" Jean Hatzfeld, *Machete Season: The Killers in Rwanda Speak,* trans. Linda Coverdale (New York: Farrar, Straus and Giroux, 2005), 24.

106 Only 7 percent "Where Americans Find Meaning in Life," Pew Research Center, November 20, 2018.

CHAPTER 9: HARD CONVERSATIONS

113 Ralph Ellison's words Ralph Ellison, *Invisible Man* (New York: Vintage, 1995), 4.

115 It comes from sailors Guzmán, *I Never Thought of It That Way,* 53.

116 respect is like air Kerry Patterson, Joseph Grenny, Ron McMillan, and Al Switzler, *Crucial Conversations: Tools for Talking When the Stakes Are High* (New York: McGraw-Hill, 2002), 79.

118 People generally vastly overestimate Proffitt and Baer, *Perception,* 38.

118 Since Proffitt first discovered Proffitt and Baer, *Perception,* 39.

119 "We project our individual" Proffitt and Baer, *Perception,* 6.

119 Proffitt's work builds on Proffitt and Baer, *Perception,* 56.

119 "We perceive the world" Proffitt and Baer, *Perception,* 20.

CHAPTER 11: THE ART OF EMPATHY

134 "Recognition is the first" Andy Crouch, *The Life We're Looking For: Reclaiming Relationship in a Technological World* (New York: Convergent, 2022), 3.

134 "The development of the soul" Martin Buber, *I and Thou,* trans. Walter Kaufmann (Edinburgh: T. & T. Clark, 1970), 28.

135 "My twin sister" Stephen Cope, *Deep Human Connection: Why We Need It More Than Anything Else* (Carlsbad, Calif.: Hay House, 2017), 29.

136 "They loved me" Demi Moore, *Inside Out: A Memoir* (New York: Harper-Collins, 2019), 69.

136 The famous Grant Study George E. Vaillant, *Triumphs of Experience: The Men of the Harvard Grant Study* (Cambridge, Mass.: Belknap Press of Harvard University Press, 2012), 43.

137 The men in the study Vaillant, *Triumphs of Experience,* 134.

137 A warm childhood environment Vaillant, *Triumphs of Experience,* 357.

137 men with a poor relationship Vaillant, *Triumphs of Experience,* 134.

137 "Whereas a warm childhood" Vaillant, *Triumphs of Experience,* 139.

138 Some children are raised Tara Bennett-Goleman, *Emotional Alchemy: How the Mind Can Heal the Heart* (New York: Three Rivers, 2001), 96.

139 a "sacred flaw" Storr, *The Science of Storytelling,* 1.

141 "rampant irrationality" Storr, *The Science of Storytelling,* 222.

141 "Jesus rejected hatred" Howard Thurman, *Jesus and the Disinherited* (Boston: Beacon, 1996), 88.

142 called "conceptual blindness" Sacha Golob, "Why Some of the Smartest People Can Be So Very Stupid," *Psyche,* August 4, 2021, https://psyche.co/ideas/why-some-of-the-smartest-people-can-be-so-very-stupid.

145 Emotions contain information Leonard Mlodinow, *Emotional: How Feelings Shape Our Thinking* (New York: Pantheon, 2022), 28.

146 A person who is good at mirroring Epley, *Mindwise,* 47.

146 high "emotional granularity" Barrett, *How Emotions Are Made,* 102.

146 unable to distinguish Barrett, *How Emotions Are Made,* 2.

147 They can distinguish between Barrett, *How Emotions Are Made,* 183.

147 Only humans can Matthew D. Lieberman, *Social: Why Our Brains Are Wired to Connect* (New York: Crown, 2013), 150.

149 "who hug you" Elizabeth Dias, "Kate Bowler on Her Cancer Diagnosis and Her Faith," *Time,* January 25, 2018.

151 Agreement with the last three Karla McLaren, *The Art of Empathy: A Complete Guide to Life's Most Essential Skill* (Boulder, Colo.: Sounds True, 2013), 13.

151 Low empaths can be cruel Simon Baron-Cohen, *Zero Degrees of Empathy: A New Theory of Human Cruelty* (London: Allen Lane, 2011), 31.

152 Borderlines make up Baron-Cohen, *Zero Degrees of Empathy,* 37.

152 They have a constant fear Baron-Cohen, *Zero Degrees of Empathy,* 34.

152 "She doesn't want to hear" Baron-Cohen, *Zero Degrees of Empathy,* 36.

152 Highly empathic people Leslie Jamison, *The Empathy Exams: Essays* (Minneapolis: Graywolf, 2014), 21.

154 "Actors walk through life" *Giving Voice,* directed by James D. Stern and Fernando Villena (Beverly Hills, Calif.: Endgame Entertainment, 2020).

154 The actor Paul Giamatti Paul Giamatti and Stephen T. Asma, "Phantasia," *Aeon,* March 23, 2021, https://aeon.co/essays/imagination-is-the-sixth-sense-be-careful-how-you-use-it.

155 people who read Dan P. McAdams, *The Stories We Live By: Personal Myths and the Making of the Self* (New York: Guilford, 1993), 243.

155 The "mood meter" Brackett, *Permission to Feel,* 113.

156 When you ask people Brackett, *Permission to Feel,* 124.

156 Brackett and his team developed Brackett, *Permission to Feel,* 233.

157 "I think people rush" David Brooks, "What Do You Say to the Sufferer?," *New York Times,* December 9, 2021.

158 "You may think that" Barrett, *How Emotions Are Made,* 77.

159 People who are scared David Brooks, *The Social Animal: The Hidden Sources of Love, Character, and Achievement* (New York: Random House, 2011), 217.

CHAPTER 12: HOW WERE YOU SHAPED BY YOUR SUFFERINGS?

160 "Having a gun pointed" Barbara Lazear Ascher, *Ghosting: A Widow's Voyage Out* (New York: Pushcart, 2021), 46.

161 "Dying was intimate" Ascher, *Ghosting,* 124.

161 "a wind began to blow" Ascher, *Ghosting,* 93.

161 "Trauma challenges" Stephen Joseph, *What Doesn't Kill Us: A New Psychology of Posttraumatic Growth* (New York: Basic Books, 2011), 109.

162 People who are permanently Joseph, *What Doesn't Kill Us,* 104.

162 When Joseph surveyed Joseph, *What Doesn't Kill Us,* 6.

164 "Reality can be harsh" Frederick Buechner, *The Sacred Journey: A Memoir of Early Days* (New York: HarperCollins, 1982), 45.

164 "We all create" Buechner, *The Sacred Journey,* 54.

164 "The sadness of other" Frederick Buechner, *The Eyes of the Heart: A Memoir of the Lost and Found* (New York: HarperCollins, 1999), 17.

164 "The trouble with steeling" Buechner, *The Sacred Journey,* 46.

165 "What I was suddenly" Buechner, *The Sacred Journey,* 69.

166 Naturally, he went off Buechner, *The Eyes of the Heart,* 68.

169 "If someone had said" Joseph, *What Doesn't Kill Us,* 70.

169 "I am a more sensitive person" Harold S. Kushner, *When Bad Things Happen to Good People* (New York: Schocken, 1981), 133.

171 "virtue is the attempt" Murdoch, *The Sovereignty of Good,* 91.

171 "The listener to Mozart's *Jupiter* symphony" Roger Scruton, *Culture Counts: Faith and Feeling in a World Besieged* (New York: Encounter, 2007), 91.

CHAPTER 13: PERSONALITY: WHAT ENERGY DO YOU BRING INTO THE ROOM?

175 extremely extroverted person Dan P. McAdams, *George W. Bush and the Redemptive Dream: A Psychological Portrait* (New York: Oxford University Press, 2011), 34.

175 the class clown McAdams, *George W. Bush and the Redemptive Dream,* 18.

176 One biographer wrote McAdams, *George W. Bush and the Redemptive Dream,* 19.

177 "dealt kindly with his world" Jonathan Sacks, *Morality: Restoring the Common Good in Divided Times* (New York: Basic Books, 2020), 229.

178 "What do you like more" Quoted in Benjamin Hardy, *Personality Isn't Permanent: Break Free from Self-Limiting Beliefs and Rewrite Your Story* (New York: Portfolio, 2020), 28.

179 We often think of extroverts Luke D. Smillie, Margaret L. Kern, and Mirko Uljarevic, "Extraversion: Description, Development, and Mechanisms," in *Handbook of Personality Development,* ed. Dan P. McAdams, Rebecca L. Shiner, and Jennifer L. Tackett (New York: Guilford, 2019), 128.

180 "I also spent" Daniel Nettle, *Personality: What Makes You the Way You Are* (New York: Oxford University Press, 2007), 81.

180 As she aged Nettle, *Personality,* 84.

180 people who score high in extroversion Danielle Dick, *The Child Code: Understanding Your Child's Unique Nature for Happier, More Effective Parenting* (New York: Avery, 2021), 92.

182 "He must spray" Nettle, *Personality,* 149.

182 If extroverts are drawn Dan P. McAdams, *The Art and Science of Personality Development* (New York: Guilford, 2015), 106.

182 If there is an angry face Nettle, *Personality,* 111.

182 They can fall into a particular Scott Barry Kaufman, *Transcend: The New Science of Self-Actualization* (New York: TarcherPerigee, 2020), 10.

183 Neuroticism is linked Nettle, *Personality,* 119.

184 They are able to keep in mind Nettle, *Personality,* 160.

185 openness describes their relationship to information Kaufman, *Transcend,* 110.

185 Artists and poets Ted Schwaba, "The Structure, Measurement, and Development of Openness to Experience Across Adulthood," in *Handbook of Personality Development,* 185.

185 One study showed Schwaba, "The Structure, Measurement and Development of Openness to Experience Across Adulthood," 196.

186 "To Jack, the cardinal sin" Quoted in David Keirsey, *Please Understand Me II: Temperament, Character, Intelligence* (Del Mar, Calif.: Prometheus Nemesis, 1998), 55.

187 personality traits predict Brent W. Roberts, Nathan R. Kuncel, Rebecca Shiner, Avshalom Caspi, and Lewis R. Goldberg, "The Power of Personality: The Comparative Validity of Personality Traits, Socioeconomic Status, and Cognitive Ability for Predicting Important Life Outcomes," *Perspectives on Psychological Science* 2, no. 4 (December 2007): 313–45.

187 very important for parents Dick, *The Child Code,* 122.

188 "Emily Brontë wanted privacy" Edward Mendelson, *The Things That Matter: What Seven Classic Novels Have to Say About the Stages of Life* (New York: Pantheon, 2006), 79.

189 "Although it is still" Brent W. Roberts and Hee J. Yoon, "Personality Psychology," *Annual Review of Psychology* 73 (January 2022): 489–516.

CHAPTER 14: LIFE TASKS

190 newborns are nearsighted Alison Gopnik, Andrew Meltzoff, and Patricia Kuhl, *How Babies Think: The Science of Childhood* (London: Weidenfeld & Nicolson, 1999), 29.

191 it's not just that your child Gopnik, Meltzoff, and Kuhl, *How Babies Think,* 37.

195 A person with this consciousness has a greater Mihaly Csikszentmihalyi, *The Evolving Self: A Psychology for the Third Millennium* (New York: Harper-Perennial, 1993), 179.

196 Her sense of herself is defined Philip M. Lewis, *The Discerning Heart: The Developmental Psychology of Robert Kegan* (Seattle: Amazon Digital Services, 2011), 54.

196 People in the midst Csikszentmihalyi, *The Evolving Self,* 38.

196 A person in this consciousness tends Csikszentmihalyi, *The Evolving Self,* 97.

197 To lose a friend Csikszentmihalyi, *The Evolving Self,* 206.

197 Thrown back onto Robert Kegan, *In Over Our Heads: The Mental Demands of Modern Life* (Cambridge, Mass.: Harvard University Press, 1994), 17.

198 "I got chills" Lori Gottlieb, *Maybe You Should Talk to Someone: A Therapist, Her Therapist, and Our Lives Revealed* (New York: Houghton Mifflin Harcourt, 2019), 174.

198 describes the furnaces Robert A. Caro, *Working: Researching, Interviewing, Writing* (New York: Vintage, 2019), 158.

199 "You can't get very deep" Caro, *Working,* 151.

199 People gripped by the career Wallace Stegner, *Crossing to Safety* (New York: Random House, 1987), 143.

200 "only when developmental" Vaillant, *Triumphs of Experience,* 153.

201 "The achievements which society rewards" C. G. Jung, *Modern Man in Search of a Soul,* trans. W. S. Dell and Cary F. Baynes (New York: Harcourt, Brace, 1933) 104.

202 When the researchers first encountered Newman Vaillant, *Triumphs of Experience,* 18.

203 He came to realize Vaillant, *Triumphs of Experience,* 20.

203 "Let me give you" Vaillant, *Triumphs of Experience,* 24.

204 "the capacity to foster" Vaillant, *Triumphs of Experience,* 154.

205 a business executive, Peter Robert Kegan and Lisa Laskow Lahey, *Immunity to Change: How to Overcome It and Unlock the Potential in Yourself and Your Organization* (Boston: Harvard Business Press, 2009), 35.

206 he felt bad about himself Lewis, *The Discerning Heart,* 88.

207 "Health is the ability" Quoted in Diane Ackerman, *An Alchemy of Mind: The Marvel and Mystery of the Brain* (New York: Scribner, 2004), 121.

208 emotion often takes the place Described in Vaillant, *Triumphs of Experience,* 168

208 "What a pity" Irvin D. Yalom, *Staring at the Sun: Overcoming the Terror of Death* (San Francisco: Jossey-Bass, 2008), 297.

208 "An inner development" Wilfred M. McClay, "Being There," *Hedgehog Review* (Fall 2018), https://hedgehogreview.com/issues/the-evening-of-life/articles/being-there.

209 "We cannot live" Jung, *Modern Man in Search of a Soul,* 125.

210 "All growth is costly" Quoted in Kegan, *The Evolving Self,* 215.

CHAPTER 15: LIFE STORIES

219 an experience of inner speech Fernyhough, *The Voices Within,* 36.

219 we talk to ourselves Kross, *Chatter,* xxii.

219 About a quarter Fernyhough, *The Voices Within,* 65.

219 Some people use their own Anatoly Reshetnikov, "Multiplicity All-Around: In Defence of Nomadic IR and Its New Destination," *New Perspectives* 27, no. 3 (2019), 159–66.

220 asked people to describe Fernyhough, *The Voices Within,* 44.

221 "Imagoes express" McAdams, *The Stories We Live By,* 127.

221 "I'm the little girl" Viola Davis, *Finding Me* (New York: HarperCollins, 2022), 6.

221 "When I won" Davis, *Finding Me,* 2.

222 "My sisters became" Davis, *Finding Me,* 67.

222 ten key scenes McAdams, *The Art and Science of Personality Development,* 298.

223 She argues that many lives Mary Catherine Bateson, *Composing a Life* (New York: Atlantic Monthly Press, 1989), 6.

224 "My childhood was" James Hillman, *The Soul's Code: In Search of Character and Calling* (New York: Ballantine, 1996), 173.

224 "here was the rub" Stephen Cope, *Deep Human Connection: Why We Need It More Than Anything Else* (Carlsbad, Calif.: Hay House, 2017), 178.

225 "She barely knew" Cope, *Deep Human Connection,* 180.

225 **"The only way"** Quoted in Storr, *The Science of Storytelling,* 68.

226 **"Calm is a function"** Philip Weinstein, *Becoming Faulkner: The Art and Life of William Faulkner* (New York: Oxford University Press, 2010), 3.

CHAPTER 16: HOW DO YOUR ANCESTORS SHOW UP IN YOUR LIFE?

228 **"I was Mama's child"** Valerie Boyd, *Wrapped in Rainbows: The Life of Zora Neale Hurston* (New York: Scribner, 2003), 32.

229 **"Don't you want"** Zora Neale Hurston, *Dust Tracks on a Road: An Autobiography* (New York: HarperPerennial, 1996), 34.

229 **"A saddle horse!"** Boyd, *Wrapped in Rainbows,* 14.

229 **"Jump at the sun"** Hurston, *Dust Tracks on a Road,* 34.

229 **"For me, the store porch"** Hurston, *Dust Tracks on a Road,* 46.

230 **She picked up glints** Hurston, *Dust Tracks on a Road,* 104.

230 **"Essentially everything"** Boyd, *Wrapped in Rainbows,* 25.

231 **"All water has"** Toni Morrison, "The Site of Memory," in *Inventing the Truth: The Art and Craft of Memoir,* ed. William K. Zinsser (Boston: Houghton Mifflin, 1998), 199.

232 **"I had knowledge"** Boyd, *Wrapped in Rainbows,* 40.

232 **"In the midst of play"** Hurston, *Dust Tracks on a Road,* 66.

232 **After her mother's death** Boyd, *Wrapped in Rainbows,* 75.

233 **"Oh, if you knew"** Boyd, *Wrapped in Rainbows,* 110.

233 **"I'm getting inside"** Boyd, *Wrapped in Rainbows,* 165.

234 **"Memory, history"** Danté Stewart, "In the Shadow of Memory," *Comment,* April 23, 2020, https://comment.org/in-the-shadow-of-memory/.

235 **"My interest lies"** Hurston, *Dust Tracks on a Road,* 171.

235 **"If you have received"** Hurston, *Dust Tracks on a Road,* 192.

237 **Between 1997 and 2002** Joseph Henrich, *The WEIRDest People in the World: How the West Became Psychologically Peculiar and Particularly Prosperous* (New York: Picador, 2020), 41.

238 **are complete outliers** Henrich, *The WEIRDest People in the World,* 156.

238 much less conformist Henrich, *The WEIRDest People in the World,* 45.

239 groups of three things Proffitt and Baer, *Perception,* 195.

240 who are descended Esther Hsieh, "Rice Farming Linked to Holistic Thinking," *Scientific American,* November 1, 2014.

243 "I am an infidel" Theodor Reik, *Listening with the Third Ear: The Inner Experience of a Psychoanalyst* (New York: Farrar, Straus and Giroux, 1948), 64.

CHAPTER 17: WHAT IS WISDOM?

247 Roosevelt was hosting Robert Caro, "Lyndon Johnson and the Roots of Power," in *Extraordinary Lives: The Art and Craft of American Biography,* ed. William K. Zinsser (Boston: Houghton Mifflin, 1988), 200.

251 "This was the most" Tracy Kidder, *Strength in What Remains* (New York: Random House, 2009), 5.

252 "the gap between" Kidder, *Strength in What Remains,* 183.

253 "It was as if" Kidder, *Strength in What Remains,* 123.

254 "Maybe we should" Kidder, *Strength in What Remains,* 216.

254 "Deo had tried" Kidder, *Strength in What Remains,* 219.

256 She knew from prior Gottlieb, *Maybe You Should Talk to Someone,* 93.

257 "In this room" Gottlieb, *Maybe You Should Talk to Someone,* 47.

257 "Typically therapists are" Gottlieb, *Maybe You Should Talk to Someone,* 154.

259 "Receptivity without confrontation" Henri J. M. Nouwen, *Reaching Out: The Three Movements of the Spiritual Life* (New York: Image Books, 1966), 99.

267 "My father, mute" Kathryn Schulz, *Lost & Found: A Memoir* (New York: Random House, 2022), 43.

Index

ABOUT THE AUTHOR

DAVID BROOKS is one of the nation's leading writers and commentators. An op-ed columnist for *The New York Times,* he appears regularly on *PBS NewsHour* and *Meet the Press.* He is the bestselling author of *The Second Mountain, The Road to Character, The Social Animal, On Paradise Drive,* and *Bobos in Paradise.*

ABOUT THE TYPE

This book was set in Granjon, a modern recutting of a typeface produced under the direction of George W. Jones (1860–1942), who based Granjon's design upon the letterforms of Claude Garamond (1480–1561). The name was given to the typeface as a tribute to the typographic designer Robert Granjon (1513–89).